MORE 100% Jackie CHAN

The Essential Companion Volume 2

Edited by Richard Cooper

TITAN BOOKS

More 100% Jackie Chan:
The Essential Companion Volume 2

1 84023 888 7

Published by Titan Books
A division of Titan Publishing Group Ltd,
144 Southwark Street, London SE1 0UP

First edition June 2004
10 9 8 7 6 5 4 3 2 1

Published in conjunction with: The Screen Power Publishing Group,
PO Box 1989, Bath BA2 2YE, UK.
www.screen-power.com

Designed by Rebecca Allen / Screen Power Publishing Group

Did you enjoy this book? We love to hear from our readers. Please email us at: **readerfeedback@titanemail.com** or write to Reader Feedback at the above address.
To subscribe to our regular newsletter for up-to-the-minute news, great offers and competitions, email: **titan-news@titanemail.com**

Titan Books' film and TV range are available from all good bookshops or direct from our mail order service. For a free catalogue or to order, phone **01536 764646** with your credit card details, or write to **Titan Books Mail Order, AASM Ltd, Unit 6, Pipewell Industrial Estate, Desborough, Northants NN14 2SW**. Please quote reference JC/C2.

A CIP catalogue record for this title is available from the British Library.

Printed and bound in Great Britain by MPG, Bodmin, Cornwall.

Acknowledgments

Screen Power Publishing would like to thank the following people and companies for their support, assistance, hard work and friendship in the creation of this book.

Thanks to:
The JC Group, Dorothy Wong, Osumi Yahagi Chan, Michelle Yeoh, Ken Sawada, Keith Vitali, Teddy Chen, Jules Daly, Roger Yuan, Tan Tao Liang, Richard & Judy Norton, John Rhys-Davies, Lee Evans, Gordon Chan, Sammo Hung, Mike Leeder, Lisa Clemens, Matthew Edwards, Trish Evans, Albert Valentin, Gail Mihara, John Miller, Alex Harding, EMG, Golden Harvest Films Ltd, Golden Way Films Ltd, Jackie Chan Films, JCE Ltd, Media Asia, Star TV, and all our loyal worldwide readers of *Screen Power Magazine*.

Very Special Thanks to: Jackie Chan, Willie Chan and Solon So for their support, assistance and ever growing friendship.

Dedication

This book is dedicated to the world's most popular, successful and best loved movie star - Jackie Chan.

MORE 100%
Jackie CHAN

The Essential Companion Volume 2

Edited by Richard Cooper

SCREEN POWER

About the Editor

Richard Cooper was born on the 8th of April 1974 in Bath, England. He watched his first Jackie Chan movie, *Drunken Master*, at the age of eleven and has been hooked ever since. He graduated from the City of Bath College after two years at the age of twenty, gaining top honours in Business and Finance.

He ventured out to Hong Kong in December 1994 to approach Jackie Chan's office about starting up an official UK based Fan Club and eight months later received their full approval and support.

In late 1997 he found interests in the publishing industry and received approval from The Jackie Chan Group to publish an official bi-monthly magazine focussed entirely on Jackie Chan. Still to this day, *Screen Power: The Jackie Chan Magazine*, is well received by readers all over the world.

These days Richard still retains a strong working relationship with Jackie and his Hong Kong Head Office, and not only is Editor & Publisher of *Screen Power: The Jackie Chan Magazine*, but also Editor & Publisher of *Jade Screen* - a bi-monthly glossy publication covering the entire Hong Kong Movie Industry.

Richard Cooper can be contacted via the following e-mail address: **office@screen-power.com**

Contents

Foreword

Publishing a book on any subject or any person is not easy. Publishing any book takes a huge amount of time, energy and enthusiasm as well as a number of other things...

My passion for publishing this book is due to my own admiration of Jackie as well as my own personal friendship with him, and also I feel I have an obligation (how small it is) to the many fans out there in world who love this guy and watch his films on a daily and weekly basis.

This book is a combination of articles, reviews, movie set reports and retrospectives from *Screen Power: The Jackie Chan Magazine* — the magazine that I founded and the magazine that has been my full time love and work since 1997.

Also in this book are several interviews conducted with Jackie, his movie co-stars and movie directors. Some of these interviews and articles have already been published in *Screen Power* and some have not.

I hope with this book and any future books in the years to come that I can not only give ardent fans something interesting, fun and worthwhile to read but also, if possible, to reach out and tap into those people who are not yet aware of the man — Jackie Chan.

Because you are reading this, at home, a friend's house, a library or in a book store somewhere in the world, you are no longer one of those unfortunate individuals who are not aware of this man's incredible films, and because of this you do not have any excuse at all for not joining in the fun that is — Jackie Chan.

MICHELLE YEOH

Interview conducted by Mike Leeder

Michelle burst onto the screen in a trio of action-packed classics from D & B Films before retiring, only to burst back onto the screen and very nearly steal the show from our very own Jackie Chan in the Stanley Tong directed third installment of the *Police Story* saga, *Supercop*. The definitive female action star in Asia, the divine Ms. Yeoh was the best thing about the James Bond movie *Tomorrow Never Dies*, is currently hard at work on Ang Lee's *Crouching Tiger, Hidden Dragon* with Chow Yun-fatt, and has just signed a multi-picture deal to star in and co-produce a number of movies for Media Asia. At the urging of a certain young Mr. Cooper, I dug into the vaults and retrieved a previously unpublished interview that was conducted just after her comeback in *Supercop*. It's funny looking back at the interview, several years have passed since it took place, and Michelle is as young and lovely as ever for me - well that's a very different story...

Screen Power: Michelle, can you fill us in on some early biographical details?

Michelle Yeoh: I was born in Malaysia, in a mining town called Ippoh. I spent my childhood in Malaysia and when I was about fifteen I went to England to study.

SP: What were you studying in England?

MY: Ballet. I always wanted to be a dancer. I always wanted to be a ballerina, anything to do with ballet. So I went over to England to do a teachers course in ballet, which I did for three years, and then unfortunately I had an accident and hurt my back so I was told to give up dancing completely. I was told not to ever do any form of physical exercise that could aggravate my back, which in turn could lead to some very serious problems.

SP: (Laughing) I'm glad you took their advice...

MY: (Laughing) I took it very seriously at that time. So because of that I went back to my books, so to say, I went back to university, but I did not want to give up dance, so I went on and did a Bachelor of Arts degree in dance and drama. So I studied choreography, the history of arts, and drama, which I hated with a passion (laughing).

SP: When I studied drama, many years ago, my biggest problem was with Shakespeare. Nobody talks like that, it's so hard to get in to.

MY: Oh yeah, God, Shakespeare... Oh tell me about it! I was never going to walk on stage and do anything of that sort. I think if anybody at that time told me that one day I'd end up being an actress I would have laughed in their face. In fact if you had told my teacher at the time he would have died laughing, we all would have died laughing (laughing). So I graduated, and then I went back to Malaysia. I was actually planning to go back to England to do my Masters in dance, but then I got roped into doing Miss Malaysia.

SP: That's the thing. Whereas in the West if you win a beauty pageant maybe you can get a few minor roles in film or television, in Asia if you win this can launch your entire singing career and in movies and television.

MY: I think it's very much true here in Hong Kong, to be fair, because all of the beauty pageants are organised by the TV stations, so it is a stepping stone. In Malaysia it's more serious. Remember we come from a more religious country, a Muslim country. So even when we did a beauty pageant and things like that it was mainly for the country, the whole concept was different. I didn't really want to do it, but my mother was quite keen on it so... Also she had a good point, she said that if you didn't do it now then later on in life, it's a... How do you say?... After you pass that age, you will never be able to do it again. And she also said you are in the arts field and performance on stage and things like that.

SP: So at least it would give you exposure.

MY: Yeah, it would bring exposure, more experience, and things like that. So I figured to get her off my back I would just do it! You know, if I lose or if I end up nowhere at least she will never bug me about it again.

SP: And you can blame her for it!

MY: Of course (laughing). I had it all planned! But I went on to win that! The "Miss Photogenic" of Malaysia. And so I went on to work with them in Malaysia and London, and also in Australia. It was mainly promotional work, and I learnt a lot about my country. You know, because I had been away from Malaysia for six or seven years while I was studying abroad. So it was good for me to know more about my country and also it gave me a sense of pride to represent my country in that way. But during that period of time while I was waiting to finish off my reign I was given the opportunity to come out here to Hong Kong to do a commercial with Jackie Chan.

SP: What was the commercial for?

MY: It was for a watch. A watch commercial. So I figured that as I wasn't doing much in Malaysia - of course there was work, but there was always time off - I figured that it's not going to take anything out of me to go to Hong Kong and do a commercial and gain some more experience. So I flew out here and did the commercial with Jackie and the next day I was offered a film contract with D & B Films. Like before, at that time, the same thing went through my mind - you know, if I liked the contract and what I was doing then I could continue, but if I really hated it then at least I could go back to England. But I stayed with the contract and I have stayed here in Hong Kong ever since.

SP: Your movie debut in Owl Vs Dumbo is so different to what you are doing nowadays. I mean in that movie, you are this sweet and innocent little...

MY: Well, I was innocent and sweet and a real darling at that time (laughing).

SP: (Laughing) No, I'm not saying you're not... (laughing). Your character in the movie is like this innocent longhaired school teacher and all the troubled teens like Season Ma and everyone else are giving you trouble and reducing you to tears.

MY: That's right, they were giving me a hard time in that movie.

SP: Was it enjoyable working on that movie?

MY: It was interesting because it was the first time I had done a movie, and also at that time I didn't speak much Cantonese. English, as it is today, was my first language, so it was a problem, I could hardly understand half the things that were going on around me, you know. And then working with Sammo Hung. Sammo is a real gem. Luckily he did speak a little English, and then George Lam speaks perfect English, so it was easy. At least I had people around me who could help me. I remember the first thing George Lam said to me was, "You don't want to get into the movie industry - go home!" (Laughing) I can remember looking at him thinking, "This is very strange! Why is he saying this to me?" He was like, "You're too nice, you should go home to Malaysia." (Laughing) This experience was a real eye opener and I never realised how people worked out here, you always hear how hardworking and aggressive the Hong Kong people are, so working on that movie it was magnified five times over.

SP: Were you happy with your role in that film?

MY: I wasn't thinking about that to be honest. I was just thinking, "Let me get this over," you know, "Let me finish it and get out of here!" Because it was difficult, I didn't speak the language well, I couldn't understand what the hell was going on! And this was the first time I had to cry in front of so many people - it's not easy! Then you're scared of the Director as well! (Laughing) But he was very sweet, he was very patient and all that, and working with him I think made it easier... But it wasn't challenging enough.

SP: Yes, it seems that you were there just to look nice and that was it!

MY: Yeah... but at the time, those were the only kind of roles that were offered to newcomers into the movie business.

SP: You had a cameo in Twinkle, Twinkle Lucky Stars?

MY: That's right.

SP: Which kind of introduced you with the new look shorter hair...

MY: Actually, we were already working on Yes, Madam!... They already planned to do Yes, Madam!, in fact we were working on that and Sammo had heard from Yuen Kwai, the Director of Yes, Madam!, of how well I was doing and how aggressive and stubborn I was, so he put me in a cameo role in this other movie.

I think after they saw Yes, Madam! I could continue with this action trend and become one of the many young and upcoming talents. You know, this was a safe road to go I think. Someone mentioned the fact that I came from abroad and had a colourful background, in the sense that I had a degree in dance and drama, I did ballet and I was very sporty. It's good that they are still putting me in that kind of a role.

At that time, action movies and comedies were the two biggest sellers in Hong Kong or anywhere in South East Asia. I didn't think I had the comic look - I couldn't see myself doing one of those comedy roles with John Sham, Fung Shui-fan and Richard Ng - so the only thing left for me was the action. And that really challenged me, because I had been doing physical things ever since I was young, from ballet to sports to things that really

On the set of Supercop

Inbetween takes of *Supercop*, with co-star Jackie Chan

require the discipline and the movement. So when they suggested action, I was very eager to try it out.

It was quite challenging. I mean it was completely different because you had to switch mode from being very sweet to very aggressive, and with a powerful look.

SP: *You were literally thrown in at the deep end of action films when you teamed up with Cynthia Rothrock for Yes, Madam!?*

MY: Yes, at that time D & B gave me a great opportunity to do something like that and I didn't want to disappoint them, neither did I want to disappoint myself. So when I knew we were doing this film, the Director Yuen Kwai and his artistic team really sat down and thought, you know, "How do we change that sweet and innocent look, because we have to make such an impact on the audience that when they see her they are going to forget what she has done before and come out totally different and dynamic and take your breath away?" I think some people actually objected to the fact that women were fighting. Even today there are some people who object to the fact that women can fight like that.

SP: *If you go to Thailand, the female Thai boxers, they can't climb over the rope, they have to go under.*

MY: Yeah, it's like only a man can climb over the rope. So when we did that movie it was a big obstacle to overcome. I'm sure the Director was very happy when he was told he was going to direct an action movie, but when he was told he had to direct an action movie with two women he went crazy! (Laughing)

SP: *Before this, did you ever study martial arts?*

MY: No. I mean I dabbled a little when I was a kid, but I always concentrated on ballet. But I think I was very lucky because when I went to university to do my degree I did contemporary dance as well. Contemporary is totally different, it's a much stronger and more aggressive form of dance, so that really helped me with the martial arts. I think it made my movements more flexible and more versatile.

SP: *Watching the movie, it's so hard to believe you are not as classically trained as Cynthia Rothrock in the martial arts.*

MY: Yes, it looks like we are doing the same thing, whereas Cynthia is trained in a particular style and form. Of course that's the beauty of movie-making. And even in China now when we go there to film you have a lot of brilliant fighters, but you also have to remember that they are trained in a particular style and they can do the entire run of their style beautifully in five minutes. Whereas I was completely new, so they could just train me in whatever style they needed to put me in. And we really worked hard on that movie.

SP: *You had Dick Wei and Lam Ching-ying teaching you?*

MY: Yeah, Lam Ching-ying, Dick Wei, Ah Dan, Yuen Wah... so when we worked I literally spent like six to eight hours a day training. And also I cut my hair... that was the saddest part of my life (laughing), you know, because I have always had long hair (laughing). I was working out in the gym with Dick Wei and Ah Dan for literally the whole week, only Sunday was rest. We'd go running and then they would teach me the form and boxing.

SP: *You had Lam Ching-ying teaching you Wing Chung Kung-fu?*

MY: That's right.

SP: *I think Lam Ching-ying is quite a strange guy, very hard to talk to?*

MY: Yes he is. But once you get him going he is wonderful, he's really nice. Very straightforward and direct. He doesn't like to beat around the bush.

SP: *The first time I met him I said, "It's very nice to meet you," and he said, "I don't like foreigners!"*

MY: (Laughing) Really?

SP: *(Laughing) I just said, "Okay, I'm going now!"*

MY: I remember him teaching me the first lesson. You know, because you can be a good fighter, but that doesn't mean you are a good teacher. Sometimes it is very difficult when you are so in tune with your body to suddenly start from basics and have to teach a total newcomer. He would just do the action and then say, "That's how it is done," and you are standing there going, "Great, but where does it come from? What is the starting position?" Then he would just pick up your leg and and twist it into all these weird positions (laughing). I mean, as a ballerina I'm very flexible...

SP: *But flexible in a different way.*

MY: That's right. I'm flexible in turning out but for action movies it's all turning in, so the minute he turns you in all your muscles will cramp up! He's like, "You are

supposed to be very flexible, what do you mean you can't do this?" So I said to him, "Give me your leg." So he's used to turning in, so I turned it out and he got a cramp, so he understood what I was getting at from there on. After that we got on the same wavelength.

SP: *Then you had Dick Wei training you?*

MY: Oh, that was real tough!

SP: *I can imagine... I sparred with Dick Wei once in a gym...*

MY: He says, "I'm not going to hit you!" He always says that: "Don't worry, I'm not going to hit you." But if you whack him once - you're dead! (Laughing)

SP: *He said to me, "I'm not going to look bad." I said, "What?" He just went BANG - and I was on the floor. He was like, "I'm sorry, but I don't want to look bad!" (Laughing) Dick Wei has that reputation.*

MY: Oh I know!

SP: *So many people refuse to fight him. Like Cynthia Rothrock, she refuses to fight with him.*

MY: Yeah, every time she saw him, you can see that look on her face, it's like, "Aaaaaggghhhhhh!"

SP: *She got hit by him badly though, I mean she broke her jaw and her internal ear got damaged.*

MY: You know, that's the main problem when you are fighting in the movies, being nervous about actually getting hit. So when you are fighting you can't really have that fear. It's like, "I know I might get hit", but you have to take the chance. The more nervous you are, the better the chance you have of getting hurt. Of course accidents happen!

SP: *When you and Cynthia both launched your action film careers in the mid-eighties, and on this movie, did you have a good working relationship on this movie?*

MY: Yeah, it was fine. I mean we didn't have any problems working together. We had a pretty good working relationship.

SP: *She always said her main problem was that no-one ever told her what was going on or what to do. The prime example is the scene in Yes, Madam! where both of you resign from the police force, and then she comes down the steps with a big smile on her face and gets in the car. On the set they said, "Oh Cynthia, come down the steps, smile, and then get in the car." So she does it, and when the film comes out and she watches it, then she realises why she had to go down the steps in the first place! (Laughing)*

MY: (Laughing) Well, I think it's a problem because a lot of the crew doesn't speak English very well. They speak English nowadays of course, but this film was a long time ago.

SP: *Yeah, I remember talking to Stanley Tong and he said that was one of the main things with Brandon Lee. A lot of people were saying he was very quiet when he was making films in Hong Kong. The language...*

MY: He didn't speak a lot of Cantonese you know. He could not comprehend. We used to hang out together too, and he did say that the language barrier was the main problem. The crew would say to him, you know, "More Power, more power!" and he didn't know if they wanted more power in his facial expression, or more power when he punched and kicked... So the language barrier was too much for him working on Hong Kong movies.

SP: *In Yes, Madam! you battle Eddie Maher, Dick Wei, Chung Fat and everyone. You're blowing up cars, you do a backward head plunge through glass. Did you get hurt during the making of this film?*

MY: Touch wood, I wasn't. I was not seriously hurt. I mean I was completely bruised, but not hurt (laughing). I think that was what impressed the Director, because after the first day I came back for more. You know the opening scenes at the bank?

SP: *Yeah, you are jumping onto cars and rolling around on concrete...*

MY: I would do all the stunts, I would never question the Director, Yuen Kwai. It's the same as today - it's something that I still carry with me - and that's whenever I work with a Director or stunt crew, I get to know them before filming, because once I start working with them I have to trust them completely. Of course, sometimes there is no time to get to know people. Luckily sometimes people you have to work with are naturally just nice people, and they become good friends of yours, they are the people who you very much trust and respect and will always lend them your help if they need it. But unfortunately sometimes people who you have to work with are horrible (laughing). But I have been lucky so far to work with lots of nice people. I think you always know who the nice people are because people speak very highly of them to you and other people. So I need to know them before I trust them and will try things out like stunts.

SP: *Yuen Wah says, "I like Michelle because she is very brave and will always try everything."*

MY: Yeah?

SP: *He said that too many people nowadays won't try anything. They will even say "No!" before they have seen it. He said that he wouldn't mind if someone looked at it, had a go and then said "No".*

MY: Yes, I always will have a try, I will always go for it - of course, unless you know something is ridiculous and if you tried it you'd have a very good chance of getting seriously hurt.

SP: *Was it difficult working on the choreography, people's timing, and the amount of contact necessary in the fight scenes?*

MY: At the beginning, yes it was. But I was very lucky because Chin Gar-lok was a stunt guy at the time. I mean it was a dream fighting with him. Whenever I had to fight with someone I always asked for Gar-lok.

SP: *He's incredible. He's "Mr. No Warm Up". His kicking, flexibility and timing is fantastic.*

MY: He's great... his timing and everything. He can do it all. He's accurate. What's worse sometimes is fighting with someone who is inaccurate. Even in *Yes, Madam!* there were people I was fighting at times when the timing was a little out. It wasn't because we were not good, but sometimes it just happens.

SP: *Chung Fat said that he had to be doubled in one scene fighting you, because both your timings just clashed.*

MY: At that time it's very easy to blame the newcomer, kind of like, "God, she doesn't know what she's doing!" But I was lucky because you had all these people like Dick Wei and Gar-lok and all these people who had been working out with me and fighting with me and they knew... Even Yuen Biao came to the set of *Yes, Madam!* just to check us out to see what we were like, and he's very fast, and he tried me out and at the end of the day they all said, "Don't worry, its not you! Sometimes you fight someone and both of your timings just don't match." But you just learn to accept that working in the Hong Kong movie industry. Sometimes you try your best and it just doesn't come off.

SP: *How well was Yes, Madam! received when it was released in Hong Kong?*

MY: Oh, it was a big hit! I mean it really launched my career.

SP: *After Yes, Madam! you then did Royal Warriors and Police Assassins which were a lot darker in tone. Yes, Madam! was still just a lot of comedy as well as action.*

MY: With *Yes, Madam!* with just us two girls... It was brave for the production company, but the audience wasn't just going to come into the theatre and see it.

SP: Yeah, one thing I did notice was that D & B put big pictures of Sammo, Tsui Hark and everyone else on it, and then you and Cynthia were two smaller images lurking in the background (laughing).

MY: (Laughing) Well that's the Hong Kong movie industry. Cynthia and myself were complete newcomers to this business and the whole idea was for these big famous guys to bring us in to be noticed. Sammo, Tsui Hark and John Sham were among the three biggest comedy actors in Asia at that time, so of course it was a gimmick to get the audiences in. I mean they were still very much part of the film but also it was a launching pad for us... it gave us a good opportunity to show the audience. Once the audience is in there we can show them what we can do, but first of all it was all about, "How do we promote this movie to get the audience in to watch it first?" It was a good trick (laughing).

SP: Well it worked! (Laughing) The good thing though was the film was good, and you backed up the promotional gimmick.

MY: I think at least we were convincing. A lot of people were like, "There is no way this film will work." Also the style Yuen Kwai wanted us to use was very aggressive. In this movie he wanted to show that these woman were going to fight like men... we were going to be beaten up like men, but also they will be tough like men. It was a big challenge at the time. In Taiwan, the movie was a runaway box office success. Today even, people will always remember me in that scene when I break through the glass. When I do a scene, especially like that one, I am always very focussed, I can't think of anything else. If it was a fighting movement I would always consult with Dick Wei or Gar-lok or anybody around me that I trusted. You know in action there's a lot of different movements, they are not always the same punch or kick. So these guys that I trained with always advised me on techniques and everything. For that glass scene, I think Yuen Kwai wanted to make a point as well, he really had to think of something that the audience was going to sit up and remember for a long time. Also, no woman had ever done anything like this stunt before. I mean no woman working in these movies would ever consider throwing themselves through this glass.

SP: It was a great scene and it worked well for you because you were clearly seen doing it with no doubles.

MY: Just before I did this scene Yuen Kwai was trying to reassure me that I would be alright and that it was fake glass, sugar glass, you know. He would pick it up and put it in his mouth to show me it wasn't dangerous or anything (laughing). Actually he didn't have

to convince me that much, I was ready to do it anyway, but he thought he still had to try and reassure me. I remember that they got in one stunt guy who was fighting Cynthia on the other side, the scene where she whacked him with a pole and he crashed and somersaulted through the glass... I remember so clearly that this guy was bald because he came rushing on from another set, so they had to tie a wig on him. But Yuen Kwai told me to watch this scene when the guy crashed through this glass to show me this guy will be alright because it was the same fake glass they will be using on my stunt. So they say "Action" and he does the flip and crashes through the glass, and they shout "Cut" and the guy gets up and says, "I'm fine," and we see him walking out and he has all this blood on his back and cuts... The glass cut through his wig and cut his head (laughing). I looked at Yuen Kwai and he just walked away and was like, "Come on, let's set up Michelle's glass scene." It was funny, and of course scary (laughing).

SP: In Royal Warriors you start off the movie in Japan. The opening is funny because you play with the Kwan Dao and I remember you do an incredible leg scissors kick. You worked with Henry Sanada and his team, what were they like to work with?

MY: They were very professional. They were great to work with. Henry was very punctual, he really researched what he had to do, he would take pride in what he was doing. He had his entire stunt boy team with him... they were great, they didn't come here with an attitude like, "We are the number one stars in Japan and we better show you how this is all done." They were very humble, modest, and they would always say "Yes" to everything you asked for.

SP: I met some of Sonny Chiba's stunt guys and they can do all the stuff the Hong Kong people can do, but they just haven't worked on the choreography enough.

MY: Yeah, you're right. They can do the same things but, dare I say it, they're not as advanced as the Hong Kong stunt boys in terms of the fighting and choreography.

SP: Magnificent Warriors is a fan favourite in the West.

MY: Kind of like Indiana Jones, right? (Laughing)

SP: (Laughing) Yes, and this movie was your first team-up with stuntman turned Director Stanley Tong wasn't it? He kind of told me this joke you played on him. Would you like to explain more about this?

MY: (Laughing) Well, like I said before, when I work with people I like to get to know them first because you are going to be with them intensively for months and months, and you will be seeing each other all the time. I like to work in a happy environment, an environment where you are comfortable to walk in there, like a family almost. Of course with the other stunt boys, I had known them and had always hung out with them because stunt boys always protect you and always tell you the little things you don't know about. At that time, Stanley had just joined the stunt group and he was very quiet and reserved. So I thought I had to break the ice too, so to speak, because I will have to work with him now for a few months in Taiwan. What happened was we were all in the dressing room. There was tons of people, you know people rushing around trying to get a scene done, people putting on make-up. I had to try on my wire outfit for an upcoming scene and Stanley was at the back testing the wire, you know pulling the strings to see if it would work and whether it was tight enough. Then (laughing), I though, "Here goes, this will break the ice," so I turned around to Stanley and said, "Hey you, stop pinching my a**." (Laughing) Stanley, literally, you see his jaw drop and his eyes popping out (laughing). He stood up and everyone around was looking at Stanley and it was all quiet because I was very serious when I said it... Normally I am very happy, but this time I was serious, so everyone believed me when I said this to Stanley (laughing). Ah, poor Stanley, he was very embarrassed and said, "I didn't do anything"... Then Tung Wai the choreographer came over and said... "Okay, I will look after the wire," and then I just cracked up laughing, and then everyone else around started laughing too... Then Stanley started laughing, but you could tell that Stanley didn't really find it funny (laughing). Stanley is a nice guy, very quiet and funny...

SP: Yeah, I remember meeting Stanley on the set of Police Story 3, and I never would have realised he was the Director because everyone else was rushing around doing stuff and Stanley was just sitting there...

MY: Yeah, very serious guy.

SP: I sat down and Stanley said, "Alright?" and I

went, "Yeah," and he goes, "I'm the Director." *(Laughing)* Stanley is like a mass of walking scars, he's been there and done it all with the best of them.

MY: Yeah, he's a very tough guy.

SP: *Right, your last film for D & B, Easy Money, was a complete change of pace wasn't it?*

MY: That was like my bonus... It was kind of like a paid vacation if you like, really.

SP: *Was it your idea to go in that direction, or was it D & B?*

MY: It was D & B's idea. They wanted to branch out with more ideas for movies, not just martial arts action movies but different kinds of action movies. I think also Dickson Poon saw a James Bond movie at that time and he liked all the different locations used and all the crazy stunts. It was great for me because we filmed this movie in Switzerland, Greece, France, London, everywhere.

SP: *When it was released though, it kind of shocked most people because there was no fighting. It was more of a holiday postcard! (Laughing)*

MY: *(Laughing)* Yes, it was very picturesque and I drive a Ferrari. I liked it! *(Laughing)*

SP: *Was it a success when it was released in Hong Kong?*

MY: It did quite well, it wasn't a huge hit, it was just okay. But I think people were disappointed when they saw it because they expected a Michelle movie where I come in and beat the hell out of the bad guys.

SP: *After this movie you shocked a lot of people and broke a few hearts because not only did you announce that you were going to marry D & B boss Dickson Poon, but also that you were going to retire from filmmaking. There were a lot of rumours about your retirement, one such rumour was that you had to retire due to you being crippled on a stunt and not being able to walk.*

MY: Actually, I was quite badly hurt when I was filming *Magnificent Warriors* in Taiwan.

SP: *What happened there?*

MY: I was doing a scene and I ruptured an artery. It was kicked until it ruptured. It was hurt so bad, at one stage they thought I would never have any more feeling in that part of my body, just below my shin. I was limping for a long time too. Actually, that's what made me do *Easy Money* as well, to give me a break, a holiday. But the main reason why I wanted to retire was because once you're married you want to have a normal family

life. You can't have a normal life being in the movies. But it was a mutual agreement between me and Dickson.

SP: *When you retired and got married you were completely out of the public eye for about four years. What were you doing?*

MY: I was away for about three years and I was trying to fit into a new lifestyle of being married. You know, everything I was doing, it was completely the opposite of what I was doing before with my movie career. I had a husband who was very busy and spent a lot of time overseas, so I was in and out of Hong Kong all the time. So of course I was busy, but I had nothing really to latch onto. Also, I have always been very independent and hardworking, but I had nothing to do really.

SP: *You burst back onto the screen and into the limelight big time thanks to Jackie Chan, with Police Story 3: Supercop. So how did this all come about?*

MY: I had spent some time thinking that I wanted to come back into the movie industry, but because I had been away for so long... You know with the Hong Kong movie industry if you are gone for a while, you are totally forgotten about. It's not like anything else where you can do something and then come back a few years later and do it again. I am lucky though, because the Hong Kong audience, the Hong Kong reporters, the Hong Kong people have all been my encouragement. They have been my support, and I think if it wasn't for them I don't think I would have come back. I think also in life if you get an opportunity then you can either turn around and walk away from it or just take it in both hands and go for it and say, "Hey, what the hell!"

SP: *A few projects had been announced during your absence but never came about, and also a lot of people wanted to pitch projects to you but just didn't know where you were.*

MY: No one knew where to find me, I know. But I was always so touched by people's sincerity about wanting me to come back, and I think the clincher was Stanley Tong. I mean, even when I was married I still saw and spoke to Stanley and other people in the industry from time to time and I remember promising Stanley a long time ago that I would make a film with him if he ever became a Director. So Stanley approached me and told me that he had a big break and he was so excited. Of course I saw some of the movies he had directed and I was impressed with his technique and saw he had great potential.

He then told me he was going to be doing this big movie with Jackie Chan, and Golden Harvest were going to give him a good budget and an opportunity. And he really wanted me to be in this new movie with Jackie. Golden Harvest liked the idea of me being in this movie because it was good publicity because this was my first movie back from retirement. But I decided to do the movie because Stanley and me are good friends, this was the reason more than anything else.

SP: Were you nervous stepping back onto the screen in such a big way after a long break away?

MY: It was at the back of my mind constantly, you know, "You have to be better than before." so I agreed to do the movie and I met up with Raymond Chow and other people at Golden Harvest and they were all very sincere and kind. But also there was the thought that this movie was a "Jackie Chan Movie" and it would be a good, if not the best kind of movie to return onto the screen with. I mean Jackie is so established and very very famous in not just Hong Kong but all over Asia. So I though it was easily the best project I could do, because Jackie is the biggest star in Hong Kong movies and I was very grateful, and still am, to Jackie for that opportunity with *Police Story 3*.

SP: One thing I liked in Police Story 3 is how they build up to your character's first burst of action. First you are in the training camp and everyone thinks, "Hey, is she going to fight or not?" Then after a while everyone is thinking, "Perhaps she doesn't fight in this film!" Then suddenly there's the scene where Jackie and Yuen Wah are getting arrested and you burst out with all this impressive martial arts. Was it difficult getting back into the action with this film after being away from movies for those few years?

MY: Actually no. Because luckily when I was away I still kept quite fit. I mean I am a very sporty person, so I played tennis, and water skiing, going for a run, so I was very active still. But before we started the movie with Jackie, both Stanley and I agreed that we were going to have to train for this movie. Especially because it was a Jackie Chan movie. I mean Jackie is a crazy trainer, he works out so much before a movie, just like a professional boxer would train for a championship fight, you know. Before this movie Stanley got two of his guys to come in every day and train me for kicks and different things.

The difficult thing is, I think, that while I was away I lost that kind of tiger's eye, that's difficult getting that back. You can be all relaxed, then suddenly you are thrown back in front of the camera and are expected to have that special look. Quite tough, but I think I did okay.

SP: Yes, that was one thing I talked to Stanley Tong about. I asked him why you eclipsed people such as Moon Lee, and he said that you have that special look, and Moon Lee even when she is fighting is still kind of smiling, so although she is a great martial artist her face doesn't show it.

MY: She's so damn cute!

SP: Yes, but when she kicks it's not very believable with her facial expressions.

MY: Actually, when I see me on the screen, I get scared! (Laughing) Wow, look at my face, it's so damn aggressive. (Laughing)

SP: We all see in the outtakes of Police Story 3 that you fall off the front of Jackie's car and the scene with the bike. Were you injured during filming?

MY: You know, touch wood, I have always been very lucky. I don't know, maybe someone up there is looking out for me. I have always been lucky, I mean there have been so many times where I have fallen and could have been so badly hurt, but I have been okay. Of course I have been badly bruised but I have been able to get up and say, "Hey, can we do that shot again?" In that movie I think the biggest person who was worried was Jackie. He would come up to me sometimes and say, "You're not doing this stunt! It's crazy, it's too dangerous!" That scene when I was hanging on the front of the car, Jackie said, "You are not going on it! I have told Stanley that he doesn't need you in there, and you are doing it!" That scene was dangerous, because it wasn't just one car, you had to rely on another twenty cars in that scene. And a couple of times the van stopped too soon and I was flying all over the place.

SP: *When they show the outtake at the end of the movie, you hit the front of Jackie's car and fall off and another stuntman is grabbing for you to help you.*

MY: Yes, that was one of Jackie's stuntmen, Man-ching. [Best known as the Red Indian in *Rumble in the Bronx*, and longtime member of the Jackie Chan Stuntman's Club or Sing Gabon.]

SP: *When I spoke to Stanley about that scene he mentioned than Man-ching got hurt more than you in that scene.*

MY: Yes, he got hurt more than me. He was in the hospital. Poor guy.

SP: *How did you find filming and working with Jackie?*

MY: I enjoyed working with him. He's funny and we had some great laughs on location at the set. I mean we were all together in Kuala Lumpur for like two months. He's very easy to work with, and also very particular on things he wants for the movie. Sometimes he is angry and sometimes the opposite. He's just a normal guy who has a tremendous amount of success. He's a good friend.

SP: *I remember going to Golden Harvest on set for Drunken Master 2 and he was in such a bad mood. I looked at him and said, "Hi Jackie," and he just looked at me and said, "Fifteen years ago I make part one, fifteen years later on I make part two!" And he just sat there not talking at all (laughing). But he was under a lot of pressure for that movie.*

MY: (Laughing) Yes, of course, when it comes to filming Jackie is very serious and concentrates a lot. Everyone has good days and bad days.

SP: *Yes, and what was funny was that the next day we went back to the set and he was like, "Come here!" He wouldn't let me and my friend leave (laughing). He was like, "Oh no, you have to stay a little longer!" We were like, "No, sorry Jackie we really have to go now," and he said, "You don't like me?" We were like, "Course we do!" He said, "If you like me you would stay longer!" (Laughing)*

MY: (Laughing) Yes, that's Jackie! Of course, all of us have bad days and we just move away and deal with it on our own... but Jackie can't do that, because he is always with his crew and other people, so he's never really on his own, so of course when he's in a bad mood you see it. Jackie is always in the public eye and therefore always under pressure. But he handles it all very well. Very modest. I think a lot of people would not be so nice if they had his fame and success.

SP: *Of all your films so far, which is your favourite?*

MY: Oh, that's very difficult. You know every time you make a movie a major part of you goes into that movie. I have good memories of most of the movies I have done. I think I will have to say that all my movies are my favourites because I spent so much time and effort on them all.

SP: *Do you have anything to say to the Western fans?*

MY: Keep on supporting us in Hong Kong. Watch this space, we are going to be coming out with a lot more better movies. I think the most important thing is that we hope to bridge that gap between the East and West and make movies together and work together.

Promotional shot for *Supercop*

THUNDERBOLT

Matthew Edwards explores the 1995 Jackie Chan car racing action movie

Initially conceived as a small-time production about auto racing that showcased two of Jackie's loves, cars and filmmaking, Thunderbolt *soon ballooned into the most expensive Hong Kong picture ever, at a cost of HK$160 million.*

Buoyed on by the critical and phenomenal success of Rumble in the Bronx *in Asia, the film found strong backing from Mitsubishi and Kirin who, once they got wind of the concept, saw this as an outstanding marketing opportunity and funded heavily into the project. This is exemplified by the amount of vehicles Mitsubishi and Kirin allowed Jackie to destroy or maim in his pursuit of entertainment.*

Intended as a Hong Kong version of Tom Cruise's Days of Thunder, *this is a film that shows more enthusiasm and inventiveness than its Hollywood counterpart. The film had a lengthy and problematic shoot, and by the time filming finished boasted no fewer than five directors. Gordon Chan, Sammo Hung and Yuen Kwai were credited with handling the action set-pieces, whilst Frankie Chan was the architect in realising the film's numerous racing sequences, and finally our man Jackie oversaw the whole production.*

With Thunderbolt's *release date looming, the film was rushed through production, thus the film suffered slightly from weakened editing and continuity. Likewise, the film's flat and thinly conceived plotline made the film at times illogical. The overall tone of the film is also more violent and grittier, more akin to* Crime Story *than, for example,* Armour of God, *and as this is the case, some fans may be put off because the action is more visceral and bloody.*

INCREDIBLE GIFT

Jackie plays a car mechanic (oddly enough also called Jackie!) who has the incredible gift of being able to hear the most minor of repair requirements on vehicles. Working in tandem with the police he also helps find illegally modified vehicles. The film opens with Jackie studying at a Japanese Mitsubishi driving school, whereupon we learn he has just graduated. After assisting a young lady in finding her lost earring, and almost breaking his hand when the young lady accidentally slams the door on it, we are suddenly propelled to the dusty sands of Salt Lake in the USA.

Here we are introduced to Cougar, a big time gun smuggler and money launderer with a penchant for racing. Amidst a blanket of chalky dust, Cougar pulls up in his rally car after a practice run. Greeted by an entourage of henchmen, Cougar invites one of his informers for a ride, where he duly uncovers the informer as an undercover police officer, Lt. Victor. Strapped with rope around his hands and tied to the back of Cougar's sports car, Cougar then cruelly drives off at full pelt with Lt. Victor's body in tow.

Next we switch to LA where Cougar has set up one of his shady deals outside the dead lieutenant's police headquarters. Laughing about the insidious deed, Cougar announces that he is off to Hong Kong to do some racing.

WRECKED CARS

Working in an unsophisticated body shop with stacks of clapped out and wrecked cars, Jackie and his crew are hassled by some arrogant punter who wants Jackie to illegally modify his car with a giant exhaust. Declining, the disbelieving punter storms off in his fluorescent yellow sports car. At this point Jackie's two younger sisters (played by Daisy Wu and Man Chung Man respectively) return from school. Stepping out of a small store, both girls are subjected to harassment and intimidation from two seedy louts. When one smacks one of the girls on the bottom, Jackie returns to exact revenge, demanding an apology. One lout makes a move for Jackie, whereby Jackie grabs his hand and smacks him around the head. His colleague makes a move for a stool but Jackie deals a deft blow to his head before spinning and sending a catapult kick into the guy's midriff, and he is sent sprawling into a small table draped in a red and white checkered cloth.

By now the other lout makes a quick dash at Jackie but he quickly extinguishes his feeble attempt by sending him into a stack of empty coke crates. Momentarily the lout picks up an empty coke bottle but thinks better of it when Jackie approaches with a spade. Threatening the pair with the spade, Jackie demands to know which one touched his sister. Weeping pathetically, one of the creeps owns up. Jackie threatens to break both the lout's hands but ultimately repents, instead giving them both a stern warning before leaving. At this point two police motorcyclists arrive and notify Jackie of an operation in the city to flush out illegally modified vehicles, whereby Jackie agrees to assist the police.

DARK NEON STREETS

On the dark neon streets of Hong Kong a huge police presence is in operation, with countless officers manning roadblocks and pulling in random vehicles. A quick cut suggests Cougar has hit the streets, as his vehicle is seen speeding down Hong Kong's inner winding streets, causing havoc as two cars career into each other.

Arriving at the scene is young wannabe reporter Ms. Yip (played by Anita Yuen) looking for the next big scoop. Following her around is her nerdish cameraman, who seems more interested in filming the attractive female police officers.

At this point Jackie's genius father Uncle Tung (played by Chor Yuen) arrives in a pickup truck to inspect the numerous vehicles the police have pulled in. Wandering down what seems like a car showroom (anyone with an appreciation of fast, bright and elegant sports cars will love this film), Uncle Tung pinpoints all the vehicles' illegal modifications with the merest of glances and orders them to be taken away.

While the cars are being inspected, Cougar's car comes racing down the road, and flashes past the police roadblock. With Jackie and the reporter looking on, the police quickly give chase and they all disappear out of sight. Toying with the police, Cougar suddenly reappears heading back towards the roadblock. A lone police motorcyclist is ordered to block the road to prevent Cougar from passing. Realising the danger, as Cougar shows no sign of slowing, Jackie dives towards the officer, dragging him off his bike and out of the path of the oncoming car

SLOW MOTION

This scene is played out in slow motion, as we witness Cougar ramming into the motorcycle. From a camera positioned inside Cougar's vehicle we witness the officer crash into the nearside left windscreen, shattering the glass. As Cougar speeds off with the police in hot pursuit, both Jackie and the officer roll along the ground, whereby their colleagues come to their aid. However Cougar escapes when the pursuing police car takes a sharp bend too quickly and then flips over in a marvellous fashion. Along with Jackie, Uncle Tung and the police we all give off an almighty groan!

After a police briefing on our "mad as a lorry" villain Cougar, given by hard as nails Inspector Steve Cannon (played by Michael Wong), and a brief scene showing Jackie at home with his family, we are again back on the streets of Hong Kong in search of Cougar.

Seated inside their pickup truck, Jackie and Uncle Tung wait for developments. After Ms. Yip confronts Jackie for an interview by thrusting a camera in his face, Jackie tells them to clear off. Jackie and his father, on police instruction, are then told to pack up. Then as Uncle Tung pulls off, Ms. Yip's cameraman cuts across Uncle Tung's path, much to his disgust. Ironically, further up the road Ms. Yip's vehicle breaks down, so Jackie stops to give the vehicle the once over to establish the fault, whilst Uncle Tung berates the cameraman for his reckless driving.

Sat in the luxurious soft black leather seat of Ms Yip's car, Jackie nervously starts the reporter's car up again, all under the watchful gaze of Ms. Yip who is sat in the passenger seat (she's got a thing for our Jackie!). At this point, just as Jackie revs up the vehicle's motor, Cougar flashes past in his black metallic sports car. Without warning, Jackie gives chase, with Ms. Yip as a terrified passenger.

HEART-PUMPING CHASE

What then erupts against the backdrop of Hong Kong's splendid skyscrapers and long weaving freeways is a heart-pumping chase scene that recalls the grandeur of computer and arcade simulations. The endless rows of lampposts shining streams of light and dark onto Hong Kong's concrete jungle and the city's eerie fuzz of distant streaky neon as the cars whizz by also help convey this feeling.

Twisting and turning in a stark silver sports car, Jackie hounds Cougar, ready to stifle his panther-black vehicle. As the chase intensifies, Jackie dodges (and hits) numerous roadworks and canisters, slamming his foot on the brake before again hitting the accelerator. Ms. Yip meanwhile looks petrified as she tries to inform the police of Cougar's position via her mobile phone.

Without warning Cougar's vehicle comes to a grinding stop. Unwinding his window, he smiles at Jackie. In a tranquil and almost surreal moment a dove lands parallel to the vehicles. Then like a starter's pistol, the dove rises and the race resumes.

This time round Cougar means business. He rams Jackie's vehicle up an embankment, scraping his offside as sparks cartwheel around the vehicle. After regaining control, Jackie is then shunted from behind and sent flying over the embankment into oncoming traffic, where he has to dodge two 7.5 ton rigid lorries with a feat of skillful manoeuvring. Payback time ensues as Jackie returns the compliment by slamming into the back of Cougar's vehicle, throwing him forward in his seat before his vehicle is amazingly sent flying over a cordoned off area of roadworks and then bounces back onto the freeway.

The police by now have set up stinger nets to puncture Cougar's tyres, but in order for Jackie to reach his compatriots he first does a 180 degree turn, and with the sound of screeching rubber on tarmac he heads off in the opposite direction. Cougar oddly follows, and again rams Jackie's vehicle in the rear, caving in the bodywork before Cougar is at last trapped when he is sent spinning into police stingers and is arrested at gun point.

However, Cougar is soon released when his passport states he is not Cougar, and Jackie cannot identify Cougar as the driver that hit and nearly killed the police motorcyclist, as it was the car, not the driver, that was seen.

Cougar then informs Jackie that he wants to race him. Jackie retorts that he is not interested but instead is committed to putting Cougar behind bars. To make matters worse for Jackie, when he returns home he finds reporter Ms. Yip with his sisters, going through pictures of him as a nipper! Shying away from the publicity, Jackie declines to be interviewed about saving the policeman and helping to catch Cougar, and Ms. Yip scuttles off to speak more to the sisters.

Next up, Cougar's henchmen arrive at Jackie's workshop, where they attempt to bribe him to keep quiet about Cougar. Intimidating Jackie by roughing up his co-workers, they wave a bundle of notes in Jackie's direction. In a flash of brilliance, Jackie kicks the money out of the thug's hands before scissor kicking him amidst a shower of notes.

What happens next is familiar Jackie style action, with all those clever moves we have become accustomed to over the years. Using bars and poles to execute his fights, Jackie once again bounces and glides across the screen delivering brutal blows and stunning spinning kicks to disable his enemies. In one great moment, Jackie jumps from a bar onto a hanging lampshade before swinging onto the opposite staircase. Once at the bottom, one of the henchmen makes a descent down the steps with a flying kick. However Jackie unleashes a thunderbolt kick to send him crashing down to the ground. In another great scene, he sends another henchman over his shoulder onto the glass roof below, shattering it.

SURROUNDED

Trapped on the bottom floor, Jackie is surrounded. However, within two jaw dropping minutes Jackie has disposed of all his aggressors in a wonderful feat of martial arts that is both bruising and electrifying. Using headlocks, cracking kicks to his opponents' heads, scissor kicks and volleys, each henchman is sent crashing inside the workshop's spraying room, where he duly covers them all in yellow paint! Coughing and wheezing, they all leave. As for the viewer, well you just sit there gob-smacked and try to comprehend what you have just witnessed!

After this, Jackie testifies against Cougar, landing him therefore into police custody. However, this does not last long as Cougar's lawyer has other plans. What then transpires is a bloody and explosive jailbreak. Two guards are cruelly shot dead at close range. Inside the cell, Cougar's lawyer uses Semtex to blow open the jail door. Using Uzis and explosives they storm out of the building, escaping in a black van.

This well choreographed sequence is somewhat of a departure from usual Jackie films, as it contains some graphically violent Hong Kong action. Several henchmen and police officers are shot in the head and chest, whilst simultaneously jetting out rivers of crimson blood. The police station becomes a blood soaked battleground as both factions lay siege against the other, diving for cover under upturned desks or crashing through plate glass windows. Inspector Cannon at one point in the intense shootout shoots dead Cougar's lover/lawyer, thus prompting Cougar to sling a grenade towards him that by sheer luck he and his partner only just avoid.

Revenge for Cougar is swift. As dusk falls over Hong Kong, Cougar and his henchmen arrive at the car yard, attaching giant hooks from a nearby crane to Jackie's two storey pre-fab building. Toying with Jackie, Cougar lifts up Jackie's accommodation and decides to spin it around his neighbours and into the stacks of derelict cars as his helpless family look on horrified. Flying out of his door and holding on for dear life, Jackie is sent crashing around like a rag doll in the wind, where at times he is left hanging suspended above the ground.

GREAT STUNT

At one point Cougar tips the building up vertically, and we see Jackie fall in slow motion from one end to the other with his bed and personal items. By now Jackie is covered with deep purple bruising and blood from the shards of glass sprayed along the building's interiors.

Meanwhile Jackie's two sisters are not fairing too well either, as they are also sent flying through windows, onto chairs and left hanging from ledges, saved only by Uncle Tung grabbing their feet!

Cougar then sends the building at the rest of the family home, and in a great stunt Jackie, perched on a ledge, then jumps from his building into the family home, where he pulls himself through a metal bar before coming to the rescue of his sisters.

By now Cougar has ripped Jackie's home to shreds, as finally he lifts the building high above their home's glass roof before releasing the pre-fab building to fall onto Jackie and his family below. In a great shot we see Jackie and his sisters dive for cover as the building crashes through the roof and down to the ground in a downpour of crystallised glass. And then Cougar appears, kidnapping Jackie's sisters and blackmailing Jackie to race him in Japan. With no option, Jackie is forced to comply. Uncle Tung is taken to hospital where he sadly dies in what is the climax of a truly exhilarating and excellently choreographed action sequence.

After upsetting Ms. Yip before an emotional reconciliation, Jackie and his crew set about building a race car capable of beating Cougar. He then gives the car a brief practice spin on the streets of Hong Kong (with police co-operation), where he also manages to smash into the rear of the Ambassador's car. Then it's off to Sandai Hi-Land racecourse in Japan for the showdown with Cougar.

Whilst Jackie is speeding around on a practice run, Ms. Yip spots some of Cougar's henchmen and follows them. Riding on a small moped, she discovers their hideout is situated in a candy coloured pachinko arcade. Ms. Yip promptly calls Jackie, and he rushes over, set upon finding his sisters.

PSYCHEDELIC

Wandering through a vast array of cyber, psychedelic and techno colours, Jackie enters a small tranquil spa, decorated with antique Japanese artifacts. Ken Sawada, Ken Low and a whole bevy of Yakuza fighters suddenly appear and surround Jackie. To make matters worse, a scantily clad group of tattooed heavies also appear from the spa, and both groups in tandem move in to attack Jackie. What then erupts is one of the most awesome and brilliantly choreographed martial arts set pieces to have ever been conjured up.

Headbutting three fighters, Jackie quickly escapes from the spa and begins smashing up the array of gambling machines with a novelty pink hammer. Armed with stools, Ken and the others attack but are immediately sent crashing into various machines. Incorporating many stylish manoeuvres, including an awesome backward summersault that slams into two unfortunate Yakuza heads, Jackie beats off his attackers with every conceivable method.

Heads smash through glass, while other bad guys meet the full brunt of Jackie's fist, kick or swipes with the hammer. Suddenly the two Kens become involved, and they end up battling on top of the arcade with the magnificent Ken Low delivering some of his trademark pulsating kicks with his spider-like legs, before he is ultimately sent crashing into the arcade machines below with the rest of his fighters. What makes this scene more incredible is the remarkable stunts that unfold right in front of our eyes, and it's a wonder that none of the performers were killed while executing these stunts in order to satisfy Mr. Chan's vision.

TATTOOED HEAVIES

After Low and Sawada double up against Jackie and he clothes-lines Ken Sawada, Jackie is then attacked by knife wielding tattooed heavies. After unleashing brutal blows, numerous kicks and over the shoulder slam-dunks onto the hard marble floor, Jackie then proceeds to tie up the tattoo brigade with a white bandana.

This action set-piece was filmed in the smudge motion look and is clearly influenced by Wong Kar-wai's seminal 1995 Hong Kong arthouse film *Chungking Express* (every true Hong Kong film fan should be made to watch this film!). It certainly conveys a new sense of dimension and

surrealism to a Jackie Chan fight scene, and though so many have failed in copying Wong Kar-wai, this scene certainly succeeds.

After enduring what seems to be a very uncomfortable bear hug, Jackie heads upwards, and ends up fighting on huge multicoloured tarpaulins (reminiscent of the rubbish sun loungers your parents may have had back in the early eighties) that are suspended from the ceiling. After bouncing around still intent on kicking the living daylights out of one another, Jackie, Ken Low and Ken Sawada bring down an advertising hoarding and send millions of silver pachinko ball-bearings pelting across the screen and swamping the floor below the three fighters. Emerging from a sea of ball-bearings, Jackie is confronted by Cougar, who oddly frees one of Jackie's sisters before declaring he will see him at the race tomorrow. How jolly dee of the man!

SHOWMANSHIP

The real key to the scene is the extraordinary feats of showmanship and acrobatics from all the participants. The use of richly coloured arcade machines incorporated into the fight scenes works well, especially when used as springboards to escape oncoming attackers or unleash a scissor kick. It's also great to see the whole of Jackie's stunt team up against Jackie, making this perhaps the film's highlight.

Next up is the big race. Whilst on a practice lap, Jackie's car decides to blow up, whereby a frustrated Jackie escapes from the flaming car, and whilst still on fire, grabs a fire extinguisher and rushes back to try to save his car. With no car, the race is surely lost, but then the

girl from the beginning of the film (the one who lost her earring) turns up, and rather generously gives him two new Mitsubishi cars and rescues our disheartened Jackie! Confused? Well so was I, but who cares about motivation, and we get to see Jackie strap up ready for his grudge match with Cougar.

Formula 1 fans will "lap up" the final scenes as we see Jackie whizzing around the track, whilst his other competitors seem intent not on racing, but on crashing into walls or each other! I can't remember this many crashes or car explosions in Formula 1 last time I watched it! There's even pit stops (timed of course), and mini shots of Jackie as he waits for the all clear. Ms. Yip does her best, but unknowingly hampers Jackie when she causes him to be penalised for ten seconds, and later she holds up a sign saying "I Love You", whereby Jackie almost crashes!

PURSUIT

Dirt flies, cars crash and Jackie and Cougar weave their way around the course in pursuit of each other. However, they both end up stuck in the gravel trap. As the minutes pass (and the viewer wonders where the third place vehicle has got to), Cougar's vehicle breaks free and heads towards the checkered flag. In one last wheel spinning effort, Jackie spins his vehicle, becomes free of the gravel, and remarkably crosses the line simultaneously with Cougar. Or so you would think, but on the action replay we see Jackie has actually crossed the line about a foot ahead of Cougar, thus winning the race and the challenge, and saving his sister's life.

However, for the jubilant Jackie the race is far from over as Cougar breaks his deal and tries to escape. Hot on his tail, Jackie is determined to nail his man. After more ramming, and more aggression from Cougar than a road rage nutter, Cougar finally succumbs when his vehicle is hit up the rear and he is sent flying through mid-air, before rolling to a standstill. This all comes after a great stunt where Jackie's vehicle is sent hurtling through a lookout tower, before debunking again on the ground. We are treated to numerous angles of this stunt, and see two of the guards dive for their lives as the car rips through the tower, before landing on a stack of tyres.

REUNITED

Whilst this has all been going on, the police rescued Jackie's sister from the clutches of Cougar's henchmen just before they killed her, so the family is finally reunited, and Ms. Yip gets in on the hugging action (so Jackie was playing hard to get after all!), then it's time for outtakes as the credits roll.

Despite the lack of an end fight sequence, Thorston Nickel's rather bland turn as arch villain Cougar, and not to mention the at times rather stagnant and repetitive final race scenes, the film itself is still a valuable addition to Jackie's repertoire of work. The fact that the film is somewhat diverse adds something extra to the production. The action scenes between Cougar and Jackie, especially in Hong Kong, are both gritty, and beautifully and skillfully staged. The pachinko parlour is also a truly remarkable moment. *Thunderbolt* is a perfect Friday night movie, and it's also great to see Jackie explore alternative avenues. It also demonstrates he doesn't have to only use his fists to conjure up exciting, fast paced action sequences. Let's just hope that Jackie doesn't drive like that for real in Hong Kong, or we're all in trouble!!

Jackie and his stunt team pose on the set of *Thunderbolt*

KEN SAWADA

by Mike Leeder

Japanese action actor Ken Sawada made his international debut in the big budget but sadly disappointing Jean-Claude Van Damme release *Street Fighter*. But followed it up with a flashy kickfighting role in Jackie Chan's *Thunderbolt*. He then played an honourable Japanese kickboxing champion doing battle with singer Aaron Kwok in *Somebody Up There Likes Me*. I caught up with Ken in between shots on the new Bruce Law movie being produced by Jackie Chan's Golden Way Films: *Project B/Extreme Crisis*, for the briefest skipchat.

Screen Power: Sawada-San, can I start off by asking you for some background details, where you grew up and how you got involved with the martial arts?

Ken Sawada: I'm Japanese, I grew up in Japan (laughing)! My first introduction to martial arts was when I was very young and I saw a Bruce Lee movie. I thought, "Whoa! I want to be able to do stuff like that!" So I started training in Japanese Shaolin Temple Kung-fu when I was 11 years old. I attained a fourth degree black belt before changing styles when I was 20. I like Shaolin Kung-fu, but it's more of a defensive art and at the time I was being a wild boy getting into fights almost every day (laughing). So I thought I should learn something that was a bit more aggressive, so I took up kickboxing. Now my style is very much a mixture of different arts and bits and pieces that I've picked up here and there, but nowadays I only like to fight on screen.

SP: How did you first get involved with action movie making?

KS: After I graduated from university when I was 23, I had the opportunity to begin an acting career on Japanese television. I worked on a lot of dramatic shows, but had very little chance to do any action and this disappointed me very much, because I wanted to fight on screen. Then I had the great opportunity of meeting Jackie Chan when he came to Japan to do some promotion for one of his movies. I was very happy and honoured just to have the chance to meet him, but he said to me, "One day, we should work together!" He really said this to me. Of course I was very excited and this inspired me to train harder. About this time I began to think that maybe if there wasn't much chance for me in Japan, maybe I should think about going to another country to follow my dreams. So in addition to my training, I started working at improving my English, because I thought maybe one day I would try to go to Hollywood (laughing) - and about five years ago I heard that an American company was going to turn the Japanese video game *Street Fighter* into a big Hollywood movie. I knew the game characters were of different nationalities and this made me think it might be a good chance for me. I flew to LA, with no appointments or introductions, and I went to the production offices and started knocking on doors. "Hello, I'm a Japanese actor, I speak English, I can fight! Please can you give me a

Ken (left) with fellow *Thunderbolt* co-stars, including Jackie Chan and Ken Low

job!"(Laughing) I think they all thought I was crazy, and at first nobody would open the door, but I kept coming back and eventually I was rewarded with a supporting non-fighting role alongside Jean-Claude Van Damme in *Street Fighter*. It was a very big production, and I had the great opportunity of meeting with Benny 'The Jet' Urquidez during the making of the film.

SP: After your non-fighting role in Street Fighter, you made quite an impact as the high kicking Yakuza boss taking on Jackie Chan in Thunderbolt. How did you feel getting to finally work with and do battle with Jackie?

KS: It was one of the most incredible and hardest experiences of my life! We were shooting the big Pachinko parlour fight in the middle of a really hot, really humid Hong Kong summer. The studio had no air-condition, it was an effort just to stand or sit around the set without melting (laughing) - and we were fighting! It was crazy, the whole Panchinko scene lasts about ten minutes in the finished film but we were shooting for about a month. The schedule for the whole film was rush, rush, rush. Jackie was running from set to set to set. He'd come in, film part of the fight scene with us, and then go off to film something else on another location, then come back and film some more with us. Working with Jackie was very demanding, and Sammo Hung was the supervising action director for this scene - he was very demanding. They worked everybody very hard to get the scene done the best they could. I like the finished scene, it's exciting, but it was very hard to shoot and I don't like thinking about it!

SP: You're currently filming the new Golden Way actioner, Project B/Extreme Crisis for another

Thunderbolt co-Director, Bruce Law, who's making his full directorial debut on this film. It's a big production with some incredible set pieces. Chua Lam showed me some footage this morning in his office and it looks incredible. Tell us about the film and the role you play?

KS: I play a Japanese policeman trying to track down a Japanese religious cult that has come to Hong Kong. The cult are terrorists like the ones who tried to poison people on the Japanese subway a few years ago. They come to Hong Kong demanding the release of their leader and plan to attack Hong Kong with poison gas if he is not released. I team up with a Hong Kong policeman, Julian Cheng [Media Asia's *Theft Under The Sun*, *G-4*], to track them down and there's plenty of action! (Laughing) I think you'll like it! Bruce Law has a very interesting style, and his action is big and interesting. We've had a lot of visitors to the set while we've been filming. It's very wild, the police come, the fire brigade, ambulances. It's wild and I like that!

SP: What's next for Ken Sawada?

KS: I'm developing some ideas of my own. I want to try to do something that isn't Japanese style or Hong Kong style, my own style (laughing). I'm writing a script now and I hope people like it. Keep watching.

And with those parting words, Ken Sawada was called back to return to action on the set of Project B/Extreme Crisis. Thanks to Chua Lam at Golden Harvest for inviting Harold Weldon, Michael Miller and me to the location. Thanks to Bruce Law for allowing our intrusion. And special thanks to Ken Sawada for taking the time to talk to me, and for remembering me when he ran into me in the supermarket a couple of weeks later!

THE 36 CRAZY FISTS

Chan Teams With Brothers Of Legendary Stars

By Albert Valentin

In 1979, Jackie Chan was asked to become the fight choreographer for a film that was going to be directed by his good friend Chen Chi-hwa. The film would be titled *The 36 Crazy Fists*. The film is not only known because of Jackie Chan's Kung-fu work on the film, but also because the two major stars of the film are the real-life brothers of two legendary Hong Kong filmmakers.

LEGACY

The stars of *The 36 Crazy Fists* are the brothers of two 70s icons in Hong Kong cinema. Tony Leung Siu-hung, who used the pseudonym "Hsiung Kuang", is the real-life brother of Bruce Liang Siu-lung, and Jimmy Liu Chia-yung is the little brother of legendary filmmaker Liu Chia-liang.

Tony Leung would go on to star and appear in films such as *Five Superfighters* for the Shaw Brothers (where he really got to show off his awesome kicking prowess) and *Duel of the Seven Tigers* for Goldig before becoming a successful action choreographer and film Director. He would also become the chairman for the Hong Kong Stuntman's Association in the 90s. Some of his best work can be seen in two American films, *Superfights* and *Bloodmoon*. Jimmy Liu would make an appearance in what many say is Jackie's best film, *Drunken Master II*, and the horrible sequel *Drunken Master III*.

MINI-DOCUMENTARY

In 1981, independent distributor 21st Century Film - who would distribute Chan's earlier work, *The Master With Cracked Fingers*, as *Snake Fist Fighter* - used a mini-documentary to start the film out, with Chan showing his techniques to stars Tony Leung Siu-hung and Jimmy Liu for the opening sequences of the film, which would have the two stars duking it out for the fans. The shocking thing about the mini-documentary is that Chan is seen with a cigarette in his mouth! Chan admitted that he smoked during his days as a stuntman and he has dropped the habit. Many international prints contain the Chan footage.

POOR WONG

The film begins with two Shaolin monks, Fung and Li, going through a town full of merchants. They see a young man (Tony Leung Siu-hung) getting beaten up by a group of gangsters. Despite warnings from their master not to get involved, they can't see the youngster get

beaten up, so they help out by fighting off the gangsters. They take the youngster to his house, where they are introduced to the youngster's sister. She tells the monks that her name is Wong Fei-ying and the man she helped was her brother, Wong Tai-kwong. She says the reason why Wong was beaten up was because he was trying to avenge his father's death.

A flashback is shown of Mr. Wong arguing with the gangsters and being brutally beaten as a result, later dying in bed, with Fei-ying witnessing his death. Fung suggests that Tai-kwong should learn Kung-fu as a way to be able to defend himself and fight the gangsters. Tai-kwong agrees to learn Kung-fu, so the monks take Tai-kwong to Shaolin.

REJECTION AND APPROVAL

When they reach the Shaolin temple, the Abbot refuses to have Tai-kwong learn Kung-fu from the temple because the monks brought Tai-kwong in without permission and the Abbot feels Tai-kwong isn't strong enough to learn. The monks think of someone who can train Tai-kwong. They turn to a former Shaolin student named Master Li (Ku Feng).

Master Li has Tai-kwong do chores first. This will remind you of another Chan film. Can you say *Snake in the Eagle's Shadow*? One day, on his way to get water at the river, he is tripped up by an old beggar (Wang Suen Suen). An angry Tai-kwong tells the beggar he knows Kung-fu and can beat him up. The beggar responds by just laughing at him and tells him that he sees the Shaolin students and that he has no skills at all. An angry Tai-kwong walks away and goes back to the school. He tells Master Li that he has to learn Kung-fu. Master Li finally accepts.

FIRST LESSONS

Tai-kwong is finally enrolled in the school and Master Li has Tai-kwong fight him. Tai-kwong is afraid but is obliged to do so. Sadly, Tai-kwong is defeated by Master Li, who shows Tai-kwong the Kung Tse Fist. At the river, Tai-kwong washes his shirt and he finds the beggar again. This time, an angry Tai-kwong begins to attack the beggar who dodges every attack. When Tai-kwong asks if he was afraid, the beggar says he is bored. After a short fight, Tai-kwong is beaten by the beggar as the result of the beggar using his stick to make the youngster look like a dog urinating.

Tai-kwong complains that the beggar used his stick. So, as a result, the beggar gives Tai-kwong the stick. As Tai-kwong begins to swing the stick towards the beggar, the beggar dodges the stick, using acrobatics like the good ol' days of Sam the Seed in *Drunken Master*. After losing again, Tai-kwong realizes he can use the techniques that the beggar used as a way of learning.

REMATCH

With his newfound skills, the young Tai-kwong goes back to the school and challenges Master Li in a rematch. When Tai-kwong gets the first shot in, the students look shocked, as does Master Li. Master Li and Tai-kwong engage in some hand-to-hand combat as Tai-kwong uses his skills to make Master Li look like a dog urinating. Embarrassed, Master Li gets up and finds a way to defeat Tai-kwong. Li asks Tai-kwong where he learned his Kung-fu. Tai-kwong says he learned it on his own. In disbelief, Master Li leaves Tai-kwong alone.

While fetching water, Tai-kwong runs into the beggar again. This time, instead of getting mad, he begins to show respect towards the beggar. After some convincing, the beggar decides to train Tai-kwong in Kung-fu. However, he must train with one man. That man is the beggar's number one student, Shin Ho-kung (Jimmy Liu). The spar between Tai-kwong and Ho-kung results in Tai-kwong getting totally annihilated, but Ho-kung says he will help train Tai-kwong in the 36 Deadly Fists. The beggar warns Tai-kwong that if he tells anyone that he is learning Kung-fu from him, he will never teach him again.

Back at the school, Master Li sees Tai-kwong sitting on the stairs. When Tai-kwong says he wants to leave the school, Master Li says he must fight him to leave. Using his skills the beggar taught him, he finally defeats Master Li. When Master Li asks where he learned the style, Tai-kwong keeps quiet. He has Tai-kwong fight a monk, in which if Tai-kwong defeats him, he will be free to go. The monk, who uses one arm to block and hit Tai-kwong,

defeats the youngster and the youngster is beaten by Master Li as a result.

ESCAPE AND REVENGE

Tai-kwong escapes and goes home to his sister. His sister is pleased to learn that her brother has learned a new form of Kung-fu. When she asks what style he has learned, he says it is a 37-form style. She is distraught because, she tells Tai-kwong, the gangsters are cheating people out of money.

An angry Tai-kwong proceeds to beat up gangsters in a casino, in the woods, and in an outdoor gambling place. One of the bosses, Master Nam, is infuriated and challenges Tai-kwong to a fight in town. When Tai-kwong accepts and meets Nam in town, Nam asks Tai-kwong where he learned Kung-fu. Tai-kwong keeps quiet and a fight ensues between Nam and Tai-kwong. In Chan fashion, the use of the tables as blockades and platforms are used in the fight as Nam begins to beat up Tai-kwong. A group of villagers tell the combatants that people must make a living, and they must stop destroying their businesses. Tai-kwong agrees and asks Nam to give him two weeks before they fight. Nam reluctantly agrees. Tai-kwong found this as an opportunity to train more because he was about to die.

HELP IS ON THE WAY

As a result of what happened, Tai-kwong tries to go to Master Li, but Master Li, angry that Tai-kwong has left, refuses to help him. In fast camera action that is meant to be comedic, Master Li is screaming at Tai-kwong who is tortured and leaves. As a result, Tai-kwong goes back to the monks, begging for their help. The monks suggest Master Li, but Tai-kwong said he already went to Master Li with no acceptance. The monks decide they are the key.

The monks teach Tai-kwong the Dragon Style of Kung-fu. It takes a few days, but combined with his kicking prowess, Tai-kwong is ready for his rematch with Nam. The two combatants fight atop a mountain. Nam's partner, played by Chan Liu, says that Tai-kwong will attend his own funeral. However, with his new skills in Dragon Fist, he is able to rip the shirt off of Nam and with his kicking skills, he is able to finally defeat Nam.

ATTEMPT AT REVENGE
Victorious from his battle with Nam, Tai-kwong goes into town with his sister. Tai-kwong finds Fung and Lee in town as well and the monks ask Tai-kwong whether he defeated Nam. Tai-kwong replies that he did, and at that moment a messenger arrives with a letter for Tai-kwong. It turns out that Nam's brother Lu Ying (former JC Stuntman Fung Hark-on) has challenged Tai-kwong and the fight must be a weapons match. This worries Tai-kwong as he has no idea how to use weapons.

In their first match, Lu Ying uses the chain whip and Tai-kwong uses the butterfly knives. Lu Ying repeatedly beats up Tai-kwong with the chain whip. Fearing he may get killed, the monks fake a sickness and Tai-kwong asks Lu Ying to have the rematch in three days. Lu Ying agrees. Fearing they may no longer be able to help Tai-kwong, the monks can only rely on one man, Master Li.

They trick a hooker into going to bed with a sleeping Master Li. As she gets into bed and takes off her top, Master Li wakes up and becomes really shocked. He gets out of the bed only to find the monks "catching" him in the act. Master is worried that his good name will be tarnished, so he asks the monks to keep quiet. In a little tale of blackmail, the monks agree to keep quiet if Master Li teaches Tai-kwong how to stop the chain whip master Lu Ying. Master Li tells Tai-kwong he must resort to tricks. During a training session, Master Li has Tai-kwong using the chain whip on him. After the training, Master Li shows Tai-kwong that he used some padding to prevent being cut. Knowing that this tactic may work, Tai-kwong has the rematch with Lu Ying. In the rematch, Lu Ying gets his hits in the fight, but it is Tai-kwong who uses Master Li's tactics to not only defeat Lu Ying, but also ultimately kill him. Despite the shock from the gangsters, as well as Tai-kwong, the monks are happy that justice has been done... or has it?

SHOWDOWN
Sitting at the dinner table, Tai-kwong, his sister, Master Li and the monks are celebrating Tai-kwong's victory over Lu Ying. A messenger arrives and gives Tai-kwong a challenge letter from the master of Lu Ying and Nam, Mao Do-tak (*Once Upon a Time in China*'s Yen Shi Kwan).

When Master Li hears the name, he is shocked and begins quietly praying. He tells Tai-kwong that Mao is the leader of the entire gang and that he has no chance of winning.

Upon training for the showdown, the beggar and Shin arrive to see Tai-kwong train with Master Li. They laugh at Master Li and the beggar finally confesses that he was the one who taught Tai-kwong his Kung-fu. The beggar challenges Master Li, and Master Li proceeds to begin fighting the beggar. After a few minutes, Shin takes over for his teacher and begins wailing on Master Li until Li realizes that he cannot beat the student. This is especially seen when the student performs the 36 Crazy Fists, which is a trick move that involves moving your arms in big circles, taunting and then proceeding to hit your opponent.

After a month of training, the showdown is on, as Tai-kwong comes face to face with Mao, who is assisted by Chan Liu. At first, Mao, who looks like your typical white-haired villain of the old chop socky genre, seems to be a phenomenal fighter. He gets Tai-kwong every chance he gets. When it seems that Tai-kwong is no match for Mao, enter Shin, who proceeds to take over for Tai-kwong before Tai-kwong joins in the fight. Chan Liu tries to jump in using a knife as he slashes Shin in the leg. A furious Tai-kwong proceeds to beat and kill Chan Liu with his own knife.

As Tai-kwong and Shin try to fight off Mao but to no use, the beggar tells them they must use the 36 Crazy Fists. The two begin circling the villain with their 36 Crazy Fists as they take turns dodging and hitting the villain. Then, as Mao is getting annihilated, the duo pulls off a spectacular move. They grab Mao by his head and legs as they kick underneath him, and when they drop Mao they perform one last stomping move before Mao falls dead.

The Abbot of Shaolin arrives and decides to take in Tai-kwong. Master Li still wonders why Tai-kwong's Kung-fu was excellent and learns that the beggar is the Abbot's older brother. Finally, with the chance to go to Shaolin, Tai-kwong jumps in happiness.

FINAL THOUGHT
Despite fans avoiding the film because it is not a Jackie Chan picture, the fights show some of that Chan-esque comedy that would be seen in his later and earlier work. The cast of fighters, from Tony Leung Siu-hung to Yen Shi-kwan were not good in acting, but their fighting skills made up for it. Ku Feng even provided some of the comedy that would be like Chan in films like *Young Master* and *Dragon Lord*. Despite what the cover says, Jackie did not direct the film. He was only the Kung-fu Director. Furthermore, he wasn't the star. Nevertheless, the film is still an enjoyable film to watch in my opinion, if you want to see some early work from Chan and his stars, Tony Leung Siu-hung and Jimmy Liu Chia-yung.

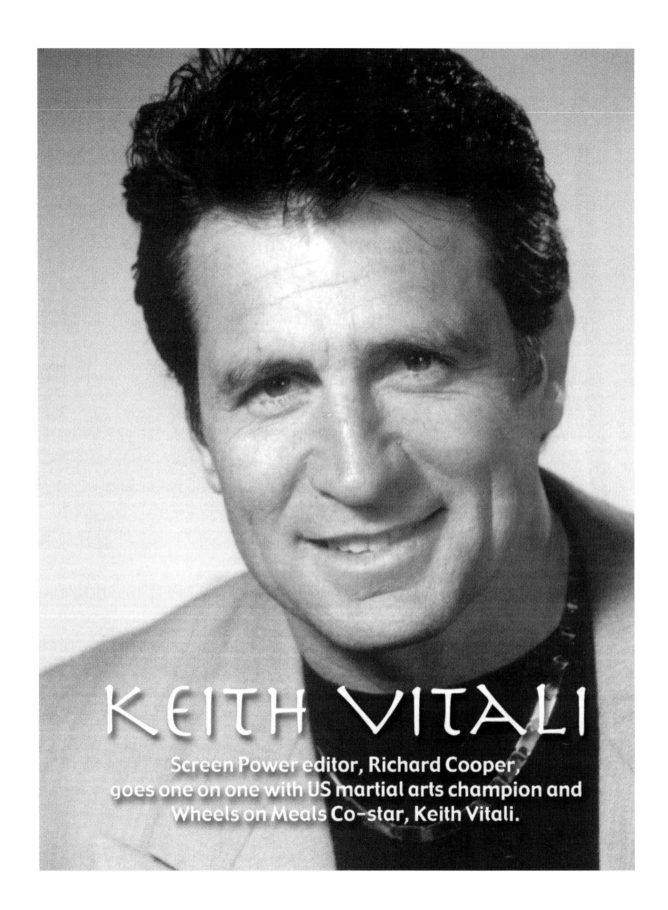

KEITH VITALI

Screen Power editor, Richard Cooper, goes one on one with US martial arts champion and Wheels on Meals Co-star, Keith Vitali.

Many moons ago (way before I had heard the name of Jackie Chan), when I was a young boy of ten or eleven, I can remember spending every Saturday morning in my local video rental shop. I loved martial arts movies even at that early age, and although most of the videos I wanted were for people over the age of eighteen, the old guy who owned the shop still allowed me to rent out the likes of *Revenge of the Ninja* starring Sho Kosugi and Keith Vitali (if you havent seen it, go rent a copy!).

I can honestly say that Keith Vitali was the one guy on film at that time who made me want to be able to spin kick people in the head! Hmm... that does seem a very long time ago considering that I am now a very young twenty-six year-old. Nevertheless, despite the fact that the old video shop has now disappeared, after all those years, my admiration for this US tournament bootmaster hasn't. It is my great pleasure to publish the following exclusive interview for all of you in everyone's favourite magazine...

Screen Power: *Keith, let me start off by asking you some background information. Where were you born and raised?*

Keith Vitali: I was born in Columbia, South Carolina, and at the age of three moved to Rome, Italy, where my father was stationed in the military. I lived in Italy for four years, began school there and moved back to Columbia at the age of seven.

This phase in my life in Rome had a tremendous impact on my future as a martial artist. As a child I actually played in the Coliseum in Rome and it was at that time in my life that I developed a love of adventure, travel and excitement. From my earliest memory as a child, I fantasized often that I was a Roman Gladiator pitted in fantastic death matches with thousands of Romans cheering me on in the Coliseum. Other kids dreamed of being Superman or a famous movie star, perhaps a famous athlete, but I was always Spartacus. Years later, I can remember many a tournament or full contact fight where my adrenaline was fueled by those same gladiator memories I had as a child.

SP: *What first attracted you to the martial arts, and when did you start your training?*

KV: In 1971, a friend of mine who had just begun studying Tae Kwon Do invited me to visit his class taught by his Korean instructor, John Roper, at the University of South Carolina. What I saw changed my life as I knew it. I walked into the class and was absolutely captivated. I watched two fighters sparring and what I saw was pure aesthetic aerial beauty combined with precision movements producing incredible power. What impressed me most was that a diminutive green belt student was displaying their prowess against a taller mightier adversary. That was the shining moment.

Immediately I was emotionally captured by the martial arts. Captured, because I fell in love and became, as many, obsessed with my training and infatuated with the arts. An example of this was the fact that I was attending another university at the time on a track scholarship (distance runner) and immediately dropped the scholarship and transferred to the University of South

Carolina (History Major) and entered the Karate program. It took my parents years to understand this, as you might expect (laughing).

SP: *Do you still teach martial arts in the USA?*

KV: I no longer teach in a dojo/studio, but continue to work out and teach seminars from time to time. I was recently invited by Chuck Norris to teach his 800 black belts at his convention in Las Vegas. It was a wonderful experience, especially since Chuck was one of the fighters I emulated while competing. I still enjoy teaching and training in the martial arts and I work out each day to stay in shape.

SP: *How did you get the part in Golden Harvest's 1984 movie, Wheels on Meals?*

KV: Pat Johnson, fight co-ordinator for movies such as *The Karate Kid* and *Batman*, recommended me for the part to Golden Harvest. I had worked with Pat on *Force Five* and he called me personally to give me a two day notice to take the part. Two days later, I was on a plane to Barcelona, Spain. At that time, I was the number one tournament fighter in the USA and Benny Urquidez was the number one full contact fighter and they needed us to play the villains in the film.

SP: *What was it like working with Jackie Chan?*

KV: It was a dream of a lifetime working with Jackie. I had just begun my movie career and had previously worked in films with talented martial artists such as Benny Urquidez, Joe Lewis and Richard Norton in *Force Five*, and Sho Kosugi in *Revenge of the Ninja*. But nothing quite prepared me for the experience of working with Jackie, Sammo and Yuen Biao though. It was a unique time for me, especially because Jackie was working on his English and spent a lot of time practicing by speaking with me. It was a wonderful time to be able to talk to Jackie on a daily basis and hear all about his life and dreams. He was very warm and open and I found that quite refreshing.

The first impression I got working with Jackie was that he was fearless in his approach to anything he attempted.

Jackie's personal safety seemed to take a back seat to creating the best scene possible at times. I remember one time filming at the castle in Barcelona the scene requiring Jackie and Sammo to enter the castle without the bad guys detecting them. Jackie asked me how I would film this scene. "How would they all enter the castle with walls at least 30 feet high?" he asked. I could only suggest, after looking at the wall, that it was impregnable and that they would have to figure a way to get in through the large front gates. Jackie smiled after hearing that he couldn't go over the wall and then produced a couple of short strong sticks about 4 feet long. Without the slightest hesitation Jackie ran towards the wall and up the wall (laughing). I can't tell you how high up the wall he ran. Running up the wall, he then placed the stick into one of the holes in the 1000 year old castle exterior. Next, he swung over the stick like a gymnast, stood on it and looked back at me smiling. To this day I don't know if he already had going up the wall planned that way or if it was just something he thought of at that moment. I was impressed regardless. He used that stunt in the film, going up to the top of the wall, and never used anything resembling a safety device. It was just second nature to him to try a stunt like this. One slip and it would have all been over but because he knew so well what he could do, he carried it off in the first take.

SP: *The Hong Kong martial arts or action choreography is totally different to the American choreography. Did you have any problems with Jackie and Sammo Hung's choreography?*

KV: Jackie and Sammo's style of choreography excited me on our first scene together. I love this story and this had an impact on every film I've worked on since. Jackie and I were going to do our first fight scene and the cameras were almost ready to roll and not the first word had been said to me about what the fight was going to look like. Normally the way we shoot fight scenes in America is that we rehearse over and over until we're ready to shoot.

Jackie could tell I was getting anxious about not knowing what we were going to do and then Jackie said he was ready to begin putting our fight scene together. Jackie said, "Keith, throw a few kicks for me." I threw a few moves, stopped, looked at him and said, "What next?"

Jackie looked at me and then began drumming out a beat on his thigh with his hands. It was as if he was playing the drum on his thigh. I asked him what he was doing and he replied, "First I create a beat, a rhythm in my head, and then apply our movements to the beat I create." He went on: "Keith, if you have the two best fighters in the world in a fight scene in a movie and there is no rhythm or beat to the movements, you will not like the fight. You will not even know why you don't like a fight, but it's because your subconscious mind has detected no rhythm. So I first create the beat and then when we fight, your subconscious will like it."

That was the most incredible information that I have ever received on fight scenes in movies and I still follow his philosophy in my films today.

As far as having problems with the choreography, it wasn't that tough for me because I loved the creative movements they were putting together. It's not that I didn't have trouble with their choreography at times, anyone would have, but I loved every minute of it and eventually pulled off every move they asked of me.

That was tough at times, especially when you are fighting multiple people at one time and one of them has a weapon. In one scene, I fought Sammo with his spear weapon (Kwan Dao) and Yuen Biao at the same time. It took two changes of clothes and about 30 takes (laughing). For example, I had to break Sammo's spear with a jump spinning hook kick in the middle of a complex fight with the both of them. I'm not sure which take it was, but on one take I missed the spear and caught Sammo squarely on his head with my jump spinning kick. He went out unconscious and none of us in the scene could move until we heard the command from the Director, "Cut", but Sammo was the Director. We all just stood there for almost 30 seconds, and when Sammo got back onto his feet, I knew I was fired. Instead Sammo hugged me and said, "Good power". Sammo loved techniques with power. He then began screaming at his stunt assistants in Chinese, and I can only guess that he was saying to them that if he can take it then he expects them to take it as well.

SP: *Did you shoot the movie entirely in Barcelona?*

KV: Yes, the entire movie was shot on different locations in and around Barcelona.

SP: *What was your opinion of Jackie as a martial artist when you were filming with him?*

KV: I had a two-fold opinion of Jackie as a martial artist. First, I recognised his skill at any movement he attempted. One phenomenal kick he pulled off in the film was in a fight scene with Benny. I wish I knew what the kick was called and how in the world he pulled it off. It's almost a cartwheel type of kick that is thrown with his back leg upside down. I've never seen this kick used in films before or since. Now, at this time I considered myself to be a Korean kicking specialist and soon to be voted the best kicking technician in the USA by my peers. I can't tell you how humbling an experience it was to see Jackie pull off kicks I could only dream of doing. Still to this day after working with so many of the greatest athletes in the world, I consider Jackie's sheer athletic ability the best worldwide.

On the other hand, Jackie as a martial arts fighter is another thing. Jackie never had the fight training in his career to ever consider jumping in the ring with Benny

Urquidez for example. It has been written about before that Benny and Jackie exchanged some tense words during one scene, and Jackie jokingly talked about putting on boxing gloves and going a few rounds with Benny. I was in the middle of that encounter (laughing) and I remember telling Jackie that the ring was a different world than the movies and he wanted nothing to do with Benny.

First of all, Benny wasn't even human at times! In one fight scene I remember Jackie was continuously hitting Benny with full force to his head. Each time Benny would smile and would reply to Sammo's concerns with a "No problem". All of the Chinese stuntmen couldn't believe how Benny could take those blows over and over. Even I would go to Benny and ask if he's alright and he would just laugh and say he was fine.

But overall, if Jackie had chosen the path of fighting in the ring instead of movies, he would have been one of the best. I was a world class runner, world class martial arts fighter, and played tennis, golf and baseball competitively. I considered myself a world class athlete until I met Jackie. Up until that time, I always considered

the martial artist who used to train with Bruce Lee, Mike Stone, the best athlete I had ever seen. Now Jackie has taken his place.

SP: Jackie's a very funny guy on set at times, so there must have been some funny happenings while you were making Wheels on Meals?

KV: There were some funny things that happened and some scary things as well. It didn't take too long for me to offend the entire crew with my sense of humor after only being in Barcelona for a short while. Benny and I were the only Americans on the set day-to-day and there were about fifty in all that made up the Chinese crew that were there. Being Italian in heritage and not liking Chinese food, I found myself surrounded by all fifty Chinese eating their Chinese soup after working long hours on the set. Maybe I was just tired, but when all of them began making more noise than I thought humanly possible, smacking as they ate, I showed my ass. I said something like this real loud to everyone: "Hey, for God's sake, close your damn mouths when you eat, you're driving me crazy." Of course, I thought they would all just laugh, but it was like I called each and every one of their

Keith (left) with *Wheels on Meals* co-stars:
Yuen Biao, Jackie Chan and Benny "The Jet" Urquidez

mothers a foul name (laughing). I made no friends that day I promise you. Jackie pulled me off to one side and explained that it was Chinese traditional custom to make as much noise as possible while eating as a compliment to the chef. Culture shock was what it was (laughing).

It only took two weeks to get back into their good graces! That wasn't easy, especially after what happened next. In my next fight scene I had to execute a running type of side kick and land it on Jackie's chest. Jackie had to be hit right before he landed on the ground after doing a jump spinning hook kick over Benny's head. This took incredible timing, but I loved this choreography and was pretty well known in my country for having a strong effective side kick. I also had the control with my right leg to control the impact, and when Sammo asked if everyone was ready, I was as confident as ever.

There was only one hitch. Jackie rehearsed one last time with Benny and said to me, "And before I land like this, hit me here (indicating high on his chest) with your side kick." "No problem" were my exact words. As we started to film, Sammo says, "Keith, change sides and use your left leg." Let me see; time the kick perfectly at a flying object (Jackie) and catch him at the exact spot on his chest with my left leg and of course not hurt him. (Laughing) Not in this lifetime, I was thinking.

I quietly and diplomatically pleaded with Sammo to allow me to use my right leg instead. Sammo assured me that it was non-negotiable and I had to do the kick with my left leg. Jackie could not put on any type of pad under his shirt for protection because he was wearing a sleeveless gym shirt.

There was additional pressure as well with all of the people on the set. There was a bus-load of Japanese fans brought in to view the filming for the day, not counting all of the Spanish bystanders and crew. There were over 300 people watching the scene, along with David Chan, the big producer from Golden Harvest.

So on the first take I hit my mark and Jackie goes flying backwards. I drop Jackie with a full force side kick and he's on the ground in total agony. All of the stuntmen are looking at me like I killed their best friend while they assist him in his pain, the spectators are close to attacking me at any moment and David Chan is yelling things at me in Chinese. I looked at Sammo and this is the honest truth, Sammo smiles and says, "More power" (laughing). On the next six takes, I drop Jackie each time as if I had killed him and each time Sammo repeats the command, "More power". On the final take I catch Jackie in the throat and I almost kill him. He was in incredible pain and I knew I was only minutes away from getting fired, but again they kept me on. Of course, that's the take they kept in the film, the one hitting him in his throat.

Sammo had an idea the same day all of this happened. He wanted to display my power with the side kick, so he had a Volkswagon bus brought over to the set. He then had a bed mattress set up on the inside of the bus against the back wall. In this next scene Sammo asked me to kick one of the stuntmen while they stood on the ground in front of the bus and see if I could propel him back into the bus against the mattress and make the bus shake.

"Make the bus shake," Sammo says. Now this was more like it. I hit the stuntman with my side kick and the next moment he hit the back of the bus and the bus shook like Sammo wanted. The stuntman was out cold and I knew that was the end of the scene and started to walk away. Sammo asked me where I was going, and I said, "The stuntman is out cold." Sammo laughed and said, "We have more Chinese." I'll never forget looking at the line of Chinese stuntmen as they waited their turn to be kicked by me. I did this scene over and over and I can't tell you how many stuntmen I went through. Oh yes, it's a little different filming with the Chinese (laughing).

One last story. During the final fight scene with Yuen Biao, I kicked him a little too hard and took his breath away with my back leg round kick. So in the course of making this movie I had somehow managed to dish out a considerable amount of pain to the three big stars and they had a plan to get me back. It was payback time. The final fight scene called for me to chase Yuen through the castle and for us to land in couch chairs sitting across from each other with a table between us. On the table sat some wine glasses and a ceramic glass vase filled with wine. Yuen was supposed to grab one of the wine glasses filled with wine and toss the wine in my eyes. Next, while I struggled to wipe my eyes clean, he was to strike me over the head with this ceramic vase.

I noticed everyone, including Jackie, Sammo and the entire crew, were there to watch the scene. Sammo then showed me a table with about five ceramic vases for the scene and he wanted me to do this entire fight scene in one take, including the end where I get hit over the head, otherwise we would have to go through the five vases.

It was a very intricate scene with many fight moves and the timing had to be just right. Yuen was an incredible athlete, as Sammo and Jackie were as well, and I loved working with him. I grabbed the vase I was going to be hit over the head with carefully since I knew it must be a breakaway type of ceramic and I didn't want to break it (laughing). You should have seen my face when I felt it and saw that it was an actual vase. I asked if they could do anything to make this a little bit safer and everyone started laughing after Sammo interpreted what I said. One of the crew took out a knife and actually began chipping away at some of the ceramic on the inside to appease me. Think about it, if you get hit in the head with a gallon of water in a plastic jug it would still do damage. Just imagine what a vase filled with wine would feel like! Well, we began shooting the scene and it actually came off without a hitch until the point where I had the wine thrown in my eyes. It really burned my eyes and while I placed my hands over my face to wipe away the wine, I prepared myself mentally for the blow to come. It came down with such force that I'll never forget it the rest of my life. I remember hearing the entire group around me as I was actually passing out - all of the Chinese laughing and clapping. The last thought on my mind was how stupid could I be to allow anyone to hit me like this, and I actually grinned as I went unconscious. In reality, I had it coming and never complained.

In the USA, a video was produced of the best fight scenes of all time, and of course Benny's fantastic fight scenes with Jackie are on this video, but they also included this last fight scene with Yuen and me as well. I consider this my best scene ever in a movie. I'll never forget how wonderful the actual fight scenes between Jackie and Benny were to watch. Remember, when I was watching, no editing or music had enhanced the fight scenes yet, but they were still unbelievable to watch.

SP: Did you and Benny Urquidez train with Jackie, Sammo and Biao during filming?

KV: We would all go to the gymnasium together and stretch and do exercises. At times, they would want to see some of my moves and they would have me do some of my favorite techniques for them. Once in a while we would throw kicks back and forth, but of course we never sparred. I learnt a lot from each of them about timing and movement. They were all so fluid with their movements and of course just watching Sammo move amazed me. He was as fast as any of us.

Benny and I would spar and that was no easy matter. Benny loved to train with intensity, and while I was better known as a tournament fighter, I was rated about 4 or 5 in the world as a full contact fighter as well. I fought my full contact matches in the USA and all of our kicks had to be above the belt. Benny on the other hand was more of an international kickboxer and his style allowed kicks below the waist to the legs. The first time I fought Benny in one of our workouts, I peppered him at will with an array of techniques. I hit Benny full power with a back leg roundhouse squarely against his head and thought I broke my foot. He didn't even stagger. Impossible, I thought, but I was still hitting him at will. He then asked me if I was ready now, and of course I didn't like the way he phrased that question (laughing). I nodded yes and thought to myself, hell, I've been fighting, what's he talking about? I picked my leg to kick him and the next thing I felt was the crashing sound of his right shin against my supporting leg. I've never experienced pain like that. I called time out, and Benny said you can't do that. I smiled and said I just did. He said we have to continue fighting and you can't just call time out when you feel like it. I said, well I just did, and another thing, if you ever kick me in my thigh like that again, I'll stab you with a pencil in your eye. Benny laughed, thank goodness, and then began working on leg kicks with me

(laughing).

Between our days filming, Benny and I toured other martial arts Dojos every chance we had in Europe and would fight anyone willing to fight us. Benny just loved walking in to these Dojos and watching the instructors' faces when they saw us coming in with our Gis. Benny is one terrific fighter.

SP: What's the difference between making a Hong Kong movie and an American movie?

KV: As I mentioned before, American action movies are very different than Hong Kong movies. The movements in the American movies are almost choreographed in slow motion compared to Hong Kong movies. I did *Blood Brothers* for Ng See-yuen, a famous Chinese producer. Many of the crew there had worked for Jackie's movies in the past so it was very comfortable working with them.

There were things I liked and things I didn't like doing the Hong Kong way. Let's take *Blood Brothers* for example. In a typical fight scene I would throw 40 or 50 moves and regardless of how many blows I landed on the bad guy, he would just keep jumping back up and continue the fight. In our culture that actually makes your techniques look like they have little or no effect. Now the fight moves and techniques are wonderful and the beauty of the fight is there, but the power is lacking. Steven Seagal on the other hand breaks and crunches the bad guys with each technique and they never get back up. So in our culture Seagal is the toughest of all the American stars and my son, Travis, who is 15 years old, swears I am the weakest (laughing).

SP: You've had some great success with books on the martial arts, Keith. Tell us about that?

KV: I wrote four of them in the 80s and they did very well. My tournament fighting book was the one I was quite proud of. Over the years it has been a real honor to hear stories relating how my book and fighting strategies impacted their training as well.

SP: What projects are in the pipeline for you now?

KV: I'm now producing films and videos as well as acting. As an actor, I played one of the leading roles, an Italian Godfather, in a film that should be released on video soon, entitled *The Cut Off*. I also just did a role for TV for the *Nash Bridges* show where I had a terrific fight scene with a famous wrestler, Stone Cold Austin.

My company Trajen Pictures is slated to produce a film entitled *Jack's World* about a young man that lives in a fantasy world and is visited by his Guardian Angel. It's a $4 million budgeted action film slated to begin filming hopefully in the fall of 2000. It's the first script I've written for a major motion picture and wish to continue writing

Keith, Jackie and Benny on the Barcelona *Wheels on Meals* set

for future films as well. I'm now writing a historical fiction script on the American Frontier that I have been researching for a few years.

Most people think my company, Trajen, was named after the Roman Emperor, and it was, but the name also comes from the "Tra" from my son Travis, and the "Jen" from my daughter Jennifer. Travis is 15, and my daughter Jennifer is 17 and getting ready to attend Georgia State College.

My video company, Trajen Video Productions, is now in production on a kids' safety video series. My first video is entitled *Stop the Bully*. I'm very excited about this kids' safety series. In our country, bullying and kids' violence in schools is a major issue and I believe that these videos will have a tremendous positive impact on kids.

I am also currently involved working as a film lobbyist in South Carolina trying to get favorable film bills passed in the legislation, and still write for a martial arts magazine, Karate International.

As you can see I am still quite busy and love what I do. I am so glad I dropped that track scholarship earlier in my life and made my new love martial arts. It has endured in my heart and always will.

SP: *Keith, it has been a real pleasure talking with you. All the best with your future projects, thanks for talking to Screen Power, and keep in touch.*

KV: Richard, you are very welcome.

Roll of Honour

Here are a few of Keith's impressive achievements during his competition days:

Top 10 fighter of all time, Black Belt magazine
Three time martial arts national tournament champion
Inductee: Black Belt Hall of Fame (1981)
Inductee: Legion of Honor

By Lisa Clemens

What happens when an average salesman who is bored with his average life, dreams of getting involved in some excitement, intrigue and adventure? Does the phrase "Be careful what you wish for" ring a bell?

In *The Accidental Spy*, Jackie Chan plays Buck Yuen, a lonely salesman who is nagged by his boss, spends his lunch hours alone and who spends time at home chatting on the Internet. He is an orphan who dreams of his parents but only remembers an early, unclear memory from his babyhood of them holding something shiny before him. Once he had ambitions of being more than what he has become: a police officer or even FBI or CIA in the US. He always had a powerful intuition which would help solve crimes. But when he learned that the person who would train him at the academy was a bully from the orphanage, he turned away from this more interesting life, and he seems to have always regretted the decision.

One day his intuition serves him well and he manages to help nab some bank robbers during a typically exciting and funny scene that utilizes all of the choreography and humor we expect from this kind of Jackie Chan film. When he makes the local papers he is approached by Many Liu, who tells Buck that he is a private eye sent to find orphans born in 1958 for his client. (But is he really the mysterious friend on the Internet that Buck has been telling of his babyhood memories?) Eventually Many convinces Buck to meet with his client, who may be his birth father.

Buck takes a chance and meets with him, and soon he is thrown into more of an adventure than he had bargained for as he learns that the man who may be his father was a spy and that he has hidden a deadly biological weapon (called Anthrax II) somewhere in Turkey. Soon Buck is caught up in searching for it and keeping it out of the hands of a villain called Zen who thinks nothing of controlling his girlfriend, Yong, by getting her hooked on drugs. Meanwhile the locals also want the Anthrax II and Buck, blaming him for having it and testing it on the local villagers. Eventually Buck is faced with a difficult choice. Zen offers to allow Buck to take Yong away from him to save her life in exchange for the Anthrax II. But should he make the exchange, Buck knows Zen would not use it for peaceful means. As he says in the film, "If someone awaits your rescue but saving her means others may die, would you do it?"

Accidental Spy was filmed in Hong Kong, Korea and Turkey in 2000 and is directed by Teddy Chen, whose credits include being a writer for *Black Mask* and directing *Purple Storm*. Chen has also had several acting roles in his career, including an appearance in *Infernal Affairs 2,* the prequel to the award winning *Infernal Affairs*. Ivy Ho was a writer for *The Accidental Spy*. Her credits include being a writer on *Gorgeous* and *July Rhapsody*. The music is by Peter Kam, the creator of great music for films like *Purple Storm*, *Gen Y Cops* and *Golden Chicken*. However, if you see the US version by Dimension, his wonderful music has sadly been replaced. I wish I knew the reason for this change. The original music was fitting and beautifully matched the mood of the film, adding to the tension and sense of adventure and occasional comedy. Dimension did the same thing when they released *Drunken Master II* as *Legend of Drunken Master*. They removed the original track and replaced it with a generic Chinese music soundtrack. But at least in both cases one can be thankful that a hip hop soundtrack was not used to appeal to younger audiences, as was done in parts of *Supercop*'s US release.

Among Jackie's co-stars in *The Accidental Spy* you will find some new faces as well as several more familiar ones. Eric Tsang, who plays Many Liu, is an actor and comedian who has appeared in films with Jackie such as *My Lucky Stars*, *Twinkle, Twinkle Lucky Stars* and *Twin Dragons*. He recently won acclaim and a Hong Kong Film Award nomination for his role in *Infernal Affairs*. (Co-star Anthony Wong went on to win for his role in the same film, however.)

An actor who has also appeared with Jackie in the past is Alfred Cheung Kin-ting who had a cameo in *Twinkle, Twinkle Lucky Stars* and played Yung in *Twin Dragons*. He also appears as a Chinese professor in *The Medallion*. In *Accidental Spy*, he plays the lawyer for Park, who may be Buck's father. Another familiar face was Athena Chu Yun in a cameo as the lady Buck tries to get interested in buying some sporting goods. She was in *Project S* aka *Supercop 2* as May. Hong Kong film fans may know Wu Hsing-guo, who plays bad guy Zen, from such films as *God of Gamblers 2* and *The Soong Sisters*. The tragic character of Yong is played very effectively by Vivian Hsu, whom Yuen Biao fans may remember from his directorial debut, *Dragon From Shaolin*. Less familiar is newcomer Him Min as Carmen, the character who helps Buck along the way to learning more about his father.

While Jackie did not write a diary for *The Accidental Spy* as he did on *Shanghai Knights* and *Around the World in 80 Days*, he did write a letter to his fans which was posted on his website. He told of how he dealt with a bad slip and fall during the Turkish Bath scene: "Fighting wet and naked in the bathhouse is hard, but not as hard as keeping your balance running around on a slippery marble floor. In one particular scene, I had to run and slide to the other side of the room. After finishing several shots, the Director thought I didn't look stressed out enough; after all, I was being chased by killers! I tried harder, and that was when things went wrong. One! Two! Three! Action! Running as fast as I could and sliding with my leg out, I lost balance and fell back with my leg in front of my neck. I could only think about protecting my recently injured lower back, hurt while shooting *Shanghai Noon*. I saved my lower back, but the back of my head hit the marble floor hard. I lost consciousness for a few seconds, but recovered almost instantly and sat up straight away. Having had a lot of experience dealing with pain, I knew that if I could tolerate it, stay awake and not faint, I would

recover quickly. Sitting on the floor with my head in my hands, I determined to fight the pain though it really hurt. The shooting scene fell deadly silent, watching me. After five minutes, the pain began to lessen and I shouted, 'Back to work!'"

He learned an important lesson about the use of spices as body paint as well. In the letter to fans he told of his painful encounter with the spice barrels: "Once, I fell into a barrel of spicy powder and came out all red. The Director said the effect of the shot was great, but what he didn't know was that it was chili powder and it makes you very itchy. Can a naked man scratch his butt in front of 200 people? Of course not! So I distracted the Director by talking to him about the next shot, and while he and the shooting crew were busy adjusting the equipment, I secretly took a quick shower in the washroom to wash away the spicy powder. Lesson learnt: never put spicy powder on your butt!"

In the *Making of Accidental Spy* feature that came with the original soundtrack CD, as well as on the Hong Kong DVD, Jackie is shown looking quite miserable as the camera zooms in on a close up of his very unhappy face. He says "I don't want to talk right now." Who can blame him as at the time he is having his posterior attended to! Yet he does go on to talk for a moment (in Chinese without subtitles unfortunately) about the spices.

Some beautiful locations were used for scenes shot in Turkey, including Istanbul's famous Pera Palas Hotel which was built for the passengers of the Orient Express, as well as the Aya Irini Kilise (Church of Divine Peace) used for the scene with the whirling dervishes.

The Accidental Spy ran in theaters in Hong Kong from January 18, 2001 as a Chinese New Year release and ended it's run March 7, earning a tidy HK $30,009,076 before going on to a DVD release.

If you have a choice between buying the Hong Kong DVD or the US version put out by Dimension Films, by all means go the extra mile and stick with the original. As I mentioned in my article "A Tale of Two Spies", there were many, many changes made to the original Hong Kong version. So many in fact, that it took two issues to list them all! Some of the changes made that really hurt the US version include cutting scenes in half. The whole sequence of events from the point where Buck is eating lunch and discovers the plot to rob the bank, right

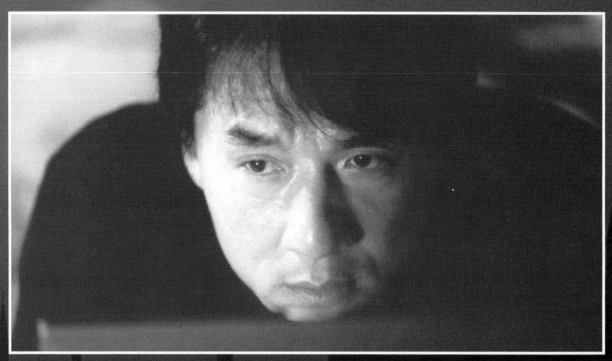

through the scene of the crane swinging through the office building, has been severely diced and edited. Even the actual crane stunt was cut in half. Another drastic cut is the scene where Buck sees Yong for the first time from the lift, and follows her through the hotel and down to the lobby until she reaches her car. In the original version, this scene had a lovely dream-like quality to it as Buck was lead through the hotel, seeming to be entranced by her and the mysterious scarf that she wore, bearing the same words that were carved into his mother's headstone, "Wait For Me". In the Dimension version, the scene is again halved and Yong's singing has been changed to a lesser quality. Jackie now merely sees her in the elevator then arrives down in the lobby, without the shots of him viewing her through the ornate windows and hallways. The enchanted feel is gone and the scene suffers greatly for it.

Some changes make bad continuity errors. In the US version, you will see Jackie follow Yong from the hotel, telling a cab driver to follow her. Yong enters the Aya Irini Kilise where she is to meet her boyfriend, Zen, and immediately goes up to the balcony. She turns a corner and boom! Jackie is already there! Neat trick if he didn't know who she was or where she was going. In the Hong Kong version, you will see that after entering the building, she goes immediately to Zen and sits with him a while to watch the whirling dervishes, not leaving until she is dismissed by him. This gives Buck plenty of time to catch up and observe her from the balcony.

The ending has also been drastically cut, sliced and diced. The US version does not have the hilarious scene between Jackie and Eric Tsang as Many mistakes Park's ashes for cocaine and then freaks out when he learns what he has just sampled with his tongue. Also gone from the Dimension edit is the epilogue after the outtakes, which is something never before seen in a Chan movie. This is too bad as it sets up a possible sequel. In the scene we find out that Many contacts Buck again and talks him into doing a job for him. And the payoff of seeing Jackie in disguise at the end is a lot of fun too.

And speaking of outtakes, what really adds insult to injury here is the fact that Dimension has not only dubbed the outtakes but changed most of the words spoken by Jackie and the other actors. Poor Pang Wing-sang, as the old man in the bank who offers to help Buck take out the robbers, has been given a ridiculously cartoonish voice as he squawks, "Here I am! You want help?!" followed by an insultingly goofy laugh. They might as well have cut out that outtake. After all, his scene was not even in the Dimension version at all!

Thankfully one of the few scenes to remain uncut

was the incredible market fight scene where Buck Yuen manages to fight off his attackers while simultaneously trying to keep his naked self covered. The timing and choreography used in this scene is mind boggling. And let's face it, if Dimension had actually been stupid enough to cut anything from this scene they would have had to deal with not only fans of Jackie's incredible fight choreography, but also Jackie's sizeable contingent of female fans who just love to see him "in all his glory!"

For a full list of changes made, please refer to "A Tale of Two Spies" in *Screen Power* Vol 4 Issue 6 and Vol 5 Issue 1. (Yes there were so many differences it took two issues to list them all!)

One of the most enjoyable aspects of *Accidental Spy* is the drama. While there is plenty of comic relief, the parts that stand out the most are the dramatic scenes, most notably the demise of Yong. In most of Jackie's other films, Jackie's character always rescues the ladies and all is well. But here, Buck is double crossed by Zen. Even though he has decided to rescue Yong from Zen and give him the Anthrax II, she has been poisoned by him and dies. Jackie's performance as he carries her in his arms and realizes that he has failed to help her, is very moving.

Although known for his light hearted comedy, it would be wonderful to see more drama coming from Jackie in the future. And he does seem to be moving in this direction more and more. During an interview at the Beijing premiere of *The Medallion*, Jackie mentioned that a project with Zhang Yimou is in the planning stages. One which he promises will be all drama and in which he will not even throw a single punch.

I am sure that among the die-hard action fans who still crave the action style of twenty to thirty years ago, this may not be welcome news, but for those, like myself and many others, who enjoy Jackie's dramatic skills and support his decision to reinvent himself yet again, this is wonderful and a long time coming. He has stated that he has been looking for the right Director and script for some time. He has talked with Ang Lee, Edward Yang and others about just such a project. Yes, Jackie has had many films which have had less action than drama. *Heart of Dragon* and *Crime Story* are perfect examples. But one without a single fight, where Jackie must use his dramatic skills to carry the film would be something new indeed. And knowing what a wonderful and expressive actor he is, I truly hope that this new project comes to fruition and Jackie Chan will get the chance to do what he wants. If the more serious side of *Accidental Spy* is an example, then we are in for a treat.

Candid shot of Jackie on-set in Istanbul

ISTANBUL SET VISIT

Report by Matthew Edwards

For Jackie's new Hong Kong picture, *The Accidental Spy*,
Istanbul in Turkey was chosen as the location for the majority of the film's action.
And *Screen Power* was there to bring you an exclusive report from the set.

Sunday 2nd July 2000

In the early hours of Sunday morning we arrived at Heathrow Airport to check in and wait for our scheduled flight to Istanbul. After a couple of hours wait on a tired green couch we then proceeded to check our luggage in before sitting patiently in the departure lounge, awaiting our call to board the plane. By this time my face had become paler than the Arctic Circle as I began to get nervous and apprehensive about the upcoming journey. This was the first time I had flown by plane for over ten years.

The flight itself took three hours, and we flew over, among other places, Romania and Greece viewing some of the breathtaking sights. Rich knew better than to eat the food on the plane, however I was made to learn by my mistakes (the worst chicken curry I've ever had).

Thankfully the journey went well and we landed around two and proceeded to go through the standard immigration controls as well as paying a compulsory Visa just for the privilege of stepping into the country. Here we met our holiday representative, and afterwards we stepped out into the glorious summer's sun and bustling streets of Istanbul and were taken to our hotel.

As we were driven to our destination I noticed that Istanbul's high rise flats and housing were badly maintained and not completed (various houses had no windows, while others had partial roofs with bits of debris lying everywhere). It turns out that many Turkish homes are not fully completed and left in disrepair, as they have to pay a housing tax when their homes are complete.

By late afternoon we had arrived and checked into our hotel that lay on the fringes of Sultanahmet. Our hotel was positioned on the corner of a small incline with its fascia tailored in a soft powder-yellow decor. Inside, a small wooden reception immediately greeted us, whilst a small seating area and drinks cabinet lay adjacent to the right. A small TV hummed in the corner relaying the local news. The breaking news seemed to have been coming from Istanbul's hospital as groups of reporters laid siege around its grounds.

After being given our key, attached to a robust metal fob, we climbed the spiralling staircase decked in a dark rouge matted carpet. Somehow the hotel attendant had managed to carry both Richard's suitcase and mine without falling back down the stairs. We entered the room, whereby it was immediately assessed.

Our feelings were at first hard to sum up in words. It suddenly brought back memories of the film *Midnight Express* by Alan Parker, starring Brad Davis and John Hurt. By Turkish standards this was meant to have been quite a good hotel, although it became apparent quickly that this was not your average holiday resort suite (I would have hated to be staying at a one or two star hotel).

With a window that would not shut, a toilet with no lock, a room the size of a matchbox, a shower that possessed no hot running water and a closet with enough space for one jacket we lay silently on our beds. After an hour of regret we suddenly felt defiant as the main purpose of the trip was not the conditions but

the exclusive opportunity of reporting from the set, and for myself the chance of meeting Jackie. With this attitude we ventured outside to check out the local sights. Finally we settled down in a nearby bar/restaurant (that soon became our local haunt) where we enjoyed a meal and a few drinks. Around ten we wandered back to our hotel for an early night so that we could prepare for our first day on the set.

Monday 3rd July 2000

We awake early Monday morning and set about getting ready for the set. It soon becomes apparent how rotten the shower and toilet really is. First up, we have to put a chair behind the door so the toilet is locked and secondly the shower has a two inch rim along its base that doesn't stop the water overflowing and flooding the floor.

At around ten we order a taxi and head off for the day's shoot at the Peta Palas Hotel in Taksim. We arrive at the hotel around ten-thirty after a mad taxi journey. The taxi is an old robust model and painted in canary yellow, and weaves in and out of the busy morning traffic like nobody's business. The scariest thing is that they all seem to pull out in front of each other without indicating, and they constantly beep their horns. We arrive on schedule outside the nostalgic looking building. Various film vans are parked outside that reassure us that we have found the right place.

Once inside the hotel we immediately spot the J.C. Group crew setting up the film's next shot. As we walk into a large dining room with overhead chandeliers and long wooden floor panels we are confronted by the brilliant light swooping down from the huge rigged lighting equipment.

After gathering our bearings Rich soon spots Jackie in the far left-hand corner with Director Teddy Chen. They sit on old deckchairs watching a previous shot to see if it had turned out satisfactorily. Jackie is decked in light stonewash trousers, a white T-shirt and a khaki jacket. Rich and myself go over to see Jackie, whereby he shakes Rich's hand and is introduced to myself. Jackie offers good hospitality by offering us a drink, before joking that an old guy sat in the corner is his stunt double!

As we wait for our drinks the Director Teddy Chen, of *Purple Storm* fame, comes over for a small chat. Rich asks him how the filming is going and whether he likes it in Istanbul or not. Teddy informs us the shoot has so far gone well and that he has enjoyed the opportunity of working with Jackie. Teddy also mentions the Euro 2000 football final in Holland, and how Italy had been winning one-nil up until the last minute when France equalised and went on to win in extra time. He also states that he would be more than happy to conduct an interview with *Screen Power*. It goes without saying that Rich is delighted that he arranged an interview within the first hour. Things get even better five minutes later when we take pictures of Jackie holding the magazine (sadly, due to the overhead lights, when they were developed the glossy front cover was partially ruined by a brilliant glow of white).

By 11:30 the next shot had been set up ready for filming to commence. We all piled into a small room with a small wooden table designed with figurines praying along its base and a glass unit on top. The walls were painted with a mustard tinge with brown arch panels intricately placed around the room. Around the table sat Jackie, American actor Tony Jones and the film's young Korean actress. Teddy's monitors lay in the

left corner of the room with Teddy's trademark deckchair.

The scene in question had Jackie being probed by a C.I.A. agent on whether or not he recognised a wanted suspect. After a smooth morning shoot - and countless members of the Turkish crew telling us we couldn't take pictures, only for Jackie to have a go at them, saying we could take what we liked - the shoot took a break at lunch time.

For the afternoon shoot it was back to the same room to finish off the day's scene. In between scenes Jackie started looking at the *Screen Power* magazines Rich had given him. At one point Jackie fluffed his lines when he started laughing at my *Hand of Death* article and the amusing old pictures of himself. Teddy Chen then told Jackie to stop laughing, as this was a serious scene! The most amazing thing about being on set was the fact that we were right behind the camera and next to Teddy Chen and the J.C. Group in a crowded sweltering hot room.

In between camera set ups we spoke briefly to American actor Tony Jones, who said we were funny guys and gave us his extensive filmography that included *My Girl* 1 and 2. Also we watched the antics of Jackie in between takes that included Jackie creeping up on his personal secretary Dorothy like a tiger, feeding cake to his co-star like a child and, when he became bored, deciding to have a rest by lying on various tables. The best part though was Jackie looking at the *Screen Power* magazines and telling the Turkish crew not to nick them.

By now it was late afternoon and the heat had taken its toll. One of the interesting aspects of the day's shoot was watching Teddy Chen's methodical direction and Jackie's acting and his tendency to, when shooting finished, read *Screen Power* instead of talking to his co-actors. When he did speak to them he seemed to talk about the magazine. Another good aspect of

the shoot was the banter on the set created when the young Korean actress could not pronounce one of her lines, much to Jackie's delight.

At around four-thirty the shooting came to a close. We felt we had experienced a wonderful day watching the world's greatest action star on set and what goes on in between scenes. However, our day was not quite over. After the shooting had wrapped, Director Teddy Chen approached us and asked us whether we wanted to conduct the interview now. Of course we jumped at the chance and we moved into a quiet side room where Rich set about interviewing Teddy whilst I took various photographs. After an excellent and open interview from the fantastic Teddy Chen that lasted an hour, we took a few personal snaps and said our goodbyes.

We quickly flagged down a taxi and set off for our hotel, trying to comprehend the amazing first day we'd had. Needless to say we got lost on the way home but that did little to dampen our spirits. That night we made a few calls and went out to celebrate.

Tuesday 4th July 2000
Today's shoot is not scheduled until 21:30 in the evening so we get the chance to catch up on some sleep. At around one Rich decides to steal my passport. When searching through my belongings I notice it has gone missing and frantically begin looking high and low for it. At this point Rich has covered his face with his handkerchief to conceal his laughter, and after a while reveals to me his prank, much to my relief. Apparently this is part of the *Screen Power* initiation, and Rich only let me sweat for fifteen minutes when this usually lasts two hours!

After finding a lovely Korean restaurant around the corner we enjoy a lovely Chow Mein before setting off for the evening shoot. Tonight's shoot is planned to take place at Instanbul's train station.

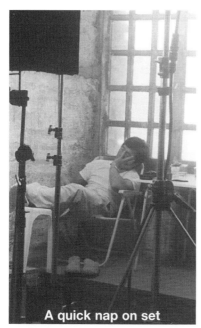

A quick nap on set

However, we learn that Istanbul has two stations, one on the European side and one on the Asian side. Of course in our Confucian wisdom we opt for the wrong station.

Convincing ourselves that they couldn't possibly be filming on the Asian side, we head to the European train station that takes five minutes by taxi. When inside the taxi, the driver decides to make small talk with his broken English. "Why do you want to go to the train station?" the taxi driver asks, whereby Rich responds "because we like looking at trains" in a sarcastic voice. I cringe in my seat thinking we are about to get chucked out, however it seems the driver didn't understand sarcasm. Thank God!

We arrive at the busy station at 19:30 and wait patiently for their arrival. Sitting in a small cafe it soon becomes apparent we have gone to the wrong destination. At 21:10 we arrive back at the hotel and beg with the hotel staff to organise a taxi for us to the Asian train station. By 21:20 we are on our way crossing over Istanbul's connecting bridge to the gateway to Asia. By 21:50 we arrive at the station and in a new continent.

When we arrive we learn the night's

shoot has yet to begin. The crew rush around setting up camera angles and lighting. The interior for the shoot takes place near the booking offices and has rows of wooden benches. The walls are filled with lavish architecture that is scrolled on the soft pink and magnolia walls, as well as featuring high prominent arches with decorative patterns and stained glass windows. Bemused people wander around like ants on the marbled floor panels trying to figure out what's happening. Above the main doors is situated a large clock that gives the room more character.

At around eleven Jackie appears ready for the first take. A mass of huddled people stare through the station's window trying to catch a glimpse of Jackie. Small Turkish children run around the set waving at Jackie with excitement. One young girl calls to her mother, "It's Jackie Chan", thus representing the universal appeal of Jackie world-wide. It also shows how language is no barrier when uniting him and his fans together with his movies.

The scene tonight has Jackie sitting next to Jackie's young co-star. First up Jackie enters the frame and sits next to her. The camera pans to the young girl, whereupon she gets up and leaves. At one point a local Turk disrupts the filming when trying to get money out of a cash dispenser. Oddly he just stops and stares blankly at the camera as the crew wave frantically with hand signals for him to get out of the way.

Jackie seems rather sombre tonight and mills about quietly, although he still finds time to wind up Dorothy and his co-actress. This may be due to the amount of takes each scene is taking, somewhat slowing up the process. In contrast, Teddy Chen is very energetic. His direction seems sharp and precise, trying to maximise his vision to the fullest.

At 23:45 the crew set about changing the camera angles ready for the next shot. Meanwhile Jackie again demonstrates his commitment

to his films by going through the rushes with Teddy on the playback monitors. Even when he is not filming it seems he is still committed to talking through the recently shot images and to discussing the upcoming scenes.

Wednesday 5th July 2000

It is gone midnight before the next scene is ready to be filmed. The scene is again an extension of the scene filmed earlier. The crew also drafts a local in to do some sweeping in the background in order to make the scene more realistic. By now a whole bevy of odd-looking people had decided to sit on nearby benches and have fallen asleep! After more takes the crew are happy with the shot and proceed to redesign the set and lighting. The crew at this point decides to take a break and chill out with a bite of food.

Rich uses this opportunity to have a chat with Jackie and Teddy, whilst I am not so lucky as a group of Turkish people decide they would like to have a conversation with me. They ask me if I like the country and general questions like that. By the time I escape, Rich has finished talking to Jackie, and Teddy orders us to help ourselves to some food.

At around two in the morning we cannot keep our eyes open any more. We decide we have obtained some good material, so we say our goodbyes and attempt to flag down a taxi to our hotel. Needless to say we get lost again! By the time we reach our bed it's 3:00 and we look forward to a nice sleep.

However, we were awoken at 6:00 by the nearby Blue Mosque as they sing their prayers that are projected out through loudspeakers intricately placed around the mosque. This loud bellowing racket was again repeated at 8:00, 10:00 and at 14:00, as well as two evening slots. Needless to say Rich and I were not impressed.

Due to the night shoot no filming was scheduled for the next day. Instead we decided to take a wander around the grounds of the Blue Mosque (a huge 17th Century dome surrounded by six beautifully designed minarets) and marvel at some of the marvellous architecture. After a wander around the famous Hippodrome racetrack, surrounded with tall columns and monuments with strange cryptic symbols upon them, and a pleasant stroll in the hot sticky heat, we decide to head back for a few drinks and a lovely meal (and boy did we indulge!).

Thursday 6th July 2000

Today's shoot is only a five minute walk away and we make it to the set around ten, whereupon we were stopped by one of the Turkish crew saying we could not enter. When he had been informed that we were from Jackie Chan's Official Magazine he soon let us in and apologised. When will they learn! The scene takes place in the Aya Irini Kilise (Church of Divine Peace), a Byzantine church. The place is haunting, creepy but somewhat majestic, more suited to a horror movie than to a Jackie Chan film. Its stained glass windows, ruins and ageing arches and staircases help convey this image. Huge eye-catching tapestries are draped over balconies awash with bright and

beautiful patterns. A small seating arrangement upon a raised stage is carved out of rock at the far end of the hall with a large crucifix etched into the wall. The nave and rows of seating preceed it.

We walk in and the second unit are filming a scene with Turkish dancers spinning in their long traditional costumes with their hands held aloft. As the dancers twirl in perfect synchronisation they chant an ancient prayer - as we find out later from Teddy, they are spinning to communicate with God. This scene boasts over two hundred extras that infuriate the production team with their antics of getting up and wandering outside for a drink or smoke.

After a small climb up a long circular staircase and balcony, we reach the top floor where Jackie and the production are camped. This floor is very run down and bare, however it features a very prominent balcony and silk curtains that overlook the whole of the church hall. This is where the majority of Jackie's scenes take place today.

As for Jackie, he is on top form today. At one point he starts playing on a grand piano that is situated at the far end of the floor. The opening bars sound like he is playing 'Imagine' by John Lennon, but I can't be sure. As the morning wears on he gets Dorothy to fan him with a piece of cardboard. Before long Jackie has a sun bed and then an electric fan! Around this point Brad Allan arrives, decked in a black T-shirt and Walkman, and says hello. Rich also manages to hook up an interview with him in the afternoon. At around one-thirty Teddy comes over for a chat and declares he would love to come over and visit England, whereby we do our best to persuade him to do so.

In between shooting Jackie also starts playing with a coat hanger, finding something oddly fascinating about it. The crew stands and marvels at his comical exploits, at once keeping the production crew's

spirits up during the long hours of filming. However, the best aspect comes during filming. Teddy is filming on the floor below (a group of aristocrats sit eating lunch on posh decorative tables) whilst Jackie mills about on the top floor. As filming begins Jackie starts playing with a cardboard tube, flicking it around his body like a staff, whereby he drops it on the stone panels and then blames the crew, shouting "Quiet". Clearly amused, Jackie sneaks off!

At around three, Rich seizes his opportunity and has a chat with Jackie and we pose for a few snaps. Rich comments that it is hot, whereupon Jackie replies he's been far worse. He also mentions he would like to go back to the Sahara to film *Armour of God III*. As I get my picture taken with Jackie it suddenly becomes apparent how bizarre this really is. Here I am in Istanbul on the film set of his new movie. Unbelievable to say the least!

At around four, Brad Allan approaches, ready for his interview. We walk off to a quiet secluded area next to two giant wooden doors and a small arched window with diagonal black bars criss-crossing the dusty pane of glass. Before the interview begins Rich has trouble with his Dictaphone whereby he cannot get the thing to record. After a couple of minutes of toying with the Dictaphone it suddenly works. Rich then pulls out his list of posing question, anticipating a good interview.

Here on Brad gives an honest and informative interview, going into great detail of how he became involved in the J.C. Group and detailing his upcoming projects. As the interview progresses I take various shots of Brad next to Rich. Brad comes across as a warm and friendly person with an excellent sense of humour that he confirms at the end of the interview. After taking a few snaps of Brad, Rich decides to take a comical picture of him strangling Brad, to which he obliges! After the interview we shake hands

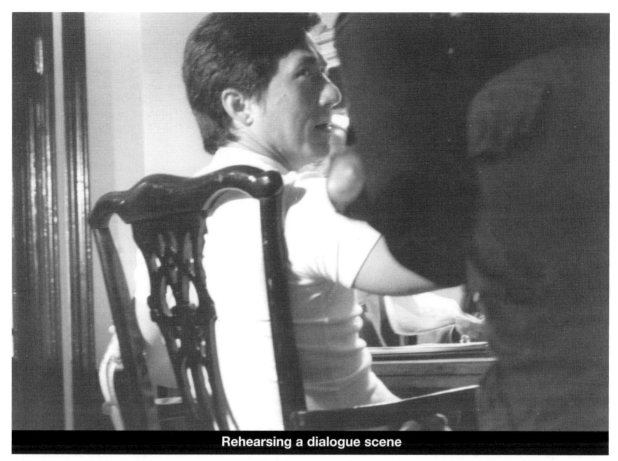
Rehearsing a dialogue scene

with Brad and thank him for his graciousness and we demand he comes to England for a special screening of *Gorgeous* next year.

After watching another hour's worth of filming we decide to call it a day. We say our goodbyes to Jackie and the crew before walking the short distance back to our hotel. Here we have a nice relaxing evening, pleased with the fabulous wealth of material we have again obtained. We decide to go to bed although Rich decides to attack me with our electric fan!

Friday 7th/Saturday 8th July 2000
We awoke Friday with a relaxing day ahead of us, knowing that as filming was over two hours away by taxi it was nigh on impossible for us to get there. We spent most the day sightseeing and being pestered by the locals to tempt us into buying a carpet or postcards. At one point we

sat under a terrace filled with primroses sheltering from the hot sticky sun when an elderly gentleman approached. He sat down and smiled at us, commenting in English on what a nice day it was and how Istanbul is. Richard wisely saw through his ploy, whilst I, thinking he was a pleasant local, kept on chatting. After a while he opened a small case that he was carrying and pulled out a toothbush and proceeded to try and clean my "Vans" trainers. Knowing my trainers were suede and that he was expecting money, I declined, whereby he kept insisting to clean them. I suddenly snapped and said I didn't want them cleaned, whereby he shot back shocked. Feeling guilty, I apologised and patted him on the back. Rich found this whole episode highly amusing!

In the afternoon we popped over to Jackie's hotel, where Rich dropped off a few presents from Bath in the

production office. Rich also left a whole bevy of *Screen Power*s for the production team and crew to read. The production room had its walls plastered with photos of Jackie, props and co-stars of the film. I also caught a glimpse of various storyboards that depicted a man clinging onto a speeding vehicle. This no doubt whetted our appetite for the movie.

After one last meal in our favourite restaurant and a couple of farewell drinks in Istanbul we called it a day. In the morning we packed our bags, took a few more pictures and had one final meal before it was off to the airport. With a smooth flight back home, reaching London Heathrow around four, we made it back to Bath for 20:00, tired and weary but pleased with our trip and the wealth of material we had obtained.

THE RUSH HOUR MOVIES
The East Meets West of Buddy Pictures
By Patricia Evans

What is it about buddy pictures? More specifically what is it about Jackie and buddy pictures?

Many of us find ourselves bemoaning the fact that Jackie always seems to be sharing the star spotlight. Many feel he can and should be left to carry the film's central role on his own. Why should we settle for less Jackie?

Buddy pictures have been around almost as long as films have been in existence. Some of the most classic and beloved movies have been buddy pictures. A few of the more memorable teams are Stan Laurel and Oliver Hardy, Bud Abbott and Lou Costello, Bob Hope and Bing Crosby, and Dean Martin and Jerry Lewis.

Each really successful team has had one thing in common: one straight man and one funny man. Although both men were funny, one always seemed to be the jokester, the more verbose of the team or the physical clown. If you have ever heard the classic comedy sketch "Who's on First?" by Abbott and Costello you'll see what I mean. Straight man Bud has all the answers and confused Lou is the one getting the laughs. Burly straight man Hardy was stoic and impatient while the timid and accident prone Laurel always seemed to land them in trouble. With Abbott and Costello, Lou was a very physical comedian, always taking a hit or pratfall. With Hope and Crosby, Bing was usually the straight man while Bob cracked the jokes. Dean Martin crooned the tunes and played straight man to Jerry's motor-mouthed sidekick. Jerry was also very physical, always falling, tripping, and generally leaving disasters in his wake. In that same tradition the *Rush Hour* movies were born.

With the added appeal of the cop teams popularized by such shows as *Dragnet* and *Starsky & Hutch*, and movies such as *48HRS* and the *Lethal Weapon* series, a new team was created. As *Rush Hour*'s tag line summed up: "The fastest hands in the East meet the biggest mouth in the West". And so, Jackie Chan and Chris Tucker began their roles as detectives Lee and Carter.

It is in part this same sort of teaming that made the *Rush Hour* series such a box office smash. In part one Detective Lee (Jackie) comes to the US at the request of the Chinese Consul Han (Tzi Ma). Han's daughter (Julia Hsu) has been kidnapped and is being held for a $50 million ransom. The FBI is in charge of the case and does not appreciate the help, so they enlist LAPD goof up Carter to babysit Lee and keep him out of the way. Neither Lee nor Carter are amused by their pairing. First of all they cannot understand each other. This was an element taken from real life. Jackie and Chris could not understand each other, so Director Brett Ratner was

always having to "translate" even though they were both speaking English.

There were several aspects to their teaming that made these movies work. First, their odd couple pairing - two very different men are being forced to work together. Detective Lee is a modest professional and a man of action, where Carter is egocentric and a loudmouth. Second, Jackie took the seat as this film's "fish out of water". This ever popular archetype is played for laughs as Jackie's character endeavors to do his job when faced with the FBI who don't want his help and a partner who prefers to work alone, as well as being in a country that's foreign to him. In one scene Jackie follows Chris's lead and ends up making a cultural *faux paux* as he emulates the detective's speech.

As the case progresses we discover the kidnapper Juntao and the Consul's friend Griffin (Tom Wilkinson) are one in the same. Carter and Lee start to work as a team, bonding in several memorable scenes, including one where Carter shows Lee how to sing and dance to the song 'War'. Lee returns the favor, showing Carter a few Kung-fu moves and how to take a gun from a suspect. As the movie continues they work together to find the missing child and uncover the identity of the kidnapper.

The film, though a box office hit, does not make full use of Jackie's abilities. However, when we do see him in the fight above the restaurant or fighting while trying to save a valuable antique vase, he is on good form. The final stunt has Jackie sliding down a long banner being held by new "partner" Chris. Lee lands safely on top of Carter in the funny stunt.

As the film concludes, Lee and Carter are together on a plane to Hong Kong. Written by Jim Kouf and Ross LaManna, *Rush Hour* earned an impressive US$245.3 million in the world wide box office. It spawned a sequel, *Rush Hour 2*, penned by Jeff Nathanson and directed by the returning Brett Ratner, which hit the big screen in 2001. Jackie reprises his role as Chief Inspector Lee and Chris Tucker appears as Detective James Carter.

When the second movie opens, Lee and Carter are in Hong Kong, supposedly enjoying some time off as Lee shows Carter around his home town. Workaholic Lee just can't seem to let go of his cases, much to Carter's chagrin, and the workload escalates as Lee accepts what ends up being another huge case. Two US customs agents are killed in an explosion, and Lee and Carter immediately begin the search for Ricky Tan (John Lone). Tan heads up a particularly nasty bunch of Triads and Lee suspects he is behind the bombing.

The cast of *Rush Hour 2* is a study in diversity. Latin star Roselyn Sanchez portrays secret service agent Isabella Molina and veteran comedian Alan King plays billionaire Steven Reign, while *Crouching Tiger, Hidden Dragon*'s Zhang Ziyi is effective as Ricky Tan's henchwoman Hu Li. Brett joked that no one in the cast spoke proper English, including Chris Tucker! Roselyn talked about how Zhang Ziyi would ask her for help with her dialog, and Roselyn would laugh and decline, explaining that she also had an accent though Ziyi couldn't hear it.

Chris Tucker has a funny moment singing a Michael Jackson song in a Hong Kong karaoke bar. Jackie has his turn to shine in the scene at a massage parlor. Thanks to Carter's impulsive bravado, Lee and Carter are forced to fight their way out through a gang of Triads. Jackie flips over chairs, and does kip ups over plants, along with a flip that begins on his stomach and lands him on his feet.

This time around Carter is the fish out of water in Hong Kong. It's a culture clash in reverse as the brash Carter fumbles his way through some pretty poor attempts to speak Cantonese. What he comes up with is never what he's meaning to say and some of his lines are very funny. Also, while making his way through a fresh food market, Lee comes across a chicken vendor and rather than seeing the chicken killed he ends up buying it live in a cage. Brett mentioned in the Director's commentary that Chris was actually frightened of the chickens, so the look of fear in the market as the chicken is thrust into his face is real.

Soon the action moves to Los Angeles as Lee and Carter head off after Steven Reign. While there they go to an informant's restaurant. In one of the film's highlights Don Cheadle, in an uncredited cameo, portrays the restaurant's owner and has the chance to trade blows with Jackie in a short but impressive fight. Apparently when Brett Ratner approached him about the movie he said he would only appear in the film if he could fight Jackie. Cheadle learnt his dialogue in very authentic Cantonese, although in reality he does not speak the language.

Following a tip from Cheadle's character, the two partners wind up in the hands of Ricky Tan's henchmen and arrive unconscious in Las Vegas. There they manage to hook up with secret service agent Isabella, who uses her charm to convince them to help her outsmart Tan and put an end to a counterfeiting racket.

Lee and Carter's characters make some changes during the two films. In the first film the two start out indifferent to each other, each one resentful of being saddled with the other. Then gradually they learn to work as a team and to accept one another's differences. In the second film a sincere friendship builds, though Carter is still frustrated by Lee's non-stop work ethic. In return Lee finds Carter's impulsive nature and tendency to brag

annoying. Still, it is evident in a scene where Lee believes Carter to be dead that their friendship has grown considerably. Jackie has a wonderful screen moment when he believes Carter was caught in an explosion and killed. Lee is very distraught. However, the dramatic moment is cut short with a gag when Lee says with remorse, "All he wanted was some Mushu." "Mushu" is Carter's slang for female company.

Rush Hour 2 raked in an impressive US$329.1 million in world wide box office receipts. The success of the franchise has spawned talk of a third installment. Chris Tucker and Brett Ratner have reportedly agreed, and it's only Jackie and his very busy schedule that are holding up the project.

For whatever reason - their inability to understand each other, Jackie's serious demeanor to Chris's irreverence, or Chris's non-stop talking along with Jackie's grace and action - these two have become a standout in buddy films. Although Jackie has been paired twice with Owen Wilson, for *Shanghai Noon* and its sequel *Shanghai Knights*, and once with Jennifer Love Hewitt in *The Tuxedo*, neither have come close to the sales of the *Rush Hour* franchise. One thing Jackie's fans will always be grateful for is that *Rush Hour* finally gave Jackie what he had always dreamed of, the US market. Where his other films, *Rumble in the Bronx* and *Supercop*, opened the door for him, *Rush Hour* blasted it off the hinges. Suddenly Jackie was Hollywood A list, pulling in top dollar for his performance. Hollywood finally figured out what everyone else already knew: not only was Jackie a one man phenomenon, he was also very marketable.

Yet even though Hollywood now knows that Jackie is so marketable, he is still always sharing the limelight. And the reason why? Hollywood loves the buddy film - always has, always will. It isn't an insult to share the screen time so much as it's an insurance policy for whoever bankrolls the production. Two stars mean twice the chance of drawing the crowds. If one doesn't get them, the other one will. Plus there is a certain feeling you get when watching the interplay between the two stars. It brings you into the relationship, lets you see how they relate, how they think. And we get to watch them play off each other. Whether the moments are touching, funny or dramatic, we see a side of the person we would not otherwise be privy to. Having that other person there to play off, to get close to, gives us insight and even a depth that we could only ever guess at. Plus it's a great source for good natured teasing at each other's expense. Just like Hope and Crosby used to do.

So, when and if *Rush Hour 3* hits the screen, I'll be right there on the first day. Watching to see if Carter is still full of himself or if Lee will ever get the girl. I'll want to know how they have grown and if they are still rubbing off on each other. They are like a pair of mismatched socks - an odd pairing perhaps, yet so comfortable to have around.

TEDDY CHEN

Screen Power editor Richard Cooper interviews Teddy Chen, the Director of *The Accidental Spy*, Jackie Chan's HK$150,000,000 Golden Harvest action thriller shooting on location in Istanbul, Turkey.

Monday July 3rd, 2000, and I am in Istanbul's famous Para Palace Hotel. My colleague Matthew and I have been here since about 10:30 this morning and it's now almost 6 in the evening.

It's been a long and tiring day - mainly due to trying to keep up with the energetic Jackie and Teddy filming an English dialogue scene with the leading actress Min Him and American actor Tony Jones (of *My Girl* and *My Girl 2* fame). "This scene is very dramatic and important," says Director Teddy Chen.

The location they are filming in is actually one of the first floor meeting rooms of the hotel, but in the movie will double as an executive office. Over a big oak table Jackie is briefed about the film's main bad guy, 'The Fixer'. He is called that because he fixes everything; guns, drugs, you name it, he gets it. He also goes by the name 'Mr. Zen' - because he thinks he is some sort of philosopher!

Teddy tells it how it is...

Jackie, Teddy and the crew have been here at the hotel shooting this scene for about ten hours now. Seems a rather long time to film a scene that will only take about 2 minutes on screen, but then again this is a Jackie Chan film, where time has no barriers or meaning, just the same as the production budget!

It's now just a little after 6 and the scene is all finished. Sure, there were a few NGs ('no good' takes) but that's not a problem, as they will no doubt appear in the outtakes during the film's end credits.

Funnily enough, one NG even occurred whilst Jackie was rehearsing his dialogue scene with Korean actress Him, when Jackie started laughing at a copy of *Screen Power* he grabbed off me earlier. I hope they include that scene in the outtakes!

Everyone looks relieved that the scene is now completed. The Turkish crew are beginning to pack up the various camera equipment and taking down the various lighting which surrounds the interior set. Jackie is obviously happy the scene is over as he comes over and lies down on a dinner table next to me and starts singing one of his well known songs from his successful late eighties Cantonese albums. "Suddenly..." he sings. "You hear this song before, right?" he asks as he lifts his head up a little. "Yeah, many times," I reply. He sniggers and lays his head back down.

Teddy is still busy... he's looking over the next day's script. "Ten minutes for the interview," he shouts out to me from across the room. I acknowledge and wave back. Meanwhile Jackie is still lying down on the table next to me - he's stopped singing now, in fact I think he's actually asleep!

I'm getting ready to interview Teddy now so I'm adding a new cassette into my tape recorder and test it out by getting my esteemed colleague Matthew to say a few words into it. He does, but I won't print what he actually says...

Teddy is coming over now. I am going to tell him it's a bit noisy in the room, and suggest we move ourselves to somewhere more suitable for the interview. The hotel's main dining hall is next door - perfect.

I guess this is it. Worldwide readers, I give you world renowned Hong Kong Director Mr. Teddy Chen:

Screen Power: *Teddy, here we are in Istanbul on the set of The Accidental Spy, the new Jackie Chan movie. So first of all, what are some of your own favourite Jackie Chan films?*

Teddy Chen: Jackie has made a lot of great movies, but I think my favourite is the... How do you say the name in English? I don't remember. You mentioned it this morning... 'The Big Crime' is it?

SP: *Ah, Crime Story, with Kirk Wong.*

TC: Yes, *Crime Story*... You know why? Because I was one of the writers! (Laughing)

SP: *(Laughing) No wonder it's your favourite movie...*

TC: (Laughing) With *Crime Story* we did a lot of research for the story. The background people also working on the story with me and the others were the actual real life people of the kidnapping story the film is based around. But of course we changed their names for safety. I was working on the story for about eight months, but the whole script had taken about two years.

SP: *It was over two years before Crime story was finished. Jackie was shooting Police Story 3: Supercop by day and Crime Story by night at that time.*

TC: That's right! I think *Crime Story* was very special because it was really the only modern day film with Jackie in a serious role. Human drama. I like human drama. I like Jackie's comedy roles, but that film was more serious. *Crime Story* was a very good movie.

SP: *Crime Story is very popular with Western audiences, who like no holds barred action and gunplay.*

TC: Yes, it is a very special movie. It showed that Jackie is not only very good at comedy and action but also at just being a serious actor. Not many actors in Asia or the West can adapt to so many different roles - maybe they are good at being a comedian or an action star or playing the Triad gangster, but Jackie is one of a very small number of people who can take on any role and make it work. *Crime Story* was a big risk for Jackie and Golden Harvest, but it worked. With another actor I don't think it would have worked so well.

SP: *How different is it working on your own movie as opposed to working with Jackie? Do you see The*

Accidental Spy as more of a collaboration, as opposed to your own movies which are solo projects?

TC: I am having a good time working with Jackie. He is now more calm and relaxed during the filming because he knows me and my films. Everybody told me before this it is very hard to work with Jackie because he likes to be so much in charge. Of course, it is a Jackie Chan film so it is true that he wants it to be the best it can be, but I think those were just rumours because I feel very comfortable and Jackie gives me a lot of ideas. This is a serious movie. *The Accidental Spy* is more serious than the usual Jackie Chan movies. Jackie is quite new to these concepts, but he gives some great ideas on set. So it's great working with Jackie. Did you see that on the set today?

SP: *Yes, it's great teamwork with the both of you.*

TC: Yes, but if it comes to the stunt or the action part then I leave it to Jackie and his stunt team. But I still give him some ideas for the action to help him think more.

SP: *That's good! Jackie has always said that he likes working with a Director who is not afraid to express his own ideas. Like Stanley Tong, he worked well with Jackie on Police Story 3: Supercop, Rumble in the Bronx and First Strike because they both bounced ideas off each other. This is only our first day on set, but I see very much of that similar working relationship between you and Jackie. It all looks great.*

TC: Yeah, the action part - I give him ideas to maybe inspire and I'm learning about the action, and when it comes to the serious human drama, Jackie gives me his ideas, so he is learning about 'human drama'.

SP: *Teddy, you have worked as an actor, producer and writer in the Hong Kong movie industry. But are there any other aspects of filmmaking that you haven't ventured into or explored yet that you would like to in the future?*

TC: (Short pause) I think something more about the serious side of human drama. Actually, I was planning to do a ghost film. Not the kind of silly one...

SP: *Not like Tsui Hark's Chinese Ghost Story with everyone flying round on wires?*

TC: (laughing) No, I think more serious like *The Shining* with Jack Nicholson. You seen it?

SP: *Yeah, quite scary.*

TC: Remember, you never see the ghost! Not all the time. But it is scary. The ghost is there, but where? How? More inside the drama, instead of showing the ghost jumping out at you like "Aaaaaahhhhh" you know?

SP: Yes.

TC: I don't like that kind of film. More drama I think is better.

SP: *That sounds like a really interesting project. I think a lot of people in the West would very much like to see you doing a serious ghost film in the future.*

TC: It is like our conversation just now. The Asian film market was dropping because of the pirate VCDs, so we tried to make it better. They always give me a good comment, they say, "Oh your film is like a Hollywood film." When I hear that I say to the Chinese reporters, "Please, the difference between a Hollywood or Hong Kong film is English and Chinese." I ask them, "Why do you put it that way?" Because the Hollywood film is a serious production - good quality filming, high quality of production, good decoration, even though it is small props. Now we are more serious about making good films, but years before so many people just made bad quality films just to make some quick money. That's why we hear comments like, "Hong Kong films look like Hollywood films." The reason is because we are all now very serious, we have good quality for the production. We give them a lot in what we call Hong Kong films.

SP: *We watched Purple Storm last year. Media Asia did a London premiere. Daniel Wu, the star of Purple Storm was present and we interviewed him. I was under the impression that you were also going to attend but you didn't. But you were scheduled to attend weren't you?*

TC: Yes I was. But the version of *Purple Storm* you saw in London was not the finished movie. If you watched both versions now you would see the difference, especially with the special effects. So at the time you were watching the film in London with Daniel Wu, I was in Hong Kong working on the special effects for the final version.

SP: *Oh, I remember now. Media Asia's Bey Logan, who introduced the film, did explain that the version we were going to see was not the finished version and some special effects scenes were to be completed back in Hong Kong.*

TC: Yes, I was working on that.

SP: *We all thoroughly enjoyed watching Purple Storm.*

TC: Good, I'm pleased.

SP: *Purple Storm has already been bought up by Miramax for a US release, and I'm sure it won't be too long before some smart UK distributor snaps it up too. Purple Storm was a great success wasn't it?*

TC: Yes, mostly at the time just before *Purple Storm* Hong Kong action films were the same, you know, lots of fight scenes and every character was the same. There is a hero and a bad guy. Good is good, and bad is bad. In my mind, I wanted to make a different kind of action film. In the film we have the star who starts off bad but then becomes good. So I wanted to make a film where the character is bad then becomes a hero. So I put more emphasis on the human drama, which other action films at the time seemed to lack. Yes, there are some good action scenes in *Purple Storm*, but it has a good story too, a different kind of story with a twist. That's what I enjoyed most about the film - the drama.

SP: *Daniel Wu was the star of Purple Storm, and his character was realistic, but earlier you said that you originally had Tony Leung from Gorgeous in mind to play the main role. Why was Tony Leung first in mind - was it because he had more acting experience?*

TC: Well, I first had the idea of having the two main characters in the film as brothers, instead of father and son. One of the guys we had in the film... I can't remember his name. He had white hair, you know?

SP: *Kam Kwok-leung?*

TC: Yes, Kam Kwok-leung. So I had it in the first draft that Kam Kwok-leung and Tony Leung would play brothers. So Tony Leung at that time waited for me to finish the script, but I kept changing it to make it better. Later when I finished it Tony already had a new schedule for a new film for Wong Kar-wai. By that time two months production had already started on *Purple Storm* and so Media Asia said to me, "Why don't you find someone else instead to take over the lead?" Then we looked for a new person. We look, we look, we look, and I can't find anybody suitable for the script. Then I had the chance to have dinner with Willie Chan in Jackie's JC Group. Then this new guy turns up, Daniel Wu - he had just come back from LA or San Francisco - and Willie looks at me and says, "You like him?" And I said, "Maybe he's the one!" But the thing was that Daniel was a newcomer, he had acted in two movies but to me he was a newcomer, and the script for *Purple Storm* was a difficult script for a newcomer, it needed someone with a lot of acting experience. So I was thinking, "Could he do it?" On the other hand, in the script the main character loses his memory, just like a piece of paper with no words on it, so I thought if I provide him with a good script and something he can work with maybe he can do it.

SP: *When Daniel was cast in the role of Todd in Purple Storm and shot a few opening scenes, were you impressed? Did you think you had made a good choice in casting him?*

TC: (Short pause) It's not very fair on him because the script is a very difficult one. To him, he did a very good job. A one hundred percent very good job, but I

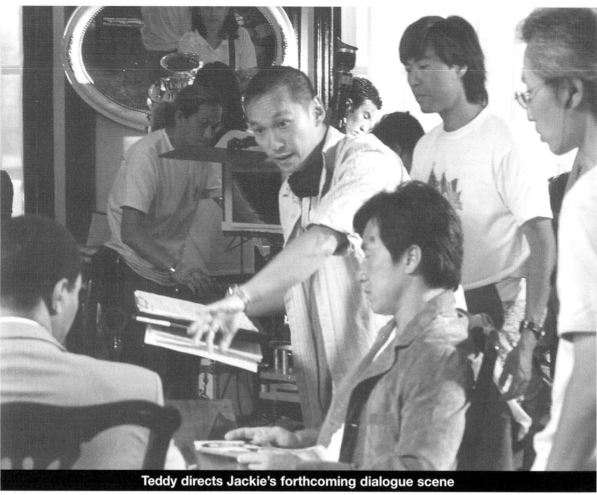
Teddy directs Jackie's forthcoming dialogue scene

think it was a very hard role for him, because this was only his third time in a leading role, but he will be better with more experience. (Short pause) I don't know, maybe I didn't do my job well.

SP: No, I asked Daniel about Purple Storm and working with you as Director and he said he had a great time working on the film and he thought you were great!

TC: (Laughing) Really? That's good. I wanted to give him some more information about the character, but I couldn't because with this script it wasn't filming scene one then two then three, it was like filming scene one then skip to scene fifty-five. So to a new guy it would be very difficult and confusing.

SP: Yes, that was one of my questions to Daniel in London. I asked him how he found all the heavy drama and working on the film with this unusual role and he said he did enjoy working on Purple Storm but he did find it difficult constantly changing from a drama scene to a fight scene to an action/stunt scene then back to a heavy drama scene again.

TC: Yes, we had the Tung Wai Action Group working very hard and planning a fight scene on one day and the next day we go to the father and son characters again, you know, with all the drama (laughing). So sometimes it was very tense on set.

SP: (Laughing) I can imagine. I did ask Daniel though what he would have liked Purple Storm to have more of or what he would have changed and he said he would have liked more action and fight scenes. But for a heavy drama film I guess you have to have a limit on the fight scenes otherwise it would have been labeled a Hong Kong Fighting Movie or something similar.

TC: Yes, that's right, I'm glad you understand. *Purple Storm* is a Hong Kong Action Movie so it has action, stunts and fight scenes, but it is also a different kind of action movie because it has a lot of drama and is geared more towards the human drama side.

SP: As I mentioned earlier, Purple Storm has been bought up for a US release by Miramax. So if the film is well received in the States, are you going to be the next Hong Kong Director going over to Hollywood?

TC: (Short pause) If there is a chance, then I think, "Why not?" Because you can learn a lot - you know, a new angle. But right now, I have just started my own company. Have you heard about my new company?

SP: *Yes I have. It's you and another well known Hong Kong Director, Peter Chan, isn't it, forming the company?*

TC: Yes, it's me and Peter Chan. The company is called Applause Pictures. We have a few ideas, so I am thinking that after this movie with Jackie I should stay in Hong Kong for maybe six months to a year.

SP: *Working on some new projects for the company?*

TC: Yes, lots of new projects.

SP: *Will these be just Hong Kong projects, or will some of them involve collaborations with Hollywood too?*

TC: No, because according to Peter... Peter has just finished his movie in Hollywood called *The Love Letter*, and he spent a lot of time talking with film people over there at the film festivals. These people were Asian filmmakers. Like, he met a guy from Thailand who made a very well known ghost story - very good movie! Broke all the records in Thailand. I think it even broke the box office record for *Titanic* (laughing). Another Director from Korea who made a film called *Christmas in August*. Very good movie. It also broke all the records in Korea. So hopefully with working with all these great Asian Directors, maybe we can achieve something good. Hopefully Hollywood will see what we are doing and will take notice. That way we can make the whole Asian market stronger.

SP: *That sounds very good. Well, at the end of the day at least the Hong Kong movie industry is taken more seriously by Hollywood and Western audiences nowadays.*

TC: Yes, but also we can work together and make the whole Asian movie market stronger as well.

SP: *So apart from all these new projects with various Asian Directors, in the future would you consider a collaboration with a Hollywood company? Especially if a US company asked you to make a Hollywood version of Purple Storm or Downtown Torpedoes?*

TC: Yes of course. Why not. That would be interesting.

SP: *What about the current state of the Hong Kong movie industry. Is it doing well? The current big movie releases over the last year have been Gorgeous,*

Gen-X Cops, Purple Storm, 2000AD, to name a few. Are things getting better?

TC: Well I think some people and companies are working very hard to find a new way to keep the industry going. The most important point is that you have a good quality film. Like at the theatres in Hong Kong now - is it worth paying to see these movies? Maybe some of the Hollywood films, even if they are too commercial and we don't even know what's going on, you still go to see it and are happy spending 50 Hong Kong dollars to see it because it is a good quality film. You know, the sound and everything, it is good quality. Some Hong Kong films come out and they are very bad, so people leave the theatre and say, "Oh I will wait until the VCD or video comes out." It's not worth it to go to the theatre and see some of these Hong Kong films. That is a fact.

SP: *Is that the general attitude of some people or moviegoers in Hong Kong then: they will not bother going to the theatre, and wait instead until the pirate VCD comes out because it is more convenient and cheaper?*

TC: Well I think that is the case with some people. One of the main problems is that the VCDs and videos of the Hong Kong films come out too quickly. Maybe you will only have to wait a month before the new film in the theatre is available to buy on VCD and video. Some films come out in only 15 days or two weeks.

SP: *That's far too soon! It takes at least six months for a film to be released onto video in the UK from its original release date in the cinema, and I imagine that it is the same state of play in the US, Canada, Europe and Australia too.*

TC: Yes, you're right. The Hollywood film companies won't release the video or VCD in Hong Kong for at least half a year. So nowadays some of us are trying to change the situation and make it better.

SP: *The two main companies I assume are Media Asia and Golden Harvest?*

TC: Yes, Media Asia and Golden Harvest. Their films are good quality and are released after at least three months to half a year. Also, nowadays in the newspaper and magazine advertisement and promotion it will say "This film will not be released onto VCD and video in the next six months". So if you miss it then you have to wait six months. But unfortunately if you don't care to wait then you can easily buy the pirate VCD. It's a shame.

SP: *The Hong Kong movie industry is known for having the most films available on pirate VCDs. I know Jackie and many others in the industry have tried their best to better the situation, but piracy still very much goes on doesn't it? Do you think it will always be possible to buy pirate VCDs in Hong Kong?*

TC: Without the government's help it is very difficult.

SP: *I would have thought the government would have helped out.*

TC: Well, they did help out a little before, but that's really not enough. The police... You know it's the customs. Maybe in the future they could look more and be more careful. But it is very difficult. Of course it is not just the pirate VCDs, but also the hi-fi, the radio, the clothes, everything. The situation is very bad. So, if the police can be more careful then I think a lot of the problems would go. If someone is selling pirate VCDs of my films then they have stolen my wealth and they should be arrested for it and sent to jail - it's illegal. Sometimes in Hong Kong you see the shops on the streets selling pirate VCDs. You must have seen it many times yourself in Hong Kong?

SP: *Yes, I have unfortunately.*

TC: The police just pass by these shops even though they see these pirate VCDs on sale (laughing). I have seen it happen many times.

SP: *Maybe some of these police buy these VCDs (laughing).*

TC: (Laughing) No, no, I don't think they would buy any!

SP: *Who are the filmmaking names in Hollywood you admire? You mentioned Stanley Kubrick earlier on from The Shining. You admire him do you?*

TC: Yes of course. I have learnt a lot from him. Especially the movie *2001: A Space Odyssey*. Wow, how many years ago was that film?

SP: *Back in the sixties.*

TC: Yeah, sixty-something. But it was incredible.

SP: *Who else do you admire?*

TC: Oh, there's Scorsese, Coppola, Kurosawa...

SP: *Kubrick was known for taking multiple shots of the same scene, and I noticed today on set you did too. It seems logical to take a number of takes of the same scene because then at least you can pick the best one for the finished print (laughing).*

TC: (Laughing) Yes! In Hong Kong some people can do it with the time, but most of the time it's really one take and that's it! Even if the shot was bad, they still use it in the finished print. Only a Jackie Chan film in Hong Kong allows for multiple takes and retakes because Jackie can command the time to make good shots.

SP: *Is that why you shoot the scene about three or four times, so you can make sure you get the one you really need?*

TC: Yes, I do, but sometimes it is very hard to tell. It's a kind of instinct. You kind of know you have missed something in the shot so you do it again. But I'm lucky I can do re-shoots because I have some very good support from Golden Harvest.

SP: *Let's talk about Hollywood again. Does the Hong Kong movie audience like the idea of stars and Directors going overseas to make films? What do they think about that?*

TC: Like Peter Chan said to me, Hollywood is a good place to learn from. I think the audience in Hong Kong don't mind because they all know we return and have some new ideas to show them. To be honest I don't think there is a great deal of difference in making a film in Hong Kong and making one in Hollywood. The main difference I see is that in Hollywood everyone has their own job - the track puller is the track puller. Hollywood has more money of course, but I think our way of making films is better in price, and with the costs it is so much better for us all to help out. Everyone will help with the camera and the lighting and the props. It saves time and money this way. I remember talking to Peter Chan about his Hollywood film *The Love Letter*. He told me about one of the trucks used for carrying equipment for the film: it was huge and cost one million US dollars. All that money just for a truck! In Hong Kong for just one million US we can make an entire movie!

SP: *Also, and I don't know if it's a waste of money or not, Hollywood productions spend a fortune on breakfast and lunch for all the crew too.*

TC: It is a waste of money really. And another thing, Peter's film used forty trucks! My last film, *Purple Storm*, used only eight (laughing). So all that is a waste of money. I would rather spend that kind of money on the film instead. Going back to *Purple Storm*, I remember that I had very good support from Media Asia who spent a lot of money on the production. We have Thomas Chung, John Chong, you know them?

SP: *No, I haven't met Thomas or John yet.*

TC: We also have Willie Chan and Solon So from Jackie's JC Group. You know them though?

SP: *Yes, Willie and Solon are friends of mine.*

TC: So we have these people associated with the movie. With *Purple Storm* we didn't have a big star to attract the audience to come to see the movie. If Jackie or Andy Lau was in the film then maybe we would have more box office but instead we had no star and spent all the money on the production instead.

SP: *Well it worked! Purple Storm is excellent.*

TC: Thank you, we were all happy with it too.

SP: *You had no star to draw in the audience on Purple Storm, so what was the advertising, marketing and promotions telling people before the film's release? Was it saying "Media Asia and Jackie Chan Presents"?*

TC: Yes, I think advertising the fact that Jackie was associated with the film did help a lot with getting the audience excited about the film, and also I would say that the Hong Kong audience knew me as well. They knew my film *Downtown Torpedoes*, they know what my editing is like, they knew about my other film *TwentySomething* - so they know what my style is like, and I think with all these things it helped to attract the audience. I take two years making a movie, that's everything from day one working on the script to the last day of filming. I made *TwentySomething* in 1994, *Downtown Torpedoes* in 1997 and *Purple Storm* in 1999. So I think the audience trusts me enough to know that I spend a great deal of time making a movie. Plus the films that Jackie and Media Asia released last year like *Gen-X Cops* and the film directed by Sylvia Chang... I can't remember the English name...

SP: *Tempting Heart.*

TC: Yeah, *Tempting Heart*... So this company makes quality films. Plus I'm an okay Director (laughing), and with Jackie's name associated with the film - the audience was excited to see *Purple Storm*.

SP: *Teddy, you had great success with Downtown Torpedoes for Golden Harvest. I hear a sequel is very much planned. Are you associated with it?*

TC: No.

SP: *It may fail if the original Director is not at the helm (laughing).*

TC: (Laughing) No, the new Director is young and talented. I like him.

SP: *I would have thought Golden Harvest would have definitely wanted you back for the sequel.*

TC: It doesn't matter. I did the first film and it was a great success. Now I can give it to the new Director. It doesn't matter. I'm not that kind of person, you know, "I directed the first film so I must also direct the sequel." It's good. Everybody's happy, especially the audience.

SP: *Well that's the main thing isn't it?*

TC: Yeah, also Golden Harvest were very good to me while I was making *Downtown Torpedoes*, they gave me a lot of support. So think of the good way, think of the good side.

SP: *Well, who can argue with that! Teddy, it's been an absolute pleasure talking with you. Good luck to you on The Accidental Spy, and if you are involved on any future Jackie Chan projects we look forward to covering it in Screen Power. In the meantime, we'll be sure to cover all your future movie projects in our new magazine coming out next year called Jade Screen.*

TC: Thank you Richard, I enjoyed talking with you too. Yes, your new magazine. I will want to see it when it comes out (laughing). Because, you know, with my new company there will be lots of different projects. Like for example I will produce a project soon with a well known Chinese Director and a Thai Director, and Peter Chan, my partner, will produce a Thai Director and a Korean Director. Later on we will work together with a Singaporean Director.

SP: *That's great. Lots of different collaborations and exciting projects to come out then?*

TC: Yeah, working with Directors from all over Asia. One project is that we have a big star like Andy Lau, serious drama actor, but he is the Phillippino equivalent of Andy Lau. So we are going to work together. Should be interesting for the audiences.

SP: *So lots more to come from Teddy Chen?*

TC: Well, I do hope to give the audience more of a choice with different films. I was going to work on a new script after this movie with Jackie but I have to produce some new projects for the new company. Did I tell you about that before, my new script?

SP: *No, what's that about then?*

TC: It's called *The Dragon Head*. It's a Chinese *Godfather* movie. Kind of like *Apocalypse Now*...

SP: *Apocalypse Now Hong Kong style!*

TC: Yeah, Hong Kong style. Because I think we really have to do more of an inside story with films nowadays. So everyone reading this interview around the world: don't worry, there's a lot of new exciting projects coming out from Hong Kong in the future (laughing).

SP: *(Laughing) That's great to hear. Teddy, thanks for the interview.*

TC: No, it's my pleasure. I enjoyed it very much.

JACKIE CHAN - THE SHANGHAI KID

THE LEGEND OF SHANGHAI NOON & SHANGHAI KNIGHTS

by Albert Valentin

In the Spring of 2000, Jackie Chan starred in one of his dream projects: the action-comedy *Shanghai Noon*. Why was this film considered a dream project for Jackie? Because he has always wanted to do a film set in the Wild West, where Chan would get to become a cowboy. For a long time, Chan wanted to work on a cowboy film. In fact, before he joined the Sifu Yu Jim Yuen Opera School, Chan's favorite outfit was in fact a cowboy suit.

After working on many period films as well as modern day films for the past thirty years, Chan has been wanting to work on a film set in the Wild West. He originally had a plan to make a film set in the West where his character would lose his memory. However, Tsui Hark did that with the film *Once Upon a Time in China and America*, starring Jet Li as Wong Fei-Hung in the Wild West. Three years later, Chan finally found the Western he had been looking for, and thus *Shanghai Noon* was shot on location in China and Alberta, Canada, in 1999 for release in May 2000.

For the film, Chan needed a partner who was the exact opposite of him, like he did with Chris Tucker two years earlier in *Rush Hour*. In order to complement Chan's

action skills, he found a partner in Hollywood actor Owen Wilson. Wilson began his career writing and starring in the independent comedy *Bottle Rocket*. However, it was his role as Chan's partner that was the breakthrough Wilson needed to make it big in Hollywood. The chemistry between him and Chan was nothing short of perfect.

In *Shanghai Noon*, Jackie plays Chon Wang, an Imperial Guard in the Forbidden City of China during the late 19th Century. When he becomes responsible for the disappearance of Princess Pei Pei (played by *Charlie's Angels* star Lucy Liu), Chon must head to Carson City, Nevada, to get her back. On a train to Nevada, he meets train robber Roy O'Bannon, played by Wilson. When he tries to stop the robber, chaos ensues and O'Bannon's gang betrays him. Having become lost in the melee, Chon helps a young Native American evade some evil rivals, and as a result Chon marries Falling Leaves (played by model Brandon Merrill).

When Chon and O'Bannon reunite, all hell breaks loose and a barfight ensues. Chon and Roy are jailed and this is where their friendship begins. They bust out of jail with

Asian promotional still from *Shanghai Knights*

Falling Leaves' assistance. Roy decides to help out not for the gold ransom, but for what he calls "chippechawa", which means "nobility". He teaches Chon how to be a true cowboy.

Chon soon learns the kidnapping of Pei Pei was orchestrated by an exiled Imperial Guard named Lo Fong (played by martial arts actor/stuntman Roger Yuan). Lo Fong ends up getting help from corrupt Marshall Nathan Van Cleef (played by actor Xander Berkeley). Now the two mismatched partners must start getting their stuff together and take on Lo Fong and Van Cleef to rescue the princess.

The chemistry between Chan and Wilson is unfairly compared to the chemistry between Chan and Tucker of the *Rush Hour* films. Chan's style of action complements perfectly Wilson's fast-talking, flirtatious train robber. They even learn life lessons from each other. Roy even learns a Chinese drinking game from Chon, which is very fun to watch in one of the film's funniest scenes.

The supporting cast give very good performances. Lucy Liu plays the princess who, despite being kidnapped, doesn't want to return to China. Roger Yuan is menacing as the traitor Lo Fong. He displays some great martial arts skills, this being his second Western. He played a corrupt foreman in the Jet Li film *Once Upon a Time in China and America*. Xander Berkeley plays the evil and corrupt Marshall Van Cleef, who gives Chon Wang the nickname of "The Shanghai Kid". He displays a bit of sarcasm to Roy during the amazing finale. Also

appearing in the film as one of the Imperial Guards chosen to get the princess is Hong Kong film star and former Mainland China wushu champion Yu Rong-Guang, who has a short but sweet fight sequence against Jackie in the finale.

Which brings us to the action sequences. The film was a reunion of sorts, as Jackie hired a really good friend to choreograph the film's action sequences. It is none other than his Peking Opera schoolmate and Hong Kong film star Yuen Biao. Yuen, assisted by Jackie Chan stuntmen Nicky Li, Andy Cheng and Brad Allan, knew what to do when it came to the action choreography. He knew he was dealing with a movie set in the Wild West, as well as knowing what his friend can do with ordinary objects. He showcased Chan in the barfight, using a moose's antlers as a weapon. In a fight against Van Cleef's boys, Chan uses a horseshoe combined with a rope, displaying a style of wushu that usually would be seen in Jet Li movies. For the finale, the weapons fight between Chan and Yu was well choreographed, and for the Chan versus Yuan fight, Lucy Liu joined in and even got a few kicks in, showing off some of the martial arts abilities she would display later that year in *Charlie's Angels*.

Three years later, in the Winter of 2003, the long awaited follow-up was released. Titled *Shanghai Knights*, Jackie Chan and Owen Wilson returned to their respective roles of former Imperial Guard-turned-Sheriff of Carson City Chon Wang and that fast-talking ex-train robber-turned-waiter Roy O'Bannon. Shot on location in London, England, and Prague, Czech Republic, in late 2002, the

Jackie battling Donnie Yen in the finale of *Shanghai Knights*

film has one of the best supporting casts in a movie, a truly international cast of actors in this fun-filled sequel.

The film, like its predecessor, opens in the Forbidden City in China. The father of Chon Wang (played by Him Chan) is the protector of the Imperial Seal, a sacred artifact that belongs to the Emperor. When Chon Lin (played by Singaporean actress/model Fann Wong) tells her father that Wang sent them a letter, the father tells her that he has no son.

Trouble comes in the form of Rathbone (played by British actor Aiden Gillen), a corrupt Lord from England who was hired by an "old friend", Wu Chow (played by the amazing Donnie Yen), to get the Imperial Seal. Lin decides to follow Rathbone, and informs Wang, who is in Carson City awaiting the presence of Princess Pei Pei, who now lives in San Francisco.

Upon hearing the news, Chon Wang heads to New York to meet old friend Roy O'Bannon, thinking that Roy has successfully been living the good life with the gold they had in the stock market, which Chon wants to use to go to England to see his sister. However, Roy has lost most of the gold on the stock market and is working as a waiter. Roy hatches a plan to get the money by sleeping with two women. However, Chon doesn't believe in that and, even worse, the two girls are the daughters of the Mayor of New York. After evading some local police, Chon and Roy stow away in a boat to England.

When they arrive in England, the duo is in for the ride of a lifetime. They meet a young pickpocket named Charlie Chaplin (played by Aaron Johnson), take on a band of

thugs, and team up with Detective Artie Doyle (played by Tom Fisher), who would later be known as Sir Arthur Conan Doyle. Roy also falls for Lin despite Wang's disapproval. They learn of Rathbone's plan to take over the Commonwealth with Wu Chow's assistance, in exchange for helping him get the Imperial Seal. Wu Chow is actually the illegitimate brother of the Emperor and was exiled from the Forbidden City. It's all one madcap misadventure after another for Chon and Roy.

Once again, the chemistry between Jackie and Owen is still there. It is as if the magic never left these two. Roy is still that flirtatious, outspoken, insane cowboy. However, instead of going after many girls as he did in the original, he ends up going after Chon Lin, much to his partner's disapproval. Even Jackie would get to show some funny comic stylings, using a line from 1970s detective Kojak.

Jackie with co-star Owen Wilson

When cheering up Roy for saying bad things about him to Lin, Chon invites a bevy of hookers into Roy's room. Chon pops up from behind and says that famous Kojak line: "Who loves you, baby?"

This time, the supporting cast mainly goes international in this action-packed sequel. Portraying the antagonists in the film are British actor Aiden Gillen as Lord Rathbone, who will do anything to get the Commonwealth to himself; and Hong Kong actor Donnie Yen, who plays the illegitimate brother of China's Emperor. Gillen, with help from a few doubles, displays some great talent with the sword and proves to be one of the best actors today, while Yen complements that not only with some of his best acting, but also his fight against Jackie Chan is well worth a watch. The beautiful model/actress Fann Wong does a great job as Chon Lin, the Kung-fu fighting sister of Chan and the object of Wilson's affections. Guys will easily fall for Wong upon seeing her, especially in a dream sequence where Roy dreams of Lin seducing him!

There are many historical references in this sequel that many people will be amazed at. As mentioned, the young pickpocket is named Charlie Chaplin, named after one of Chan's personal heroes. Detective Artie Doyle is a reference to Sir Arthur Conan Doyle, who created the famous fictional detective Sherlock Holmes. Speaking of Sherlock Holmes, Owen Wilson calls himself Sherlock Holmes when they go to infiltrate Rathbone's Jubilee Ball. Furthermore, the third Sherlock Holmes reference is the name Rathbone, which is a sly nod to the actor Basil Rathbone, who played - who else? - Sherlock Holmes. Other references include the name Chon Wang (sounds like John Wayne), and an appearance from Jack the Ripper, who gets his butt kicked into the Thames River by Chon Lin.

This time, Jackie Chan took over the action choreography himself, using some wire stunts and amazing hand-to-hand combat. The first of Chan's major fights, where he takes on a group of thugs in London, pays homage to one of his heroes, the legendary dancer Gene Kelly. Using an umbrella as a weapon, the fight paid homage to the classic *Singin' in the Rain*. In fact, listen carefully and you will hear the song playing during this elaborate fight sequence. Sadly though, the fight between Chan and Yen was cut short due to pacing. Not only was this fight cut out, but also a few other fights were cut short. However, with the release of the film on DVD, we get to see fights in their entirety as extra features.

For the past three years, Jackie Chan has lived his dream of working on a film as a cowboy. With his style of martial arts and comedy with a setting in the Wild West, Chan is truly "The Shanghai Kid".

Jules Daly

Screen Power editor Richard Cooper talks with Jules Daly, the co-producer of Jackie's latest Hollywood blockbuster, *Shanghai Noon*.

Daly, who has been in the Los Angeles 'producing game' for a number of years, has been associated with numerous videos and commercials for some of Hollywood's biggest production companies. She has, for the past ten years, worked for RSA USA Inc. and its directors, who include the likes of Ridley Scott and *Shanghai Noon* director Tom Dey. Jules is one busy lady, but extremely courteous as she kindly accepted my invitation for a *Screen Power* interview. Here's what we spoke about roughly a week after the movie's US release...

Screen Power: *Jules, test audiences reportedly gave Shanghai Noon in the high 90s. That must have made you feel pretty good. Did that come as a surprise? What do you think the reason is for such an enthusiastic response?*

Jules Daly: Yes, it came as quite a surprise. Not because the movie didn't deserve the high scores but because the scores were the highest test scores in Disney history. I think the audience responded so well because it's a very special movie. It reaches people on many different levels, it's not just an action flick.

SP: *Jackie has talked about making a western for several years. How much of this movie is Jackie's vision and how much of it came from the screenwriters? During interviews he has said that it is his screenplay, though he doesn't get a screenwriters credit.*

JD: The original story idea was Jackie's. The screenwriters were given a basic outline that they formed the screenplay from.

SP: *In interviews Jackie has said that the production was a bit Hong Kong style in that he was allowed to make on the spot storyline changes during production, something that doesn't normally happen in your typical Hollywood movie. Is this true?*

JD: Yes, this is absolutely true. Sometimes Jackie would improvise a bit in a fight sequence. Our director, Tom Dey, was very receptive to Jackie's ideas.

SP: *Beside being the star, what other roles did Jackie take on in Shanghai Noon? He's an executive producer or producer, correct?*

JD: Yes, Jackie has a producer credit on the movie. Jackie is very hands on and contributed to all aspects of the film's production. He really made himself part of the crew.

SP: *In his Hong Kong films Jackie is usually a solo act, but we've heard good things about the Jackie and Owen Wilson combination. Can you comment more on that?*

JD: The relationship between Jackie and Owen Wilson really shines. *Shanghai Noon* is truly a buddy movie in every sense of the phrase. Their chemistry is extraordinary and the key to the success of the movie.

SP: *What is it about Owen Wilson that convinced you that he would make a good match for Jackie?*

JD: When we met Owen we thought he was a talented actor who could compliment Jackie's physical and comedic skills. It was a pleasant surprise that they got on so perfectly.

SP: *The Shanghai Noon release was moved up to your American Memorial Day weekend, which traditionally marks the beginning of the summer blockbuster season. It went head to head with Mission: Impossible II, which did actually get a head start a few days before. What were the reasons behind that decision? How do you think Shanghai Noon did upon it's release, I mean how did it fare against such a heavily hyped film? What does Shanghai have that Mission: Impossible II or Dinosaur haven't got?*

JD: Disney decided to open *Shanghai Noon* on Memorial Day weekend because of their confidence in the film. All in all, the movie did respectably well against *Mission: Impossible II*. *Shanghai Noon* got far better reviews than *Mission: Impossible II* but had limited release. I think it's the perfect movie for kids too old for *Dinosaur* and too young for *Mission: Impossible II*. But it's actually a great movie for all ages.

SP: *Recently, western movies have been few and far between. Did the Shanghai Noon western format give Spyglass any reason for pause?*

JD: Not to my knowledge. *Shanghai Noon* was appealing because it is a western with a twist.

SP: *Do you think this will make the western movie fashionable again?*

JD: Jackie told me that after he wore his cowboy hat and long hair it became fashionable in Hong Kong, so who knows?

SP: *Word has it you are already planning not one*

Jackie converses with Jules (second left) and producers Gary Barber (centre) and Roger Birnbaum (right)

but two sequels. Is that true? The tone of the sequels has already been determined as being more of an Indiana Jones type adventure. Any idea when that might be in the works?

JD: All I can say is that there has definitely been talk of sequels.

SP: What was the personal highlight for you in working with Jackie?

JD: Just meeting Jackie and working with him on a personal level was an experience I wouldn't trade for the world. He is such a generous, kind hearted, hard working ingenious athlete. I feel honored to call him my friend. Not to mention how much he loves my dog, Jones!

SP: What did the American crew think about having to work with Jackie?

JD: They were all pretty excited. Jackie worked so well with the crew because he's so down-to-earth, he is very approachable, like just another crew member. Jackie has such an incredible reputation in the States, but I think he's also a bit of a mystery. Hopefully Shanghai Noon will secure his celebrity status in America.

SP: Were there any funny happenings on set?

JD: Every day! Everyone should check out the gag reel at the end of Shanghai Noon. That says it all.

SP: Jules, thanks so much for talking to me.

JD: Thank you Richard.

Special thanks to Jules' assistant Kelly Williams for her help setting up the interview and to our very own Gail Mihara for additional questions used in this interview.

SHANGHAI BAD BOY

RICHARD COOPER TALKS TO ROGER YUAN - MARTIAL ARTIST, FIGHT CHOREOGRAPHER AND ACTOR BEHIND THE ROLE OF LO FONG IN JACKIE CHAN'S SHANGHAI NOON

Screen Power: *Roger, let's first start off by getting some background information and details. Where were you born and raised?*

Roger Yuan: I was born in Carbondale, Illinois, USA, but I spent my first five years in Taiwan. I returned to the States and my family moved around quite often. I returned to live in Taiwan again at the age of eight and I spent my teen years in New York, eventually moving to San Francisco and ultimately Los Angeles. I now reside in Southern California but I spend quite a bit of time in Ireland.

SP: *You and Jackie had some great fight action in Shanghai Noon - have you studied martial arts in great detail?*

RY: My martial arts history is strange and varied. My parents felt that academics were of the utmost importance and they discouraged me from athletics and sports in general. As a youngster I trained myself in my parents' basement armed with Bruce Lee's book *Tao of Jeet Kune Do* as my martial arts bible. I read everything I could get my hands on and ingratiated myself with schoolmates that were training, even incorporating ballet exercises into my regime. I have a black belt (4th degree) in Tang Soo Do and I've also trained extensively in Wing Chun, Kyokushin, Tae Kwon Do, Thai Boxing, Western Boxing, Tai Chi and an extreme form of Shaolin Kung-fu.

SP: *Wow, that is varied! (Laughing) When and how did you get into the acting business then?*

RY: I've been in the film and television business for about fifteen years. I started out doing martial arts fights and later did choreography and second unit directing for film and television. I've been obsessed with martial arts since I was a boy watching Bruce Lee as Kato in *The Green Hornet*. I was always trying to find a way that I could parlay my passion into a vocation. Through the film fights and choreography I was afforded the opportunity to continue to train and grow as a martial artist. One man who took me under his wing was legendary kick boxer Benny 'The Jet' Urquidez. Benny introduced me to some real legends like Blake Edwards (*Son of the Pink Panther*), Robert Zemeckis (*Death Becomes Her*) and Tim Burton (*Batman Returns*), all of who I choreographed fights for. I began getting a lot of calls for acting roles

Roger on set with Jackie

that called upon my physical abilities, but it's been over the last five years that I feel like an actor who happens to have physical abilities as opposed to a guy with physical abilities who happens to act! Because my family moved around a lot I was relatively shy. Public speaking was always a fear of mine. Looking back on why I chose to be an actor, I think it was my way of confronting my fears and continuing to grow as a person and an artist. Acting has provided me with the perfect venue to face my fears.

SP: How did you get the role of the villainous Lo Fong in Shanghai Noon?

RY: It's a funny story now. The director, Tom Dey, didn't want me initially and it was the casting directors Matthew Barry and Nancy Green-Keyes that pushed hard for him to meet with me. Tom had seen my work in film and television and apparently at the time he didn't feel that I could be cold-hearted and evil enough based on my previous roles (laughing). But Matthew and Nancy never gave up on me and once Tom agreed to meet me, as they say, "The rest is history."

SP: Were you a fan of Jackie's films before you worked with him on Shanghai Noon? What are some of your favourite Jackie films?

RY: Yes, I've been a fan and I continue to admire Jackie for his ability to define his own niche. Jackie has an amazing ability to combine martial arts athleticism with physical comedy of the likes of Buster Keaton and Charlie Chaplin. My favourite Jackie film is *Drunken Master II*, which I believe to be the best Wong Fei-hung action film.

SP: What was it like working on Shanghai Noon with Jackie?

RY: It was a great experience. Tom Dey gave me a great deal of freedom developing my character and it was a lot of fun working with Lucy Liu. Of course it was especially rewarding seeing Jackie in action, up close.

He's very traditional as a martial artist and as a teacher. He was very reserved with me at first, but Yuen Biao (fight choreographer) and I seemed to click immediately. As Jackie got to know me better he seemed to get more comfortable. He was very helpful and it was terrific to work closely with him to draw from his years of experience.

SP: Action film fans remember you in Hollywood's Lethal Weapon 4 and Hong Kong's Once Upon a Time in China and America. What were those films like to work on? In fact, Once Upon a Time in China and America has just been released in the UK on video and DVD, and Hong Kong movie fans are looking forward to seeing this one.

RY: I didn't know that, that's good to know. I

Roger with co-star Lucy Liu

enjoyed my experiences on both films for different reasons. On *Lethal Weapon 4* my daughter was born during the shoot, so that's something I'll never forget. Secondly, *Braveheart* had a profound effect on me when it came out and that made working with Mel Gibson all the more special. Richard Donner was very generous and overall it was a very positive experience.

On *Once Upon a Time in China and America* I was working on a project in Texas already when I got the call about a meeting with Sammo Hung. I met with Sammo in San Antonia and then I went back to work on the project I was working on. I got a good feeling about the film and I felt that Sammo really wanted to have me on board. We had some difficulty with scheduling, but once I was finished with my other commitments I went from Dallas to the little town of Bracketsville, Texas, where they were shooting. It was interesting to work with a Hong Kong crew on American soil. When I first got there I didn't even know what part I was playing. I got the role of Dick, a man who turns on his fellow immigrant settlers by framing them for robbing the local bank.

If you see the film there's one scene where it seems that Seven [Xiong Xin-xin] and my character are about to fight. There's this intense moment where we stare each other down but we never did get to fight. I would have enjoyed fighting Xin-xin on film.

SP: *I remember the scene well, and it was a great shame that you didn't get to fight him. Now you've starred in both Hollywood and Hong Kong films, what films or industry do you prefer?*

RY: Well the truth is Richard, I just enjoy working. I've got the best job in the world. I get to see the world and work with some of the most talented people in the business. I'll gladly take the best of both worlds. I'm definitely looking forward to working on more Hong Kong projects in the future. For me, it's about the people I'm working with, the character I'm playing and the story we're telling, not necessarily in that order. I want to do quality projects and if it's a Hong Kong film or a French film or a big Hollywood movie it's all good. I've worked all over the US as well as Canada, South Africa, Thailand, Hong Kong, Ireland and France. Each project and each location ultimately poses its own unique challenges and offers its own special rewards.

SP: *Many Hong Kong directors are coming over to the West to make their action films these days. That must be good news for you?*

RY: It's very exciting news, although I haven't professionally reaped the benefits of the influx of Hong Kong directors. I worked with Sammo and Tsui Hark on Hong Kong projects, but as a fan of the genre it's wonderful to see.

SP: *Were there any funny happenings while you were filming Shanghai Noon with Jackie?*

RY: There was the night we all went out for dinner and Jackie and some of the crew were playing drinking games and singing karaoke. The whole scene resembled the scene between Owen Wilson and Jackie in the bath tubs playing the games. At one point Jackie told the producers to "stop singing, you're giving karaoke a bad name!" (Laughing)

SP: *What can people next see you in?*

RY: I just wrapped back-to-back episodes of *Walker, Texas Ranger* for American Television (CBS) which gave me the chance to work with my friend Chuck Norris. It was a bit of a homecoming because Chuck and I have known each other for years and I have a lot of friends that work on that show. Those episodes will air in the US in November. I'm also currently working on developing film and television projects, and I've got a few other irons in the fire, so to speak.

SP: *Roger, thanks so much for taking the time to talk to me. I wish you all the best in your career, and keep in touch!*

RY: It's been my pleasure Richard. Thank you very much, and I'll be sure to stay in touch.

DRUNKEN MASTER

By Matthew Edwards

When charting the career of Jackie Chan there are countless examples of how he has managed to revolutionise the Martial Arts and Action genres with his dazzling feats of athleticism, storytelling and breathtaking stunts, each time becoming more daring and spectacular. Films like *Project A*, *Police Story*, *Armour of God II* and *Rush Hour* give credence to this, at once displaying how Jackie had managed to define and perfect his art of filmmaking as his vision evolved. His knack of performing his own stunts, no matter how ludicrous or gruelling, stood him out from others. Wrapped around this he incorporated an innocent sense of humour and nice guy persona that could unite and bond both the young and old to him. Thus, when assessing his career the pivotal point can be clearly placed on a little 1979 film entitled *Drunken Master* that would in time define the genetic

make-up of all his films. Following on from the success of *Snake in the Eagle's Shadow*, *Drunken Master* captivated the world over and still remains unsurpassed, making it perhaps the most important of all Jackie's films.

Everything gelled with *Drunken Master*. The choreography, the imaginative set-pieces, the comedy, Jackie's mischievous performance as Chinese folk-hero Wong Fei Hung, the strong direction of Yuen Woo Ping and the comic antics of Yuen Siu Tien as the wine guzzling alcoholic Sam the Seed. Although the premise and narrative was essentially a reprise of *Snake in the Eagle's Shadow*, it still had enough innovative Martial Arts and set-pieces to make it stand out from its predecessor, and to make it one of Jackie Chan's most distinctive pieces, if not a masterpiece.

Drunken Master opens in a similar vein to *Snake in the Eagle's Shadow* (obviously building upon its success by repeating its winning formula and structure), whereby we are introduced to the cold blooded assassin

Jackie with the late Simon Yuen Siu Tien

"Thunderfoot" (played by Hwang Jang Lee) as he carries out a contract to exterminate Charlie Wei. As the credits roll, Thunderfoot dispatches his foe with ease, culminating in an exquisite two footed barrel kick to his opponent's chest.

The film's basic premise revolves around a young Wong Fei Hung, played by Jackie, who incurs the wrath of his father with his delinquent behaviour while a pupil at his Martial Arts school. Intent on teaching his son discipline, he sends the disgruntled Wong away to train under the notorious training methods of his uncle (Yuen Siu Tien), an alcoholic Kung-fu master with an infamous reputation for crippling his students. Wong finds the training methods gruelling, and escapes from his brutal regime only to be confronted by Thunderfoot and badly beaten. With his pride dented, Wong returns back to his Sifu and resumes his training, intent on mastering the "Eight Drunken Gods" technique in order to gain revenge on Thunderfoot, who by now has a contract to eradicate Wong's father, as issued by the evil "King of Sticks".

Aside from the comedy that had been accentuated to greater heights, the film's success can be attributed to two key areas. Firstly the two major training sequences (including Jackie learning the art of the Eight Drunken Gods) and secondly the Martial Arts action that punctuates the plot like an assassin's target as it rips through the narrative.

The first key training sequence to take place in *Drunken Master* consists of Jackie inside a small courtyard receiving his punishment from his father for an earlier scuffle. Irate with Wong's lack of discipline and behaviour, his father demands Wong undertake five hours of the painful horse stance whilst under the watchful eyes of his teacher. To make matters worse, Wong has five china cups placed around his body (one is placed on his head, one on each shoulder and one each on the tops of his legs) and filled with boiling water. If that wasn't enough, an incense burner is placed in a precarious position below him so that if he were to stray from his position he would soon know about it!

The scene turns extremely comical at this point as the teacher attempts to taunt Wong. After refilling the china cups with boiling water, he starts tickling Jackie with a feather so that he will drop one of the cups and have to complete another hour of horse stance. As his teacher returns to his table and starts picking his feet, one of Wong's mates brings him a conveniently shaped bench to perch on. Unsuspecting of this, the teacher looks on, blissfully ignorant, until Wong's father spots him in the act and kicks the chair from beneath him. A scalded Wong gives off an agonised screech! It is at this point that Wong's father informs Wong that he must now train under Sam the Seed. Also of interest, the next scene sees Jackie hanging with his hands tied around his back with a large black casket of ale hanging around his neck.

Needless to say, Jackie's face is bright red, making you realise that this isn't just great acting but also the work of a man who will inflict any sort of pain on himself to get the right shot!

This scene is the first real indication of the agility and natural ability that Jackie possesses. Although it had been hinted at in *Snake in the Eagle's Shadow*, this was the first real film to showcase his skills and his full potential as a Martial Artist. To watch Jackie undertake the horse stance is a glorious moment and one that lingers in many fans' minds for days after watching.

After Wong has attempted to escape from Sam's booby-trapped house, the second key training sequence has Sam teaching Wong the tricks of the trade. First up he shows Wong how to fall, whereby he throws Wong over his shoulder on countless occasions. Sam comments that all his pupils must learn how to fall properly. Wong on the other hand comments that Sam could break a gorilla's back! The next task for Wong is to fill and empty four large jars simultaneously with a bucket. As Wong

spins and twirls he ends up falling in, much to Sam's disgust.

Next up, against the bright lush countryside, Sam teaches Wong bamboo wrist press-ups. This entails Wong having his wrists tied with rope attached to two metre long bamboo sticks. Here Sam throws poor old Wong around again, before he is soon hanging upside down filling a small wooden bucket with two-teacups from two large water jars! After Wong cheats when fooled into thinking Sam is asleep he is made to repeat the exercise with two smaller cups! Finally Wong has to crack walnuts with his forefinger and thumb before his training exercises are over.

What both of these scenes demonstrated was Jackie's natural athleticism and dedication to his work and the film. Reports suggest that Jackie and the filmmakers performed take after take to perfect the strenuous psychical demands of these scenes and the end results prove this theory. These scenes are a remarkable testimony to Jackie and the lengths he was prepared to

put himself through in order to heighten the film's impact. His scenes of perfecting the art of the Eight Drunken Gods also indicated he was destined for the big league. Against a backdrop of green fields and hills Jackie falls, rolls and twirls like some drunken ballerina. Aptly he can only truly master the technique when absolutely soused!

The Martial Arts sequences also contribute to the film's success, demonstrating Jackie's superb fighting ability. Such classic scenes include Jackie squaring up to a sword wielding maniac in a local market, whereupon he beats him senseless and leaves him on a chopping board table, and an encounter with a bald headed freak who seems intent on pulverising Wong's chest with his head. Luckily Wong and Sam work in tandem to beat the bald headed fool by any means necessary. When a wooden board and a porcelain pot both fail, they use a pair of blue pants! Another classic scene involves Wong's second encounter with the King of Sticks that highlights Jackie's gift of incorporating objects when choreographing his fight scenes. It also showcases his Drunken Gods technique for the first time, before producing several blows to the King of Sticks' chest!

Each of these scenes displays excellent Martial Arts, however it's the added slapstick motifs that set the fight scenes apart from other Kung-fu films of this period. At times they are painstaking but always delivered in good taste and humour. The violence as always leans towards the comical as opposed to the bone cracking fight sequences of modern Kung-fu pictures.

After Wong receives a beating from Thunderfoot, Wong confronts him in an epic showdown. Quickly drinking huge quantities of wine, Wong unleashes his Eight Drunken Gods technique on the unsuspecting Thunderfoot. At one point Wong adopts the form of Miss Ho the Drunken God Flaunting Her Body, whereby he defeats his opponent with ease, at once perfecting his new-found style. This scene is laced with excellent slow-motion shots that leave the viewer begging for more long after Hwang Jang Lee lies motionless on the soft sandy ground.

The film is a true testament to Jackie's career and signifies the feel good format he would also stick to. The film also highlights his dedication to his films by performing take after take to gain maximum realism. His scenes in the brutal regime of Sam the Seed highlight this. Also the supporting acting warrants praise for Hwang Jang Lee and the irreplaceable Yuen Siu Tien who undoubtedly brings the film alive. The Director Yuen Woo Ping and producer Ng See Yuen, who took their creative madness to a higher plateau, also deserve credit. *Drunken Master* still remains unsurpassed and the turning point in Jackie's career. It would be fair to say that Jackie has used the same mould as *Drunken Master* on most of his films since, and it is this feel good nature and slapstick comedy combined with fast paced and adrenaline pumping action scenes that he has chosen to follow ever since.

Island Of Fire

By Matthew Edwards

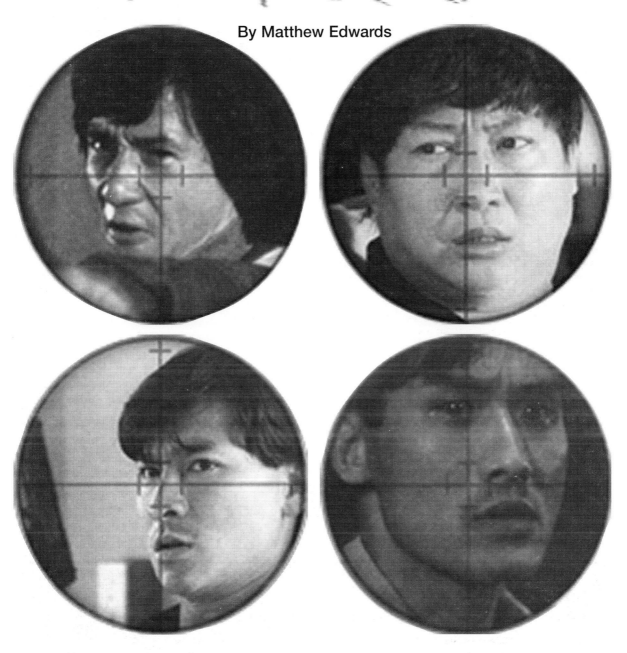

From left: Andy Lau, Jackie Chan, Tony Leung Ka Fai, Sammo Hung

Any Jackie Chan fans who were expecting great stunts and numerous bouts of tomfoolery from *Island Of Fire* were sure to be disappointed, as the film is devoid of any humour, replacing it instead with dynamic red-blooded fight sequences that had a panache for squirting out gallons of red blood. It also marked a rarity for Jackie in that his character is killed at the end, as well as the fact that he replaces his fists with guns in the film's finale.

Although flawed, *Island Of Fire* proves to be an entertaining, exciting and violent movie that also features gripping performances from its principle cast. *Island Of Fire* is one of Jackie's most daring films that will divide Jackie Chan film fans into either a love or hate relationship with the film, primarily because of the graphic violence. The film is good fodder of its kind and is best suited for Hong Kong Cinema connoisseurs.

The film opens with Andy, a Hong Kong police officer played by Tony Leung, returning to his mentor Professor Leung, his colleague Jerry and his girlfriend Sally, where he learns of a confidential operation to go undercover. Sally, who berates them for talking about work, cuts the details of the operation short, whereby Professor Leung agrees to talk more about the operation on the following day.

As the evening comes to a close, Sally offers to take Andy back to his hotel. As they become intimate in their

car, against a backdrop of torrential rain, Andy notices someone is visiting the professor. As Professor Leung answers the door he is shot at point blank range by an unknown assassin. Leaping out of the car, Andy fires back, catching the assassin in the arm. The assassin then reaches the sanctuary of his vehicle, whereupon his vehicle is suspiciously blown up by an apparent car bomb.

When looking for clues, Jerry finds the assassin's gun and a severed finger. When searching the computer records, Andy and Jerry discover that the murder suspect, Carl Chan, was in fact supposedly executed three months prior, leading them to believe there is corruption within the jail.

Andy agrees to go undercover in order to reveal the corruption by setting up Operation Hunter. In order to gain access into the penal system, he first beats up a group of young hoodlums in a trendy bar, and then waits for the police. As he waits in jail, Jerry warns him his life is at risk, however Andy vows to continue in order to seek justice on those who had killed his mentor.

Decked out in a dull blue prison uniform, Andy is thrown into prison life, where other inmates taunt him by clipping him around the head and tugging on his clothes. Andy is shown his small cell that is both dark and damp. It is here that Andy meets his cellmate Charlie, who keeps a small pet mouse. Charlie befriends Andy and offers him a cigarette, whereby we meet Sammo Hung's character John, who at first pretends he is a prison guard. John begins offering betting odds with Charlie on Andy's impending fight with the prison champ and whether or not he will last thirty seconds. It is here that Andy learns the cruel nature of prison life and gets his first taste of the corruption within.

As Andy is pulled from his cell, the prison has turned into a boxing arena with all the inmates and guards in attendance. As a small clearing is made, the fight begins with Andy taking an early beating. Picking himself up from the floor, Andy lays a few heavy punches into the champ's head, at once forcing him backwards. Rattled, the champ delivers a succession of furious blows that leave Andy sprawled across the hard prison floor.

Staggering onto his feet before the count, Andy, who by now is badly dazed and bruised, swings a bevy of wild punches into the air, before the champ finishes him off with one last punch that leaves him crumpled and unconscious on the floor. As the inmates retire to their cells, Charlie drags the injured and bloody Andy to his cell, his initiation to prison life complete.

The next few scenes flesh out John's character, where we learn he misses his son. Learning he has been sent to a boarding school, John engineers an escape from prison by offering to cook the head guard a piece of steak. Dressed in an apron and cooking hat, John begins to demonstrate his cooking skills that leave the guard literally drooling. Just as he serves up the meal he proceeds to whack the guard over the head with his cooking stick!

What follows is the film's only moment of humour as we witness Sammo struggling to fit into the guard's uniform and shoes. Whilst attempting to escape from the jail's perimeter grounds a fellow guard asks for a light and begins engaging in idle chit chat. Meanwhile the guard's dog begins licking his toes, whereupon John is forced to hit the guard and then the dog, which is sent crashing to the floor whimpering!

Whilst on the run John steals a car and meets up with his son. They spend the day together, eating candyfloss and taking photos, before John is finally arrested outside his son's boarding school and sent back to jail, where he is strung up in front of his fellow inmates and beaten by the guards. He is also forced to apologise to the dog he hit that now sports a bloody bandage around its head!

The next scene introduces us to Jackie's character Steve, a big-time pool player, who is watching his girlfriend Kiki, a model for Chanel, performing at a fashion show. As Steve watches Kiki, a mysterious businessman offers him a bribe of half a million dollars to throw his pending pool match. Steve refuses, as he is intent on winning the competition.

At the pool event, Steve absolutely annihilates his opponent with various trick shots and superb potting that would leave any professional in awe. As Steve clears the table with his impressive array of shots, his opponent steps in and places his cue in front of Steve's. In a great sequence, Steve flips his white ball over his opponent's cue, that in turn knocks in his coloured ball then the black, thus winning the competition. Stunned, the mysterious businessman leaves, unimpressed.

It's great watching Jackie playing pool in this scene as it confirms he is in fact quite a gifted player. All the trick shots are not staged and it's Jackie actually performing them as opposed to clever editing.

The following day Steve meets Kiki in a bar. As they decide where to go, the mysterious businessman and his men suddenly confront Steve. Surrounded, Steve bursts into action by beating his opponents with some deft punches and kicks. The businessman then puts a knife to Kiki's throat. Steve is suddenly beaten to the floor, and as his girlfriend tries to escape she is stabbed in the back. The businessman flees, leaving Steve to carry his injured girlfriend to hospital. Once there, he is told that he needs HK$200,000 to save her. Oddly he decides to raise the cash by gambling!

Situated around a small wooden table in a gambling den, Steve beats his opponent with a full house. Taking his winnings, Steve leaves. However, his opponent, Teddy, demands he stays longer so he can win back his money. Steve refuses, whereupon Teddy declares him a cheat. As Teddy's men surround Steve another fight kicks off. With the money in his mouth, Steve uses chairs, bottles and stunning scissor kicks in order to escape. In one brilliant sequence, Steve throws one gang member over his shoulder and through a glass door and one through a bright red telephone box.

In this sequence we are back in familiar Jackie Chan territory as he slides and bounces around the screen delivering some of his trademark kicks and punches. Although used briefly, he still manages to use a few objects in the fight sequences as well as a few slow-motion shots of villains flying through shattered glass.

As Teddy lunges at Steve with a knife, Steve disarms him before leaving with the money. As Steve turns his back, Teddy rushes at Steve, and in the ensuing struggle Teddy is accidentally killed. As the police cart Steve away, Teddy's brother and boss of the establishment Li (played by Andy Lau) vows vengeance on Steve for his brother's death. Once inside jail, members of Li's gang begin threatening and intimidating Steve with the intention of killing him.

A basketball is thrown near Steve. Throwing the ball back he notices Li's men are watching him. Strolling across the jail floor, Steve refreshes himself by drinking tap water. As Steve drinks he is attacked. Dodging his opponent's swipes he places his enemy's hand under the hot water tap, at once burning his arm. From behind him another of Li's men attacks, this time piercing his flesh. Steve turns to hit him into the prison's door. Steve is then attacked for a third time and again he is injured. Bleeding, Steve head-butts his opponent, who is sent crashing to the floor. Another one of Li's men jumps down from the balcony above, before the prison guards rush in to restore order. As the guards try to ascertain what has happened, Andy and Charlie step in and snitch on Li's men, whereby they are sent to the "hole" (a blackened cell where inmates are forced to stay when they have broken the jail's strict rules and guidelines).

This scene is played out in super slow-motion where we witness Jackie performing a few kicks and punches. This sequence is shot stylishly by Director Chu Yen Ping, especially in the way we are made to feel the full anguish of Jackie's character as he struggles desperately for his life amidst the brutal blows he receives.

The next scene introduces us to Lucas, the jail's leader, who sports a large tattoo across his back and shoulders, and who has just been released from the infamous hole. As he is returned to his cell all his inmates pick him up and throw confetti all over him as they greet him. Once in his cell he calls for Andy, whereby Andy is thrown into Lucas's cell and is accused of being an informer. With a knife to his throat, Lucas probes him on why he has been asking so many questions about Carl Chan, whereupon they begin burning his hand with torched paper. Andy withstands the torture, denying everything. Letting the injured Andy go, Lucas warns Andy that his life is in his hands.

At lunch Andy is asked how he injured his hand by a prison guard. Andy lies, telling the guard he cut it in the workshop. Not believing Andy's story, he takes away his food. Impressed with Andy, Lucas offers Andy his meal. When the guard notices, he makes Lucas eat the entire rice pot. As Lucas is being humiliated, Andy and then all the inmates join in defiantly against the guards to help Lucas consume the rice pot.

Andy and Lucas manage to get their revenge on the guard days later when working outside. When the guard boastfully claims that if they finish the work early he would turn into a pig, the inmates all rally together to complete the work two hours before schedule, at once humiliating the guard.

Soon after, a dejected John returns to his cell where he admits to missing his son. However, his spirits are soon raised the following day when he comes to the aid of a young damsel in distress whose vehicle has become stuck in mud. The lady's wet and revealing top causes much laughter and arousal from John and his fellow inmates, who talk about the incident endlessly when gambling that evening!

The joy on the floor is short lived though as Li's men return from a stint in the hole. Trying to unite the two parties, Lucas demands that Li's men forgive Steve and end the feud running between them. When one of Li's men questions Lucas about the death of Li's brother, Lucas promptly takes out a knife and cuts his forearm before declaring, "I'll bleed for him." Reluctantly Li's men make a truce with Steve.

During lunch Charlie mentions to Andy that he cannot find his mouse. When Li's men serve his meal it turns out that they have cruelly boiled his pet mouse and have buried it beneath his food. Enraged, Charlie attacks one of Li's men, whereupon he is smashed around the head by a cooking bowl. Coming to his aid, Andy grabs one of Li's men and rams his head against a kitchen unit. Stepping in, the guards smack Andy with their truncheons and drag him off to the hole.

Meanwhile, after more outdoor work, John manages another successful breakout after tricking the guards into thinking he is taking a dump. When the guards investigate they realise that he has gone, whereupon John reappears and escapes in a police car along with Lucas. Their freedom is short-lived when around a small campfire the police arrive. John confesses that he has tipped off the police in order to see his son. However, when the police arrive they murder Lucas and double-cross John by denying him access to see his son. Slumped upon John's shoulders, Lucas's body is brought back to the jail as an example to others.

It is only a matter of time before John attempts another breakout, however this time it ends with fatal consequences. When a snake causes a commotion amongst the inmates working in the long reeds, John quickly escapes in a police car, where he hits a police guard and overturns the vehicle. Unconscious, John is dragged out of the wreckage along with the dead officer. Later a judge sentences him to death.

After Andy is released from the hole, we see Li's club raided by his corrupt father-in-law, who is a high-ranking officer in the Hong Kong Police. Li's father-in-law demands HK$50,000 from him. In turn, Li first beats him, before demanding he be arrested so he can gain access to Steve within the jail.

Once Li is inside the jail the tension mounts. Steve even goes as far as to apologise to Li for the death of his brother Teddy. Li is less forgiving and he comments that he would have killed Steve's girlfriend if his girlfriend weren't dead already. Before Li leaves he also declares that he will make Steve feel the agony of his girlfriend's death before he kills him.

Sat in his cold pastel-blue cell, Li waits for his pending fight with Steve. Emerging from his cell, he throws Steve a small handmade knife. From an above balcony the guards arrive, placing bets on who will be the winner.

Peering through their cell doors, the other inmates watch as the fight kicks off.

Li attacks, sending various swipes at Steve's midriff, while Steve uses a nearby banister to great effect to dodge his opponent's attacks. After both fighters have received various kicks and punches, Steve throws Li over his shoulder and onto the dusty jail room floor. Getting to his feet, Li then pushes Steve from a balcony and they begin tussling against a black beam. It is here that Steve is stabbed in the chest. In one last bout of energy, Steve again throws Li over his shoulder and then proceeds to send a brutal kick to his head. Jumping on his opponent, he places the knife to Li's throat amidst the chants of "kill him".

Instead of killing Li, Steve attacks the prison guards and delivers several blows to the senior guard's head before he is beaten senseless by the guard's colleagues. Trying to come to Steve's aid, Li is shot by another guard and is then dragged off. As Steve lies bloody and bruised, the senior guard points a gun at his head, whereupon Andy warns him that he will report him. The guard repents and Steve is dragged off.

For a Jackie Chan fight sequence this is quite visceral and violent, and some viewers may find the level of violence not to their taste. Both Li and Steve are at first intent on killing the other as demonstrated by the anger on both their faces and by the brutal force that they deliver on one another. When Jackie attacks the prison guards it may come as a shock to some fans to witness Jackie being beaten with truncheons until his head is left in a bloody pulp.

During the New Year celebrations things begin well, until the corrupt senior officer gives one of Li's men a mysterious syringe that he injects into Andy's lightbulb. Obviously intended for Andy, it is Charlie who unfortunately goes back to his cell first, where he turns on the lightbulb and is set ablaze. His screaming burning body rushes onto the jail room floor, where various inmates try to put out the flames.

As Charlie's corpse lies motionless on the ground, Andy spots one of Li's men escaping from Andy's room. Andy begins beating him until the corrupt guard steps in and begins whacking the suspect in truly bloody style! As Li's man is dragged away he mutters he was framed and that the senior guard wanted Andy dead. Naturally this sparks a prison riot involving countless guards and inmates, with Andy pitted against the senior guard.

During the riot the guard and Andy tussle on the floor as Andy attempts to strangle him. Pushing him aside the corrupt guard attempts to shoot Andy, when suddenly

Charlie's killer steps in instead to take the bullets. Andy, who is at this point sprawled upon the ground, gets to his feet and picks up the guard's gun and shoots him dead.

Next we learn that Andy has been sentenced to death by firing squad. Blindfolded and tied against a small post, he is executed as ripples of red blood squirt from his chest. However, Andy awakes in a small cell where we learn from the jail commissioner that he has been selected to work for the jail's secret executive committee. He tells Andy that he is legally dead (he shows him pictures of his own funeral) and that should he succeed in his pending mission he will be given a new identity and passport to start over his life again. It is here where Andy and the viewer learn of deep-rooted corruption within the jail and that it is the prison's commissioner who is behind it.

Blindfolded, Andy is taken to the location of his mission, where he learns that he, along with John, Steve and Li, must assassinate Colonel Sama, the biggest drug dealer in South Asia. It turns out he is to stand trial but has paid off the judges. Their mission is simple: execute him before he gets onto the plane. The commissioner also adds that a getaway car will be on hand when they finish the hit.

Emerging from their vehicle, the quartet walk towards the plane. From beneath their jackets they pull out their handguns and begin firing. Colonel Sama is killed instantly and slumps to the floor. Steve, John and Li begin firing at the police and their bodies jerk backwards from the impact of the bullets.

Racing towards their getaway jeep, Andy recalls the death of his mentor and realises the jeep has a car bomb hidden in it. Warning his friends, they dive from the vehicle simultaneously as it explodes into flames. With nowhere to go, Steve, John and Li run off, whilst Andy, with the help of Jerry, who has mysteriously appeared, clambers onto the plane.

With our trio on the run, they start gunning down various military personnel in a frenzy of bullet-ridden mayhem. As countless army men die in typically bloody fashion there is still time for Jackie to adopt the famous Chow Yun Fatt *Heroic Bloodshed* dive whilst blowing away the enemy. There's also a great sequence when Andy Lau's character leaps at his foe and grabs him in a headlock with his legs and flips him onto the ground, breaking his neck.

In the following sequence Steve tries to burst open the air traffic control room door, however his foot goes through the door and it is nearly blown off by the returning gunfire. Needless to say, John smacks open the door and unleashes a furious burst of gunfire, killing everyone inside the room, bar one who they take hostage.

Surrounded by over three hundred army officials who are armed to their teeth (there're even fighter helicopters flying about) our trio tentatively walk out into the blazing sun towards the getaway plane they have demanded. They have all now become targets, whereupon John is shot in the shoulder, and in retaliation Steve and Li shoot dead the hostage.

By now Steve, John and Li are all scampering towards the plane whilst being pursed by the army. John is the first to fall as he jerks uncontrollably to the ballistic effects of the bullets impacting through his body. Steve and Li follow shortly as both collapse amidst a shower of bullets that penetrate through their chests, squirting ample amounts of crimson blood. Andy escapes in the plane, unable to help his companions.

Those fans that winced at Jackie being beaten earlier will not enjoy watching Jackie die in quite such a depressing or bloodthirsty manner. It also signifies a rare moment, one in which we watch Jackie die on film, something we are unaccustomed to seeing. Usually in a Jackie Chan film Jackie will save the day and it will feature a feel good or comic ending, however Chu Yen Ping scuppers any chance of that. The trio's demise at the end seems to be inspired by Oliver Stone's Vietnam epic *Platoon* in the memorable sequence when Willem Defoe is pursued by the Vietcong where he takes hit after hit before he succumbs in his somewhat symbolic death.

Arriving home, the commissioner enters his study where he finds Andy in the corner. Initially he goes for his gun but, realising it has gone, he congratulates Andy and then claims he is free. Andy sarcastically praises him for using supposedly dead convicts to do his dirty work then to have them killed afterwards. When asked why he killed both Professor Leung and Colonel Sama, the commissioner replies that Colonel Sama was his partner and that he would have testified against him in court and that Professor Leung had investigated the jail and was getting too close to uncovering his dealings.

Searching in his cabinet, the commissioner pulls out another gun and fires. However, the gun is empty. Putting a gun to the commissioner's head, Andy threatens to kill him. Jerry rushes in with the police and they arrest the commissioner and Andy is reunited with his girlfriend Sally.

Many Jackie Chan fans will not like *Island Of Fire* because of the brutality of its violence and the film's harsh and gritty nature. However, those fans who like to see Jackie take on new and more challenging roles may find the film an interesting and alternative entry in his resume. With a good strong cast that performs well, *Island Of Fire* is a good Hong Kong action film, although it never reaches the brilliance of Ringo Lam's *Prison On Fire* series or Karel Ng's Category III shocker *Jail Of No Return*. That said, fans of Hong Kong prison dramas and Hong Kong Action Cinema will surely lap it up.

DANCE OF DEATH

JACKIE'S INFLUENTIAL FIGHT SCENES IN UNDERRATED CLASSIC

By Albert Valentin

In 1980, Jackie Chan was asked by good friend Chen Chi-Hwa to be the martial arts director for a film entitled *Dance of Death*. The film starred Angela Mao [Ying], best known to audiences in the West as Bruce Lee's sister in the classic *Enter the Dragon*. Chan and Chen had done films such as the 1976 film *Shaolin Wooden Men*, and the 1978 film *Half a Loaf of Kung Fu*, the first "real" Kung-fu comedy. A year before, the two collaborated on *The 36 Crazy Fists*, where Jackie was also the fight choreographer.

In the film's extravagant fight sequences you can clearly see that it was Jackie who had done the fights. Some of the techniques had a comical element added to them, marking a difference between those serious chop-socky films of the 1970s and Jackie Chan's breakthrough genre of "Kung-fu Comedy".

IN NEED OF HELP

Fei Fei (Angela Mao), a disciple of the Five Forms School, has escaped from a group of bandits led by the Upside Down Horse Boxer Ma Fa-Chun (Sun Reng-Chi, *The Leg Fighters*). On her way, she sees a Kung-fu fight emerging between two old masters, Hu (Chin Pei) and Lu (Shiao Bou-Lo). As she looks on, she discovers that they may be the key to helping her get revenge. Upon meeting them, they tell her that they have been going at it for 20 years now to see who is the better fighter, and that every time they fight the combat always ends in a draw.

Fei Fei then has an idea that may help the two, as well as assist her in her plan for revenge. She offers to learn both their styles and fight someone else. She explains that whichever style defeats her opponent is the best of the two. The two masters have their doubts, worrying that she might use only one of their styles, but Fei Fei makes the promise to combine their styles and whichever style is the final blow, that master will be the victor.

FLASHBACK

In a flashback scene we see Fei Fei help the master of the Five Forms School, Hsu, fight off three misfit experts, Roc, Little Bird, and Big Bird. During the fight, Fei Fei uses a staff and even a wooden spoon to take out her opponents, as well as using some impressive hand and foot techniques. Hsu asks Fei Fei who she is and why she helped him. After explaining to him how she was an orphan and had learned Kung-fu on the streets, Hsu invites her to join his school. He tells her the story of Ma Fa-Chun, the Horse Fist expert who killed his master and has made a vow to kill all Five Forms disciples.

The misfits go to their headmaster, Lo Kuan-Tien (Chai Kai), who sends his disciple Bird Egg (Dean Shek, best known for his roles in *Drunken Master* and *Snake in the Eagle's Shadow*, providing yet another comedic role) to dispatch Fei Fei. When Bird Egg sees Fei Fei, the two begin to duke it out, and Fei Fei beats her opponent using the Five Forms technique.

When word of this gets out, Ma Fa-Chun arrives at the Five Forms School with Bird Egg's master. An all-out brawl occurs, with Ma using his specialized Upturned Horse Boxing combined with some pretty good kicking skills, and Bird Egg being serious as he fights the Five Forms School. When Ma and Bird Egg seriously injure Hsu, he tells Fei Fei to leave and get revenge when she has the chance. Bird Egg then strangles Hsu with his own ponytail.

TRAINING

Lu tells Fei Fei that he had seen the body of Hsu at the nearby Willow Bridge. Angered and ready for revenge, Fei Fei begins her intense training with Lu and Hu. During the sequences, Lu and Hu teach Fei Fei some of the most unorthodox techniques imaginable. Some of them involve combining blocking and counter-attacking using both the hands and the feet, and they are given odd names like "Dragon in the Seabed". Fei Fei uses one master's technique to spar with the other. When the teacher she fights counter-attacks the technique, she is taught a new technique by the other master.

After some intense training, Fei Fei is ready to fight the men responsible for her master's tragic death.

FIRST STRIKE

With her newfound skills, Fei Fei, and masters Hu and Lu, arrives in town and finds the three misfits Roc, Big Bird, and Little Bird. The deal made between Fei Fei and the two masters was that they would come along with her during a fight and they would tally up, and the master with the most techniques used by Fei Fei would be the best. At first, she begins using Hu's techniques. Fearing he may lose, Lu tells Fei Fei to use some of his techniques. She begins using some of his techniques. Using three of Hu's techniques as well as three of Lu's, Fei Fei dispatches the three hooligans as they go to Bird Egg.

Bird Egg finds Fei Fei outside with her two masters. Thinking he is the great Kung-fu expert, Bird uses the Five Animals Style to try and fight Fei Fei, but considering she is a former disciple of the Five Forms, she uses the same forms and to better effect. During the fight, in an effort to dispatch Fei Fei, he even resorts to something disgusting, most specifically breaking wind. The looks on everyone's faces prove it, with the addition of the sound effect. One thing to note is that during Bird's use of the Leopard Fist, he says "Pink Leopard" and you hear the opening to the Pink Panther theme. However, Fei Fei, using a combination once again of Hu and Lu's techniques, beats Bird Egg and his misfit gang.

THE SEARCH

Fei Fei fights the school that killed her master. She finds Lo and demands to know where Ma Fa-Chun is. Instead of telling her, he fights her. This time, Hu and Lu are not there because they are not really needed. The combatants use weapons, Fei Fei using a spear while Lo uses a glaive. Fei Fei quickly defeats Lo and he tells her that he knows where his disciple Shui Chang-Liu is located.

Fei Fei is seen in a local brothel with her masters. She pays to take one of the girls with her while the masters stay downstairs. Hu and Lu notice a dancing girl who is putting on a show for the guests. Two rowdy men try to make advances at the dancer, and she beats them while she dances, as if her fighting technique is part of the dance. She also hits Master Lu, who hits Master Hu. This scene plays a key element in the film.

Meanwhile, Fei Fei finds Shui and begins to fight him. Once again, the masters are there to tally up their techniques. Quickly, Shui is dispatched, but like the previous fights, an even combination of the masters' techniques was used. The next day, at the top of a mountain, Ma arrives and begins their confrontation. Ma seems to be too powerful for Fei Fei. The masters try to help but to no avail. Ma's Upside Down Horse Boxing is too powerful, even for Fei Fei.

REMATCH

Realizing that Ma's Upside Down Horse style is too powerful, the masters try to figure out what to do to counter it. All of a sudden, Lu remembers the dancing lady at the brothel and tries to copy what she did as Hu tries to attack to test it out. The masters agree that this new form of "dancing Kung-fu" might be the key to defeating the power of the Horse style. As Lu tries his best and successfully masters the form, Fei Fei is taught the form, but they realize that the form is more effective with music - capoeira anyone?

The next day, the rematch is on. At first, Shui fights Fei Fei again. This time, Fei Fei uses a combination of the Phoenix Eye and the Eagle Claw to fight Shui. When Ma tries to interfere, he inadvertently kills Shui. Angry, Ma tries to fight Fei Fei off. Fei Fei attempts to use the same combination of Phoenix and Eagle, but it is too little as Ma's Horse Style is just too good. The masters then begin to play a little music, prompting Fei Fei to go into dancing mode. She begins to beat on Ma with this new form of Kung-fu, a combination of swaying and the Miss Ho technique used in *Drunken Master*. When Ma sees the masters playing, he destroys their instruments and Fei Fei is stuck. However, she feels the music in her head, and she continues to beat Mao by playing an air zither. When she pretends to strum the air zither, you hear the sounds of the zither. However, Ma is once again too much for her. She develops a new technique on her own based on that of one of her former enemies: Bird Egg, of all people. She begins to make goofy faces and fights the way Bird did against her in the previous rematch. She successfully combines this "comedic Kung-fu" with the dancing style to defeat Ma. The masters agree they have drawn again and Fei Fei has gotten her revenge.

OVERALL

Jackie Chan and Chen Chi-Hwa made a wonderful collaboration with fighting female Angela Mao. She even displayed some Chan-like qualities during the finale of the film. The goofy faces are a trademark of Chan's. It reminds me of his directorial debut, *Fearless Hyena*, where he made some goofy faces while fighting the lead villain. Anyway, Chan developed some good techniques here, especially the new "dancing" form of Kung-fu. I don't know of another film that uses this technique, but it had elements of Miss Ho of the Eight Drunken Genii used in it. The Horse Boxing style used by Sun Reng-Chi was just a perfect style for him because Sun is a magnificent kicker (see *The Leg Fighters* for a real taste of Sun). A lot of the comedy went to the masters and Dean Shek as Bird Egg. They will crack you up from their first fight with each other onwards, because not only does their fighting look funny, but they look funny too. Nevertheless, if you liked *36 Crazy Fists*, or if you want to see some really great choreography from Chan, check out *Dance of Death*.

Hand of Death

By Matthew Edwards

The Lo Wei years were in all honesty a pretty risible affair for Jackie before he struck big with *Snake in the Eagle's Shadow* and *Drunken Master*. Lurking in the darkest recesses of his resume are such forgettable titles as *The Young Tiger* and *Killer Meteors*. However, *Hand of Death* (aka *Countdown to Kung-fu*), prior to this phase in Jackie's career, proves to be a little gem that retains enough gutsy martial arts to make this a welcome addition to any Jackie Chan fan's video collection.

With shotgun shogun John Woo (*Hard Boiled*, *Bullet in the Head* and *Face Off*) at the helm and also featuring a young Sammo Hung, the film acts as a kernel from which their talents were allowed to blossom. Although *Hand of Death* complies with the same formula of Kung-fu movies of this period, its energy and creativity serve as a template for the grand scale to which these three young filmmakers would later aspire.

Hand of Death begins with an offensive from the Manchu government against the Shaolin disciples. Led by renegade Shaolin disciple James Tien, they break down the doors and storm the Shaolin Temple, massacring the disciples inside. The opening action sequence also introduces us to Sammo Hung (also the film's fight co-ordinator), a Manchu General who is instrumental in the offensive's overwhelming success. Despite resistance, the Manchus prove too strong, culminating when they crudely hang one of the Buddhist monks and Tien disposes of a young headstrong disciple.

Although the action choreography here does not posses the same fluency we would expect from the classic Chan or Woo films, it's still nevertheless extremely well handled and typically violent. Amidst countless brutal slayings, Sammo and James Tien dish out enough deft blows to whet the appetite for the rest of the movie.

Escaping persecution, the surviving Shaolin members scatter themselves throughout China where they set up underground movements in order to preach their beliefs. Driven by the need for vengeance against the traitorous Tien, the movement picks its most competent martial artist, Dorian 'Flash Legs' Tan, to exact revenge.

Excelling in all Shaolin styles, we witness Tan undertaking a rigorous training regime in order to prove his worth. Within a small arena, situated inside the confines of a small forest, Tan, armed with a staff, repels superbly the efforts of four armed warriors, as well as showcasing several lethal kicks that equally render the warriors immobile. Satisfied, his master gives Tan his blessing to exterminate Tien.

Before Tan departs, his master requests he makes a detour to a village to warn a fellow disciple (Shaolin Scholar Chang), who has acquired a map showing the strength and position of the Manchu army, of a proposed ambush on him by Tien. Agreeing, Tan leaves to embark on his mission.

As Tan approaches a Manchu outpost, he comes to the aid of a young firewood merchant who is scrambling up the hill face. Pulling him up to higher ground, we realise the merchant is a young Jackie Chan. Thanking Tan for his kindness, Jackie returns to his horse and wagon where he offers him a ride.

Reaching the outpost, a Manchu guard probes Jackie on his journey. Claiming he is delivering firewood, the guard spots Tan and demands to know who he is. Foolishly Jackie says he is Tan's auntie and is subsequently thrown from his wagon and beaten. A bruised and battered Jackie is finally allowed past the outpost, after which they come across the lifeless body of a Shaolin fighter hanging from a tree.

Jackie pulls the wagon to a sudden halt, and he and Tan cut down the corpse. Picking up a bundle of firewood, Jackie sets fire to the body, giving the fighter a dignified send off. Jackie comments he won't let the birds eat the decaying corpse before he discovers Tan is also a Shaolin disciple. Returning to his wagon, Jackie turns to Tan and says, "There's two types that get themselves killed, the nosy type and a Shaolin fighter." Jackie subsequently rides off, leaving Tan in the wilderness.

Manchu warriors suddenly raid a quaint Chinese village. Peasants and locals are beaten as the oppressors run amok. From the heat haze on the horizon Tan appears. He is calm and unfazed as he strolls further into the unknown. Atop a white stallion, Sammo rides into view. A Shaolin revolutionary is dragged into the village's court as the warriors gather. The condemned awaits his fate. Tan is grabbed by an innkeeper and pulled inside. From the safety of the inn they watch. Shaolin revolutionaries lurk upon the rooftops. The executioner raises his sword. Pulling a small hollow tube from his pocket, Tan fires a dart. The executioner falls, clutching his neck. From the rooftops and smashing through the interiors of the peasants huts, the Shaolin warriors attack.

Freeing himself, the condemned Shaolin fighter quickly stabs one Manchu warrior before he is sliced across his back by one of Tien's henchmen. Both factions lay into each other in a ballet of swirling metal. Blow after blow Shaolin fighters are felled; their bodies lying lifeless upon the barren ground. With his back pierced like grinning red mouths the warrior clutches his bloody lesion before diving for safety over a wall. With Sammo's brooding presence the Manchu army quash the attack.

Pulling Tan to one side, the innkeeper comments that it must have been a trap. Tan's concentration is disturbed by the sound of someone playing the flute. It is here we catch a glimpse of a rogue swordsman played by Yeng Wei. Clambering from the blood-strewn battlefield the wounded revolutionary bangs on the innkeeper's door. Although at first reluctant to let the fighter in, the innkeeper ultimately relents. Tan quickly takes him inside where they begin nursing his injuries.

Left to right: Tan Tao Liang, Jackie Chan, John Woo

Meanwhile Sammo orders a search of the village in order to apprehend the fighter. Turning up at the inn they force themselves in and inspect the property. Two warriors make the mistake of going into the room Tan has occupied. Both are subsequently slung out, and from behind a blue curtain Tan appears. One Manchu warrior jumps from a balcony onto the wooden floor panels below and squares up to Tan. With ease and prowess Tan unleashes a brutal one-footed kick to the warrior's head, catapulting him over the bar and into an array of crockery.

Impressed, Sammo offers Tan the chance to join the Manchu movement and work as one of his henchmen. Tan rejects his offer. Sammo then invites Tan to look him up should he reconsider, before leaving the premises.

With the Manchu warriors gone, both the innkeeper and Tan tend to the injured Shaolin fighter. As they inspect his wounds Tan confesses that he too is a Shaolin warrior and that he is here to settle an old vendetta with Tien. Curious of the other guest, Yeng Wei, Tan begins to probe the innkeeper, asking who the mysterious swordsman is.

Told in flashback we learn that Yeng (nicknamed 'Zorro') also has a personal vendetta against Tien. We learn that a violent run-in with Tien in a seedy brothel led to the accidental death of a young prostitute. Plagued with guilt, Yeng descended into alcoholism to numb the pain over the young girl's death. We realise that Yeng has not used his infamous blade since.

Awakening, the Shaolin warrior thanks both the

innkeeper and Tan for saving him. Tan informs the warrior that he is here to protect him and was sent by his master. Advising the warrior that Manchu spies could be anywhere, they quickly flee from the inn through its wicker shutters. Here they both devise a plan together in order to assassinate Tien. He also informs Tan that Shaolin Scholar Chang will arrive soon with the precious map that may bring down the Manchu regime and that Tan must go and protect him.

Putting their plan into operation, Tan embarks for the Manchu palace. Here he announces that he must speak to Sammo. When Sammo appears he brings forward the wanted Shaolin warrior and demands to meet Tien. Impressed, Sammo sets up the meeting.

Gathered inside the desolate grounds of the palace and surrounded by Manchu warriors, Tan awaits the arrival of Tien, with his compatriot by his side, bound and tied. Tien finally arrives. Sat upon his throne Tien orders Tan to show his obedience and respect to him by kneeling in front of him. Refusing to show him any respect, Tien orders Tan to show his commitment and loyalty by killing the wanted Shaolin fighter. Immediately the Shaolin fighter rises armed with a sword in what becomes an audacious attempt to assassinate Tien. Sammo steps in and disarms his foe before sending a brutal kick to the Shaolin warrior's head. After a further crushing blow to the warrior's chest his foe lies motionless on the dusty ground, dead.

It is here Tan proclaims his allegiance to the Shaolin movement and announces his orders to kill Tien. Within the confines of Tien's temple an epic duel begins. After numerous brutal blows a floundering Tan realises he is no match for the superior Tien, who proudly proclaims that Tan's martial arts is that of kid's stuff.

Trapped, Tan is suddenly set upon by Tien's eight henchmen. A bald Manchu warrior then head-butts Tan in the chest before putting him into a bear hug. If Hong Kong movies are to be believed then all bald men in Hong Kong must be maniacs (there's a similar scene in *Drunken Master*). Freeing himself, Tan then dodges countless swipes from the Manchu warriors before the volume of attackers overwhelms him. Suddenly several blows pierce Tan's flesh. Despite deep gouges to his back from the swirling Manchu knives, Tan still manages to display enough subtle kicks to his opponents' heads to leave them crippled and writhing upon the dusty ground. As the fight intensifies Tan seems to be taking on the entire Manchu army as they all seem to come scurrying from nowhere (certain members even appear from the rooftops). Delivering firewood, Jackie emerges and witnesses Tan's plight.

At this stage Tien becomes involved again and beats the exhausted Tan into submission. Lying wearily upon the ground Tien holds a sword to his neck before claiming that to kill Tan would be "too damn easy".

The Manchu warriors subsequently string up Tan where he is, to be brutally beaten until he reveals the whereabouts of Chang. Sammo urges Tan to confess. Tan is warned he will be condemned to death should he not comply. Withstanding blow after blow, Tan refuses to dishonour the Shaolin movement.

In the dead of night, Tan attempts to escape. Despite hanging upside down, Tan lifts his upper torso forwards towards his bound ankles. Using his teeth, Tan unties the rope that is wrapped around his ankles. Freed, Tan's body falls towards the ground. However, underneath Tan is Jackie, who has arrived to save him. Together they escape from the temple and head to Jackie's hut.

Awakening in Jackie's hut, Tan feels the bruises from the previous day's skirmishes. As Tan stretches, Jackie returns with firewood. Tan thanks Jackie for assisting him in his escape. Tan points out that if the Manchu warriors find out Chan is hiding him, they will kill him also. Spotting a Shaolin scroll, Tan discovers that Chan's brother was a Shaolin warrior.

Again told in flashback, we learn that Chan also holds a personal vendetta against Tien, over the death of his brother. We learn both Chan and his bother were trained at the Shaolin temple, however his brother sought to wreak justice on the repressive Manchu regime by setting up small guerrilla movements to combat the Manchu army. It is revealed that Chan's brother was tortured and murdered by Tien and his men. This is played out within the confines of a Shaolin hideout.

A Shaolin warrior is sent plummeting from a balcony onto the hard stony floor panels. Manchu warriors emerge from the darkness, felling the Shaolin fighters. Despite their efforts, they are overwhelmed. Chan's brother is stabbed twice in his back. Crimson blood oozes from open wounds. A Manchu warrior slings a knife into his chest. Surrounded by a ring of Shaolin warriors, he collapses dead on the grey and ashen floor.

This scene bursts with energy, as amidst the action John Woo layers the scene with slow motion shots of Shaolin warriors crashing into shelves or over tables. Its cold and grainy feel gives credence to the overall sense of despair and sadness, whilst enhancing its authenticity in the means of replaying this sequence as flashback. Returning back to a down hearted Chan, he states he has waited three years for his revenge. He also tells Tan that in order to beat Tien, they must find a good swordsman. Enter Zorro.

Seated on a wooden table, Zorro quietly plays his flute, before being confronted by Tan. Sporting a conical shell-like hat, Tan introduces himself, before claiming he is a wanted man, and that with his help they can defeat Tien. By now two Manchu guards become suspicious of Tan's activity. Tan comments that he was not to blame for the young prostitute's death and that he is an honourable man. Rising, Zorro slices his infamous blade through Tan's hat, missing his head by inches, before turning to slay the two Manchu warriors.

Agreeing to assist Tan in his quest, they head off to Jackie's home, with Zorro claiming, "We are all fugitives now." On their return, Tan meets up with a couple of Shaolin disciples who have been sent to help bring down Tien. Back at Jackie's hut, and after the formal introductions, Jackie crafts a steel staff, before sharpening Zorro's blade.

Against the backdrop of lush secluded hilltops, the trio's training begins. In order to defeat Tien, Tan must master the Tiger Claw style, which, by using greased bamboo shoots and with Zorro's assistance, he finally perfects.

After meeting up with Chang (a small cameo role played by John Woo), the group devise a plan to overcome Tien. They learn of a proposed ambush on them, so Jackie devises a plan to create a diversion on the East Gate in order to secure Chang's safe passage. Uniting as a team they rally together, and Tan comments he would rather die than live under Manchu rule.

In the subsequent scene, a Manchu warrior spots the Shaolin flag from above the hilltops. Suspecting an attack he calls for backup. We discover it is Jackie riding upon his cart with mats attached to give the effect of an approaching army. Dismounting, Jackie wanders up to the gate's entrance, but he is pushed back.

Suddenly from an ivory silk sheet Jackie reveals an iron spear, attacking at once. Caught off guard, the Manchu warriors are quickly slain. Jackie deftly sends his weapon into the warriors' chests. At one stage Jackie is sliced along his back, but in his first action set piece he aptly and coolly disposes of the guards. As a light breeze circles around the castle walls, scarlet lesions probe from the inanimate.

Realising they have been tricked, Tien orders his troops down to the river in order to cut off Chang and Tan. Meanwhile, Jackie returns to the group, where shielding behind the long spindly rows of foliage, they attempt to bypass the Manchu warriors. Unable to escape, Jackie honourably defends their ground in order for Chang to escape, proclaiming he has an old vendetta to settle with the warrior who killed his brother.

As they approach, Jackie has flashbacks of his brother's violent demise. Fuelled by anger, Jackie impales one guard, before slinging his blade into his brother's killer's stomach. Although injured in the duel, Jackie clambers onto his horse before galloping off.

As Jackie is reunited with Tan and co, the remaining members of Tien's henchmen corner them. Zorro immediately unleashes his blade onto two unfortunate warriors, who attack him simultaneously. At one point

Zorro is impaled in his left shoulder by a Manchu spear, however he recovers quickly to defeat his attackers.

Meanwhile, Scholar Chang is beaten to the ground, whereupon Tan duly steps in, resuming his ongoing feud with Tien's bald henchman. After he is sent flying over the henchman's shoulder, Tan flips himself up onto his enemy's shoulders before grabbing his head then sending him into an embankment with a brutal kick. With blood pulsing from his head he collapses dead. Tan then grabs another henchman and breaks his neck.

Chang struggles for his life as he writhes in the grassy reeds. A Manchu warrior approaches, ready to thrust his iron spear into Chang. Realising the danger, Jackie jumps over a verge to save him. The spear pierces through Jackie's flesh. Bleeding heavily, Jackie throws his spear into the Manchu warrior, killing him instantly. Jackie tells Tan to go and secure Chang's passage to the river. Then, clutching his blood-soaked stomach, Jackie collapses, dead.

Reaching the river, they are suddenly attacked by Sammo, who is disguised as their getaway. Chang and Zorro jump onto the boat along with two Shaolin warriors. Escaping across the river, Chang informs Zorro that he has hidden the map within his hat. The two henchmen on Chang's boat turn out to be Manchu spies, who in turn stab Zorro in the back. The flailing Zorro then turns, killing both spies. Dying, Zorro throws himself into the river - his body covered by the river's violent ripples.

Back on land, Tan competently disposes of Sammo. After a gruelling duel, Tan sends Sammo into an array of China pots, where against the shattered remains he lies motionless. Chang reaches the safe haven across the river, where Shaolin disciples await his arrival. After defeating a Manchu General, and Tien's warriors, Tan finally squares up to Tien.

A depleted and barren horizon hosts this final duel. Tan repels Tien's forceful efforts. Tan unleashes Tiger Claw, breaking Tien's arm. Writhing pathetically Tien begs for mercy. With a slow-motion kick to his head, Tien is defeated. Riding off into the distance, Tan is victorious.

Hand of Death was intended as a vehicle for Dorian Tan, however he sadly slipped into Kung-fu obscurity. For fans of Jackie, Sammo and John Woo this is essential stuff. Although Jackie's role is limited, there are enough duels in the final reels to keep any Chanster happy. John Woo fans will notice the same slow-mos and narrative structure that have defined his career as one of the world's greatest action directors. *Hand of Death* is a fast-paced, entertaining martial arts flick, and despite Jackie's supporting role, it gives a clear indication of the heights he would later reach.

'Flash Legs' Tan Interview By Ken Stewart

As I pulled into the small parking lot just outside of Los Angeles, I couldn't help but feel a little nervous. Funny, considering I have spent time with quite a few big-name Hollywood actors and never once broke a sweat. And here I was, about to meet a now semi-retired Hong Kong martial arts actor and I was feeling jittery. I guess looking back on it, he was one of my first martial arts idols growing up. At a time when Bruce Lee was a more recognizable name than Jackie Chan, films like *The Hot, The Cool and The Vicious* were must-see matinees that, growing up in Oakland, I would cut school for. After settling in for the $1.50 Kung-fu double feature, I would wait impatiently for the moment the screen would explode when this amazing martial artist stepped into view. With his amazing balance, flexibility and dexterity, he would launch off 5 to 10 rapid roundhouse, hook and spin kicks without once putting his foot down. This display, usually during the well-staged opening credits, always brought scattered "hoots" from the small theater crowd. And then the name of the man would erupt 5 feet tall above us all: Tan Tao Liang!

Born in 1947 in Fusan, Korea, to Chinese parents, Tan would have an early start in his martial arts journey. At 12 years old, inspired by the martial arts showman he had encountered in his town, Tan used what pocket money he had and joined a Tae Kwon Do school. By 17, he became a Tae Kwon Do instructor at the University of Fusan. Having won the Korean Presidential Grand Champion Tae Kwon Do Cup, at 23 Tan moved to Taiwan, where he continued his career as an instructor. And it would be here that a new direction in his martial arts would take place - his film career.

To audiences in the US, his name did not ring many bells, but the titles of his films would always draw an unequivocal smile: *Countdown To Kung-fu*, *The Leg Fighters*, *The Tattoo Connection*, etc. And for many young martial artists like me, it was his face and image that would materialize in our minds as we would practice our kicks in the mirror. In the late 1980s, as martial arts films' popularity began to wane, Tan went the route of many others in his field, and faded from sight. Through this period, any fan worth his salt treasured the lucky video copy he may have owned from some late night television taping of *Challenge of Death*. So it was to my great surprise that I learned that Master Tan now lived and taught in a small Asian community outside of Los Angeles.

Catching my first glimpse of this screen idol was no disappointment. Dressed in a well worn black gi, Master Tan wrapped up his advanced class with the kind of confidence you would expect. Now slightly older, he seemed no worse for the wear! A youthful glow accompanied that familiar smile as I shook his hand and sat down to talk with him about his long career.

(What follows is written exactly as spoken by Master Tan. As this interview was conducted in English, one must keep in mind this is a recent language to Master Tan, and we were both dealing with his translation of his thoughts.)

Ken Stewart: What is the exact date of your birth, for the record?

Tan: December 22, 1947.

KS: Where did you grow up?

Tan: In Korea. There were not many Chinese there at the time. For about 40 miles, there was only one Chinese family.

KS: Really? And where was your family from before you were born?

Tan: My family was originally from China.

KS: Did your father own a restaurant in Korea?

Tan: Yes. I sometimes helped deliver for him, but I was very young.

KS: And you had brothers and sisters?

Tan: Yes. I have one older brother, one younger brother and one sister.

KS: What about school?

Tan: The Chinese people in Korea had their own school. It was only for Chinese, and I went there.

KS: Now, rumor has it that when you were young there were bullies that sometimes came to your father's restaurant.

Tan: (Smiling) Yes. That was a long time ago and many people didn't have enough food, enough money. Some people sleeping on the street. And because we were Chinese, there was some anger towards us and we would sometimes get hit to get our food.

KS: Was that part of the reason you got involved in the martial arts?

Tan: Oh, basically when I was young I liked martial arts. I saw one demonstration when I was about 5 years old. It really impressed me. They showed gun and knife stuff. They had a gun and used real bullets. Well, I don't know if it was real or not. They said it was! So, I thought, "Wow, I should learn martial arts."

KS: Then the first martial art you studied was Tae Kwon Do, right?

Tan: Yes. I learned in Fusan. At that time it was called just Karate. They later called it Tang Soo Do and then Tae Kwon Do. Tae Kwon Do has a very short history. Before Tae Kwon Do, they combined, you know, different styles. Too many different styles in Korea. But when the government took control, you had to learn Tae Kwon Do first, before learning other systems. My parents didn't like it because they didn't like

Now we know why he's called 'Flash Legs' Tan...

fighting anybody. I studied for three years before they knew. Because if they would catch me, they would burn my uniform.

KS: Why didn't they like it?

Tan: They don't like people to fight. Usually the Chinese people, they nice - they are scared, or they are nice. But the Korean people, they are strong, they can fight. That time I grew up in was a tough time. I did a lot of stuff. Even... Tizan. You know, the movie? Tizan.

KS: You mean Tarzan?

Tan: (Laughs) Oh yeah, you know, like the hoses in the trees. How do you say those?

KS: Oh, vines.

Tan: Yes. I did a lot of stuff in the jungle. Not actual jungle, kind of like mountains. You know, play around. Crazy stuff! I'm not scared at that time. Then comes the war. I was 5 or 8 years old.

KS: I heard you also trained in something called "Gecko" Kung-fu?

Tan: Ah yes, when I was young I followed different instructors.

KS: [Showing a photo of Tan from the film The Dragon, The Lizard, The Boxer where he is about 15 feet up between two palm trees.] This photo seems to be of you practicing the art of Gecko Kung-fu.

Tan: Oh, I don't think I like this movie. But my first movie (smiles), they do this very good.

KS: I will get to that soon.

Tan: This cannot really be called a kind of Kung-fu. It is more like "The Art Of Climbing Walls". Children in my vicinity and I often played the game hide and seek. Sometimes when I could find no place to hide, I would run into a lane with two walls facing each other.

With one jump, I could climb 4 or 5 feet.

KS: What brought you to Taiwan?

Tan: Yeah, in high school, the... like the Embassy, they contact me to go to Taiwan to teach Tae Kwon Do, but I was too young. After high school, I go to college, but I stop because I have problems like.... In Korea if I wanted to continue Tae Kwon Do I would have a nationality problem. I am Chinese and I wouldn't change to Korean nationality. So I move to Taiwan and I help my country to learn Tae Kwon Do. This I think is a good idea at the time. I could stay in Korea, but for a Tae Kwon Do future, I feel Taiwan is better. That's why I help Taiwan.

KS: What did you do first? Did you have your own school or teach at somebody else's?

Tan: I first teach the CIA in Taiwan, and then at 5 colleges in Tai Pei, some high schools, Tae Kwon Do Federation and my studio. Teaching at Taiwan University I had around 500 students. They paid like $15 a month. Terrible money, but good enough for me. It could take care of my life at the time.

KS: You didn't have any other job?

Tan: No, I don't have job. I teach at the colleges and special programs.

KS: How did you first get involved with the movies?

Tan: Ah, movies. Basically, I don't like movies, because I don't understand movies. When I was young, I just feel like the movies are fake, especially the action part. Too fake. So the first time they [movie producers] come to ask me to help produce a movie, I say "No". Then they say, "Can you help us find one of your students to be a movie star?" Then I say, "Yeah, I can help." Because young people, they like movies at that time. I introduced

them [to the students]. They say, "No". I put many auditions [together]. They don't like it. No one. My feelings are my students have good techniques. The have a good face, you know? A good look. Personally they are very nice. That is why I recommend them to the movie company. But they don't like them. Finally, I am angry. I say, "Forget it, I don't want to play with you guys." One day, they call me: "Please come to us." I say, "No, I'm not going to go." "This is the last time," they say. I say "Okay". I take taxi. I go inside to this big company. My picture is on the wall! [Spreading arms wide.] A big picture.

KS: Of what? You practicing Tae Kwon Do?

Tan: No. They put up like a fake one. The audition is a fake. They had a small camera that caught me. My face.

KS: So there was this giant faked movie poster of you?

Tan: Yes. A big one. I am surprised. I asked, "Why did you take my picture?" They say, "We already make a choice. You are going to be in this picture. The lead actor." I say, "No". They say, "Please". Then we have a meeting at the office. They have the best writer in Taiwan who spent two months with the director writing this movie. Every day. But the movie is good. I like it even today.

KS: Was this in 1973, after Bruce Lee died?

Tan: No, before - 1971 or 1972. We finish in 1971.

KS: This must have been Hero Of The Waterfront? The film did well at the box office, right?

Tan: Yes, very well. Almost as good as Bruce Lee at the time.

KS: After that, did you decide "Well, maybe I'll do a few more movies"?

Tan: Oh, at that time my feeling is I want to do the right kind of movie. Because I learn martial arts I want to follow the right way. I don't want to follow money. My director, after we make first movie, he got cancer. The other big companies like Golden Harvest, they tell me to come work with them. I say no. I stay with my director.

KS: *What was his name?*

Tan: Wong Shin Lee. And then almost 3 years later, director Wong's cancer is better. At that time we want to start a movie. But then he realized, no more action film. The market is bad. Already too late. Nobody is producing action movies after Bruce Lee died. That is why I go back by myself to Taiwan. So I go back to teaching again.

KS: *So what drew you back to the films again?*

Tan: The boss of a small independent company in Vietnam said that my movie did very well in Vietnam. He moved to Taiwan to try and make an action film with me. After a couple of films together, more companies call from Hong Kong. They want to make movies with only me. A one man show. I make a lot of movies. Then, a couple of years later, a lot of action movies start to come up. Like a few hundred produced.

KS: *So you went right to the top in your first film. You didn't even start as a stuntman.*

Tan: (Laughs) Not like Jackie Chan did.

KS: *It sounds like a hectic schedule. I heard you would only get a couple hours sleep a day sometimes between shooting.*

Tan: Usually at that time, too many people invited me to produce their movies. I already had 2 or 3 movies going. They would say you have to help us. You couldn't believe it. When I was young I saw big movie stars. When I make movies they are already old. And now they would come to me, on their knees crying I need help. I had to help. I can't say no. Once I took on 8 movies at once. I had a record of 27 days and no sleep. Everyday 8 hours a film, then to next film for 8 hours, 24 hours a day. My body is good, healthy. But, still very difficult. I get sick and want to stop doing movies. Too difficult.

KS: *You did Hand Of Death (aka Countdown To Kung Fu) fairly early in your career, right?*

Tan: That was in 1975 I think. This was John Woo's first movie. As an action movie.

KS: *Had you met John Woo prior to that?*

Tan: No.

KS: *What was it like?*

Tan: Good. He had no experience but he worked hard. The people helped John Woo at that time. Like Sammo Hung. Sammo is very good. Jackie Chan was a fellow member that followed Sammo at that time. There were 8 people that followed Sammo. Also Yuen Biao, Yuen Wah, all the brothers...

KS: *[Showing a photo of Tan hanging upside down next to Sammo.] You remember this?*

Tan: Oh yeah. I had a little headache (laughing).

KS: *Was this the first time you met Jackie Chan and Sammo Hung?*

Tan: Oh no, long time before. Way before, like 1970 or '71. I met them when I started movies. They were doing stunt work and action choreography. They would work in films I was producing.

KS: *At the end you are fighting James Tien and it is an amazing side kick you pull off.*

Tan: Oh yes, I remember that very well.

KS: *Did you really hit him?*

Tan: Yes, sometimes we have to make contact.

KS: *You choreograph much of your own work, correct?*

Tan: Yes. Some movies, even the action directors say to me: "Master Tan, you do your stuff. I can't choreograph your style. You do your own." I say, "No, the company pay you money, you help me!" (Laughs) So no one helps me. They respect me so much, it's not good for me. So, that is why I do so much kicking, because I know this very well. A lot of leg stuff.

KS: *Have you been injured on any of your films?*

Tan: Not really, not that many. I won't do dangerous stuff. The company says, "No, you get hurt and the company loses a lot of money!" They want to put the movies out in the summer. They have a very tight schedule and if you get hurt they lose money. I try to do everything myself, but they stop me.

KS: *What was it like being famous at that time?*

Tan: The first movie, when I go to Taiwan for the screening, at the train station where I am to premiere it is a huge crowd of people. Like Chinese New Year. Fireworks and everything. All for me! I can't believe it! Even for the President, they don't do this. It's crazy. Like thousands of people. Just crazy...

After the premiere I go back to Taiwan. One day there I checked the cinemas. There is not many people out as it is raining. I am sick this day and I go down the street a little further and see a huge crowd. I say, "Wow, what is going on?" I look up to see what the crowd is waiting for and it is my movie! I am shocked.

KS: *One of the more famous directors you worked with was Lee Tso Nam. One in particular was The Hot, The Cool and The Vicious.*

Tan: Basically Lee Tso Nam directed me for a low budget company.

KS: *I heard that for The Hot, The Cool and The Vicious, he shot it very quickly. That he didn't do too many takes.*

Tan: Yes, that is true. The action director on this was my friend, Tommy Lee. One day he talked to me: "Tan, come be an actor in my movie." Okay, I think. I'll be a bad guy and we will fight good. But then he wants me for the hero. Tommy Lee is a smart person, but on the martial arts side he is a little weak. There I helped him out a bit.

The owner of the company is Wong Tao, the film's other star. He produced it. That is why I come help. So when we all fight in the film, we already know each other well and it made it easier. That is why I think this one was good.

KS: *This was one of the first of the martial arts films to popularize the two-on-one fights. You worked with Wang Tao again in the sequel, The Challenge Of Death. At the end you had what appeared to be a complicated battle where the bad guy, using spider techniques, has to fly around on a "web". Was this difficult to shoot?*

Tan: Not too bad. In Hong Kong they are used to the wires. It is very common there. At times the timing was hard when he was jumping from the trees and we had to kick or hit him.

KS: *To backtrack a bit, when you first started working in films,* *did they pay you a lot or a little?*

Tan: (Smiling) A little. Very small. You can barely use the money to take a taxi to work! (Laughs)

KS: *By the time you got to The Hot, The Cool and The Vicious, I take it you were getting a little more.*

Tan: Oh yes. Maybe 50 times more at least.

KS: *I know you are not so happy with some of your films, but does this one count as one of your better films?*

Tan: Yes, I did like this one actually. I helped produce the sequel and what I like about doing that is working with people you like. I don't enjoy the politics of some

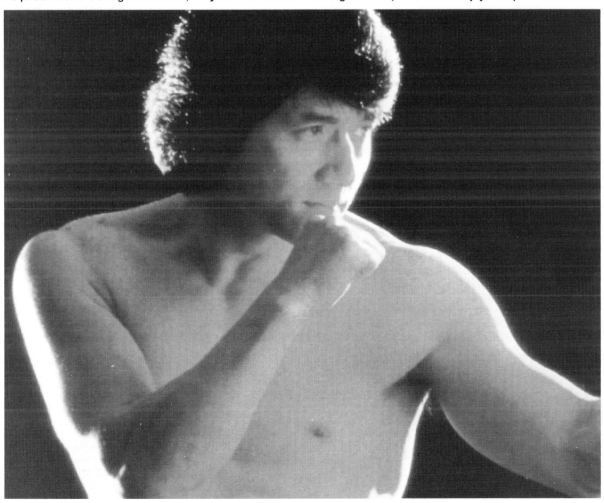

films. Wong Tao, Tommy, Lee Tso Nam and I are all friends. Much better.

KS: *You have been dubbed one of the greatest kickers in Hong Kong films. [Master Tan begins to blush.] Many people I am sure are wondering how you came about developing the "hopping" kick that you have made famous in your films?*

Tan: When I was young, competing in the Tae Kwon Do championship I felt that many times the referee is not fair. Many times I kick to the head and they don't see this, they don't give me a point. So to make it more obvious, I trained on a very special technique: when I bring my leg up to kick, I follow through with more, continue. Hopping and kicking very fast. So in the movies I try to do this technique. Usually at this time people kick once and then put their foot down. This way is kind of boring, especially for close-ups. You can't kick a face, put the foot down and then kick again. Too slow. It is much better when you keep your foot up and keep kicking. You can see the action better this way.

KS: *When was it that you were married?*

Tan: 1970. I have 1 son and 1 daughter. They were born in Chicago. I went there in 1972 or 1973 trying to get my green card. I would go back and forth while making movies. I was in Chicago, Seattle and Los Angeles. I then moved back here permanently in 1984. The movie companies back then kept yelling at me to come back and work (laughs).

KS: *Later you and Lee Tso Nam did another film together called The Tattoo Connection with Yang Sze.*

Tan: Yes, I know this movie. I can't remember what year. [Tan looks at a picture of Jim Kelly from the film.] I can't remember his name...

KS: *Jim Kelly?*

Tan: Ah, yes...

KS: *I have heard through the rumor mill that you and Jim Kelly were going pretty hard on each other during this film. A bit of a competition. I read this in an interview with Lee Tso Nam.*

Tan: My feeling is, I like Jim Kelly. His hand movement and his body is very good. His kicks are... okay. I think Jim Kelly learned from Bruce Lee. But my feeling is that Jim Kelly came to Hong Kong to do this film and he was a little cocky. But I still want to give him room because we are different cultures. But he seemed unhappy and I don't know why. We did argue sometimes.

KS: *That happens.*

Tan: For the movie we try to work together and make a good movie. Some people though just want to make movies to make money. Some want to make a good movie. Everyone is different. He was a good fighter I think.

KS: *Were you also still teaching during this period?*

Tan: No, I couldn't. It was too busy.

KS: *There was another film you did that is perhaps most people's favorite, The Leg Fighters.*

Tan: I remember I only spent about 2 weeks shooting it. Lee Tso Nam had very strong ideas and he could control the budget very well. If it is 3 million, he stops at 3 million. Never over budget.

KS: *This was one of your last movies with Lee Tso Nam, as at this point the Ninja movies began to become very popular. So was it your decision to finally leave the business?*

Tan: I decided to stop.

KS: *What is it that brought you here to America?*

Tan: My wife and my son lived here. I had a lot of friends in China, but my family is obviously the most important. So I came here and opened up a Tae Kwon Do school and it has been very successful.

KS: *Would you ever consider doing another film again?*

Tan: (Smiling) Always possible, but I am happy and don't care if I ever do another film. But last week Yuen Woo Ping did come by to talk about working on The Matrix 2.

KS: *Wow, you would certainly add to that. But you have already left a great legacy in the Hong Kong film industry either way. Thanks for taking the time to talk.*

Tan: No, thank you.

As I left the school the moon was high overhead. The mood felt somewhat surreal, as if I had just stepped out of a Twilight Zone episode where a young kid is sucked into the TV set while watching his favorite Kung-fu movie. He then finds himself standing in front of the Shaolin hero he had always emulated. The two of them take a journey together and, like a well-written script, by the end the kid walks away from the adventure a changed character.

Climbing into my car, I don't know if my character had been changed. But I did know that if there ever was a soul that had the power to reach anyone, it was the humble figure of a man standing in the small parking lot. Surrounded by a few scattered young students climbing into their parents' cars, he waved goodbye to each one for the night. And as he stepped into his studio, flicking each light switch as he went, his figure began to fade from sight into darkness. I couldn't help but think the words THE END were about to pop up, as I watched the man that had been called The Leg Fighter, The Hero Of The Waterfront and "The Hot One" once again walk on with the pride and humility of a life well lived.

THE POLICE STORY SERIES
NOT YOUR ORDINARY COP CHOP SOCKY!

By Patricia Evans

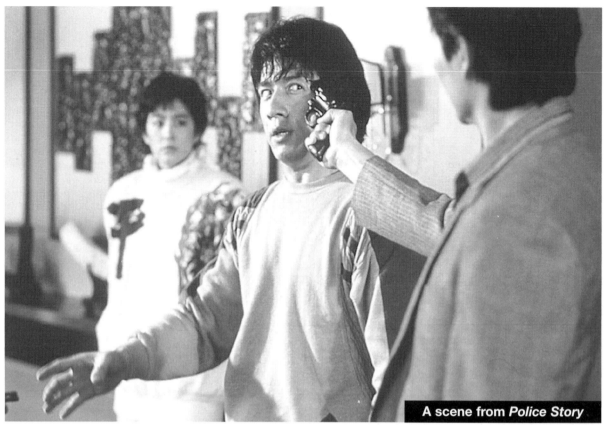

A scene from *Police Story*

It can be human nature to run and hide when something goes wrong, to give up, throw your hands in the air and cry foul. But from something we perceive as negative we can buckle under or we can rebound, come back and make it right, make it better. This is how one of the most popular Hong Kong movie series was born.

In 1985 Jackie Chan turned to Hollywood a fourth time in an attempt to win over the US market. He starred opposite Danny Aiello in a police drama called *The Protector*. The movie was far from what Jackie had hoped it would be, featuring gratuitous nudity, bad language and, to Jackie's mind, inferior fight sequences. Jackie re-shot a good deal of the film once he was back in Hong Kong, but still it rankled. He knew he could make a much better cop drama than that. So he did. In fact, not only did he make a better film, he made film history.

Police Story was filmed in Hong Kong in 1985. Written by Edward Tang, Jackie directed and stars with Maggie Cheung, Brigitte Lin, Bill Tung and Chu Yuen. This was Maggie Cheung's first outing as Jackie's girlfriend May, a part she would return to play in two of the *Police Story* sequels. This was also Bill Tung's first film with Jackie. He would go on to appear in many of Jackie's other movies.

Police Story was a groundbreaking film in the Hong Kong market. Breaking away from the traditional Kung-fu genre, this movie was a modern day masterpiece that even 18 years later still wows the audience.

Jackie plays a Hong Kong police officer who is involved in a botched raid. Ka-Kui (Jackie's character name in the original version) and his fellow officers attempt to persuade the secretary of the crime boss to testify against him. With a little trickery Jackie convinces her she does indeed have something to fear from her former employer and the police are on their way to convicting the bad guy. However nothing goes quite as planned and much confusion, fighting and betrayal follows. Jackie's character is even framed for murder.

The movie has many funny moments as well, but action is the hallmark of the film that has been nicknamed "Glass Story" due to the sheer volume of glass-shattering stunts. Some of the more memorable stunts in the movie include a car chase right through a small shantytown. It was a dangerous and expensive shot, costing HK$500,000. The impressive action left several stuntmen injured.

They were not alone. There is a famous scene where Jackie clings to the side of a moving bus, using only an umbrella to keep him from flying away while the bus makes fast, frequent turns. At the end of the bus sequence four stuntmen fly out of a double decker bus, missing their mark. Instead of breaking their fall on the car in front of them as planned, the four land painfully on the hard concrete. Two of the stuntmen where hurt badly.

A huge fight in a shopping mall at the end of the film left Jackie badly injured. Jackie slides down a tall pole decorated with Christmas lights, sparks flying and bulbs breaking all the way. Unfortunately, the power had not been reduced as planned, so when Jackie reached the bottom of the pole, all the skin had been burned off both his hands. He could easily have died from electrocution.

If that wasn't enough, during a leap into a wooden structure, Jackie dislocated his pelvis and nearly broke the seventh and eighth vertebrae in his spine, and was almost paralysed. In spite of all the pain Jackie endured for this movie, it remains one of his favourites due to the sheer magnitude of the stunts and fight choreography.

Police Story has had several scenes copied over the years. The bus scene was copied by Sylvester Stallone in *Tango & Cash*. The motorcycle chase through the shopping mall was copied almost shot for shot for Brandon Lee's movie *Rapid Fire*. And *Bad Boys II*, with Martin Lawrence and Will Smith, has a scene with Humvees crashing through a town just like in *Police Story*.

Police Story was a hit at the box office, taking in over HK$26,000,000. It received several nominations, and won awards for Best Stunt Coordinator (Jackie Chan), Best Picture and Best Action design (Jackie Chan's Stuntman Association) at the Hong Kong Film Awards.

The first sequel, *Police Story 2*, was shot in 1988. It was also filmed in Hong Kong and brought back Maggie Cheung as Jackie's long-suffering girlfriend May, and Bill Tung as Jackie's uncle and superior officer. Other cast includes Lam Gwok Hung as the superintendent and Chor Yuen as Chu Tao (the drug boss Koo). Jackie directed and co-wrote the script with Edward Tang and Ging Sang. This action-packed installment starts off almost where *Police Story* left off. Jackie is demoted to a traffic cop due to his penchant for rule breaking. While planning a romantic getaway, Ka-Kui and May find themselves in the centre of a bomb threat. Jackie steps in to help his fellow officers and makes the decision to clear the building, saving many lives when the bomb threat turns out to be real. Jackie is then reinstated to his former rank and put on the case.

Though *Police Story 2* does not have the sheer volume of stunts and fighting of the first, it holds its own very well. In one particularly awesome fight sequence, Jackie and May are attacked in a park. The playground fight that follows is a high-energy feast of the imagination as Jackie incorporates slides, swings and monkey bars into his battle against Chu's gang of thugs. Some of the falls are painful to watch as the stuntmen are laid out by our hero.

A scene where Jackie crosses the street was painful for him. After leaping from the top of one moving bus to another, and deftly dodging two low-hanging signs, Jackie plunges through a huge glass sign. Unfortunately,

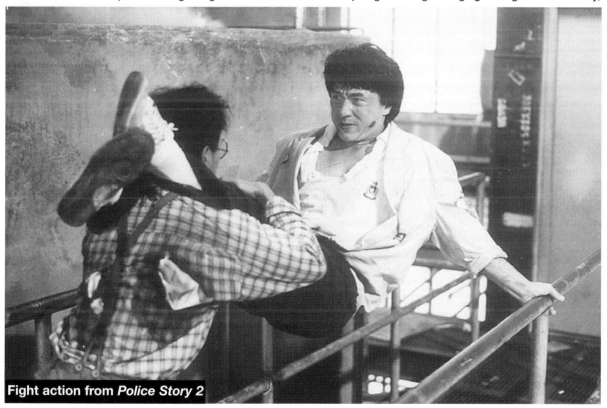

Fight action from *Police Story 2*

it was the wrong one! It was *real* glass, and Jackie found his arm had been sliced to the bone and his scalp was covered in glass shards.

Later on Maggie Cheung was injured when running through a corridor of metal racks. She had a deep gash in her scalp. Also, according to Jackie's autobiography, *I Am Jackie Chan: My Life In Action*, she cut her head badly while sliding down a chute and went to the hospital for stitches.

One thing that was different about *Police Story 2* was the glimpse into the relationship between Ka-Kui and May. Though she loves him dearly, May has grown weary of always coming second to his career. She writes him a tearful goodbye letter which ends up in the hands of the bad guys. They read the letter aloud to Ka-Kui while May pleads for them to stop. It's an emotional moment where we come to connect with May and Ka-Kui as real people. Later, when they are both tortured by being hit with very authentic looking firecrackers, we feel their anguish all the more. In one outtake, Jackie is shown getting a piece of it in his eyes. If you had any doubts these things were real, this outtake will prove how very real they were! The final fight of the film takes place in a warehouse full of fireworks and explosives. Jackie's character gets to give them a little payback by throwing the firecrackers at one of the chief antagonists. The explosion of the warehouse was the biggest stunt in Hong Kong's history. The explosion was huge and the fire lasted for hours. It was another Jackie Chan first.

The second installment of the popular series earned over HK$34,000,000. The movie received an award for Best Action Design (Jackie Chan's Stuntman Association) at the Hong Kong Film Awards.

Part three in the classic series is titled *Police Story 3: Supercop*. Released in Hong Kong in 1992, it earned an impressive HK$33,000,000. It was then released again to the US market in 1996 as *Supercop*. This film boasts a sturdy script by writers Edward Tang, Fibe Ma and Lee Wei-Yee and is directed by one of Jackie's favorite directors, Stanley Tong.

Jackie is back as Ka-Kui, but if you watch the English dubbed version you'll hear him called Kevin Chan. The lovely Maggie Cheung returns as May and Bill Tung takes another turn as the ever conniving Uncle Bill, Jackie's superior on the force. Martial arts superstar Michelle Yeoh appears in the movie as mainland security officer Hanna Yang. Opera brother Yuen Wah portrays Panther, and Ken Tsang plays his ruthless drug kingpin brother.

One of the movies that made Jackie a household name in the US market, *Supercop* boasts excellent action both from Jackie and the lady he refers to as "the toughest woman I know", Michelle Yeoh. The movie was filmed in Thailand and Malaysia (home to Michelle).

Gun play in *Police Story 3: Supercop*

The action begins when good old Uncle Bill and the Chief trick Jackie into accepting a very dangerous assignment. They let him overhear their conversation about how dangerous it is, and how he is the only one who could take the case. Appealing to his sense of pride and duty, Ka-Kui volunteers for the life-threatening assignment to go to mainland China and infiltrate a drug cartel. Ka-Kui tells poor May that he is taking light duty at a park somewhere, and the trusting May doesn't have a clue, even when Ka-Kui hands her his life insurance policy and other important documents!

One of the most amusing parts of the film is when 'Kevin' arrives on the mainland. Dubbed a 'Supercop' in his file, he is instantly immersed in a different world than what he is used to. The no-nonsense Inspector Yang shows him around and maneuvers him into the first of his many fights. Though the first fight, a demonstration for the recruits, is short, it offers up some fine moves and gives a taste of the action to come.

Jackie and Michelle go undercover to spring a con named Panther from prison. Jackie does the rescuing and manages to befriend the grateful Panther. Later Michelle joins them in the guise of Jackie's younger sister. The banter between Michelle and Jackie works well, and keeps the movie moving along between the action sequences.

Now enter May, who sees Jackie and Michelle wandering together and concludes that her long-time paramour is cheating on her. She eventually manages to blow Jackie's cover, and the fights and stunts begin in earnest.

Michelle does a good share of fighting, nearly outshining Jackie himself as she leaps, twirls and kicks anyone that gets in her way. She also holds her own in one of the movie's most dangerous stunts. She rides a motorcycle onto a moving train. It took her three tries to do it. The stuntman who tested the stunt broke his leg! Some of her other stunts are difficult as well as painful, as can be seen in the outtakes.

One of the most dangerous stunts ever filmed is the jump to the rope ladder that hangs from a helicopter. Jackie has spoken many times about how he wanted to postpone the jump until another day, but after learning he was literally surrounded by press watching him from every angle, he felt compelled to do the stunt. He runs toward the edge of the building, leaps, grabs the ladder, and clings to it for dear life. He didn't trust the safety wire he was wearing as the copter flew him 1000 feet over the city below. On one take Jackie was struck by the moving helicopter and knocked unconscious. He also dislocated a cheekbone while making *Supercop*.

The film gained Jackie the Best Actor nod from the Golden Horse Awards in Taiwan, as well as a Best Actor nomination from the Hong Kong Film Awards.

The latest installment in the further adventures of Ka-Kui is the 1996 release *Jackie Chan's First Strike*. Jackie's character, the same Hong Kong cop, is now called Jackie Chan in the US release of the film. Uncle Bill is present, once again portrayed by Bill Tung. Additional cast includes Jackson Lou as Tsui, Chen Chen Wu as Annie, Yuri Petrov as Colonel Yegorov and Nonna Grishayeva as Natasha. This film was shot in Hong Kong, the Ukraine and Australia.

Jackie is charming as ever as the Hong Kong cop on another dangerous assignment. This time though the action sneaks up on him. He takes on the simple task of shadowing a mysterious woman, following her onto a flight to the Ukraine. He takes notes, even how often she

Supercop

Special guest appearance by Jaws in
Police Story 4: First Strike

leaves her seat to go to the restroom. Once the plane lands, Jackie figures he's done and goes about his business. But he witnesses Natasha being abducted and finds himself once again in the thick of things. *First Strike* makes good use of Jackie's everyman quality of stumbling into the wrong place at the right time and then coming out of it ahead by use of improvisation and his physical ability.

While following the mystery woman, Jackie discovers a dilemma worthy of James Bond. It seems this bunch of baddies is acquiring a nuclear warhead. Jackie makes chase down the snow-covered hills while inadequately dressed. He is freezing, not acting, as he tears down the hills on a snowmobile and then a snowboard. He then leaps off a cliff to grab and cling to the runners of a helicopter. Finally, to avoid being blown to bits, Jackie lets go and drops into the freezing ice-covered water. This stunt was as real as you can get, and Jackie nearly died of hypothermia.

Once recovered, Jackie learns from the KGB that the warhead is in Australia, and they take him there by way of a submarine. Sunny Brisbane looks and feels like a paradise, especially after almost freezing to death, and our hero figures this portion of his assignment is going pretty nicely. But once he locates the people who have the warhead things get ugly again. Jackie is forced to retrieve the bomb from inside a shark tank. The water battle allows for techniques you just can't do on land and the fighting becomes a ballet of choreographed motion. Managing to fight at all under water is difficult enough, doing it without an oxygen tank made it harder. Part of the comedy lies in how Jackie manages to steal breaths from his opponent's tank.

Jackie is also attacked in his posh hotel room by two goons that are made up to look like giants. One slams Jackie straight up over his head onto the ceiling. An interesting side note is that the actor who did it actually had a broken arm, and still managed to lift Jackie up. Using his brains over their brawn he outmaneuvers them

Promotional still from *First Strike*

in a series of moves that bring laughs and smiles. Managing to escape, he realizes he's been duped and is now in the middle of more than he bargained for. Hiding from the Russian Mafia and some of their local accomplices, Jackie finds out he has been framed for murder.

Before it's all sorted out, there are plots to expose and Jackie engages in more fabulous action, including his legendary ladder fight. Anything he can get his hands on becomes a weapon as he is outnumbered and the lion dance heads, sheet rock and objects fly. At one point he resorts to using an aluminum ladder as he fends off several foes who are determined to take revenge on the "murderer".

This *Police Story* installment earned an impressive HK$57,000,000, and went on to help further Jackie's career with his English-speaking viewers. The film was directed by Stanley Tong and written by Stanley Tong, Gwai Lai, Nick Tramontane, Greg Mellor and Tong Ming Gei. Stanley Tong received an award for Best Action Choreography from the Hong Kong Film Awards. It was also nominated for Best Actor (Jackie Chan) and Best Picture.

There have been rumors and hints that another installment of the *Police Story* series may be in the works. [Editor's update note: *New Police Story* is scheduled for release in summer 2004.] Fans of Jackie and the popular movies are waiting eagerly to find out what is happening with Ka-Kui, May and Uncle Bill.

Jackie's self-assured well rounded *Police Story* character appeals to his fans. Ka-Kui has intensity, ingenuity and the skills that make the character someone to look up to and to expect great things from. This series also shows Jackie involved in a mature romantic relationship with May. A fifth outing would be a welcome reunion with a character that's become bigger than life and whose exploits we are eager to witness. Only Jackie knows if there will be a *Police Story 5*. But even if there isn't, there is enough action in these four alone to satisfy the most die-hard action fan. The series is available on VHS and DVD. The English versions of *Police Story* one and *2* were not dubbed into English by Jackie, but *Supercop* and *First Strike* are. There are several different releases of each film, so be sure to read the description as to what you are getting before you buy. Some versions have extensive cuts, or alterations to the original soundtrack.

Armour of God Explored!

By Matthew Edwards

Taking inspiration from the Hollywood hit *Raiders of the Lost Ark*, Jackie decided to make an equivalent Chinese action adventure. It proved to be a box office hit not only in Asia but also in the West (*Armour of God* received a small theatrical release in Britain). The film was shot in the former Republic of Yugoslavia, with Cantopop superstar Alan Tam as his sidekick, Rosamund Kwan as Laura and Eric Tsang directing. During the shoot Eric Tsang was dismissed and directorial duties were taken up by Jackie. However, all this was overshadowed by the now notorious stunt that almost killed Jackie.

What at first seemed like an innocuous stunt - Jackie jumping from one wall to another with the aid of a branch - backfired when the branch snapped, sending Jackie plummeting twenty feet to the ground, where he hit his head on a rock. Rushed to a nearby hospital with a fractured skull, Jackie underwent emergency surgery and stayed in hospital until he made a full recovery and could return to the set. The signs of his injury are still visible today.

The media attention the fall attracted no doubt boosted *Armour of God*'s profile, especially when the footage was famously added to the bloopers segment at the end of the picture! Sadly the film itself has always taken a back seat since, but it's a glorious romp with an international feel, especially with its nods to Indiana Jones and James Bond.

The film opens with a parody / homage of the *Raiders of the Lost Ark* opening. Jackie (sporting a fetching new haircut) plays an adventurer named 'Asian Hawk' who arrives at some abandoned ruins within the heart of the African jungle, intent on stealing 'The Sword of God'. Meanwhile its protectors, a local tribe, are performing the sacrifice of a young woman who is tied to a bamboo stretcher. In order to go undetected, Asian, with the help of his trusty crossbow, abseils down to the sword's holy shrine (the sword is situated within a giant God-like statue). Unfortunately for Asian, in his clumsiness he knocks the head off the statue and it tumbles down onto the tribesmen. With their suspicions aroused they look up and, in a comic moment, Asian pretends to be the head of the statue!

Now these tribesmen may not be the greatest thinkers of the century, but they easily spot Asian as an impostor. With lightning speed he pilfers the Sword of God before back-flipping off the statue. After dodging countless

spears and burning coal, Asian is finally cornered, so he opens a can of beer and begins to drink it! Intrigued, the locals stop and stare at Asian oddly. Asian then throws them a can of beer. However when they open the can it explodes and produces a pink fluorescent smoke, thus allowing Asian to make his getaway by swinging onto a branch from one wall to another (yes folks, Jackie did it right on that occasion).

Grabbing a handy shield, Asian then slides down a steep mountainside where the angry tribesmen pursue him on makeshift sledges. Reaching the foot of the hill unscathed, Asian then quickly jumps into a mini plane that is cleverly hidden in a bush, and flies off. However the tribesmen go from hounding to hailing him!

This pre-credit sequence sets the tone nicely for the rest of the picture, and it also highlights its nod to the James Bond films with Jackie's endless amounts of crazy inventions that pop up throughout the film. The sequence also showcases more stunning stunts from Jackie and his inventive use of comedy into these scenes.

Next up we see Asian singing in a band aptly named 'The Losers'! The band reminded me of the awful late seventies and eighties pop bands with their awful dress sense - Jackie wears a lovely sky blue top, white trousers and is draped in a Hawaiian flowered necklace - and naff songs. It is video footage, being watched by a group of nasty monks. It turns out that Asian was part of this band but left after clashing with fellow band member

Alan over Alan's ex-girlfriend Laura. It also turns out the monks are after the 'Armour of God', a relic that is split into five pieces, of which they have two, and another is the Sword of God, that Asian plans to sell at auction. They devise a plan to kidnap Laura so that Asian can be bribed into retrieving the other parts.

Intercutting images of Alan in concert, we next see the kidnapping of Laura while at a top fashion show. A group of armed monks burst in on the show and begin firing. As the audience dive for cover, a police officer goes for his gun but is cruelly shot dead, his blood-splattered body lying motionless on the floor. The catwalk is then plugged full of bulletholes before they kidnap Laura.

Upon their retreat more armed police arrive, however they are quickly cut down as the monks reel off hundreds of rounds of ammo, the police officers' bodies jerking violently as the bullets penetrate through them. After another shootout with police officers on a balcony above, the monks escape. As the audience gets to its feet amidst a scene of carnage, a fashion photographer takes a picture of the dead officers. At this point a monk returns and shoots the photographer in the eye and then the chest.

For a Jackie Chan film, this scene is quite graphic and realistic in terms of violence. When the officers are shot various amounts of blood squirt from their wounds, whilst the photographer's death is quite unexpected and crude. The intercutting of Alan Tam's concert performance is good, however his epic song seems most inappropriate for the scene overall.

Next we witness Asian at the auction for the holy sword, whereby the Sword of God is sold to a mysterious lady after a bizarre bidding war that Asian and his partner hinder rather than help. After the auction and a brief rendezvous with the mysterious lady, Asian reaches his hotel where he meets up with his old band mate Alan, who informs him of Laura's kidnap and ransom.

It transpires that the monks will only release Laura if they receive the three missing pieces of the Armour of God. At first Asian is reluctant to help, however they soon set aside their differences. Asian informs Alan that he has just sold one of the pieces at auction, while the other two pieces belong to a rich Count, whom they immediately go and visit.

Sat around a wooden table in a large decorative room, Asian and Alan explain their problem to the Count, and enquire whether or not they could borrow the two pieces. The Count asks why he should trust them, and talks about borrowing the Armour of God break down. Instead of leaving, Alan takes up the Count's offer to look at his antique collection. It is here that Asian and Alan learn the history behind the Armour of God.

It turns out that long before Christ, evil was rampant throughout the land, and that the true God waged a war against these forces and won. The weapons they used were known as the Armour of God. However some evil cults have resurfaced, and they believe if you destroy the Armour of God then religion will perish and the dark forces will take over! Asian dismisses the story as rubbish, whereupon the Count invites them to stay the night, an invitation Alan readily accepts.

Interestingly, the reciting of the history of the Armour of God is told in flashback, where we see Medieval looking clans clashing in the dead of night, before a gloomy morning-after shot of a corpse-ridden battlefield. This is a nice touch and although not shot on an epic scale, the small fight sequence is well staged.

As Alan and Asian relax in their room, Alan informs Asian that he intends to steal the Armour of God, thus prompting an argument between the pair. As Asian sleeps he has a weird dream, before he is woken up by one of the Count's butlers, who informs him that the Count wishes to see him. When he enters the room the Count is seated on a couch surrounded by dogs, with Alan cowering in the corner - he tried to steal the pieces but was obviously caught in the act!

At this point the Count's daughter, May, enters the room. To Asian's surprise she is the same lady who bought the Sword of God at the auction. The count informs the pair that he has called the police, but Asian quickly talks him out of turning the pair of them over to the authorities. They come to a gentlemen's agreement whereby the

Count agrees to lend them the three pieces, on the condition that the pair return with all *five* pieces of the Armour of God, and that May goes along with them. From here Asian, Alan and May set off towards a remote guesthouse, where they wait for the impending meeting with the kidnappers.

The following morning sees the trio arriving in town in readiness for the meeting, carrying the Armour of God in a black bag as requested by the kidnappers. Alan informs the others that he has to meet them alone. However, they agree that Asian and May will stay close by to keep an eye out. We learn May is a champion rifle shooter, so naturally she takes a key lookout position on a nearby rooftop.

From the crowded marketplace a monk approaches Alan, producing a photograph of the captured Laura. Naturally Alan follows the monk through the winding cobbled back streets. Here they demand the Armour of God, and wrestle the bag from Alan. Opening the bag they find the contents are fake and subsequently drag Alan off. Luckily Asian is nearby and he quickly frees his pal with a lightning kick. After a brief tussle, with May also involved trying to shoot the bad guys, the monks escape. Giving chase, Asian and Alan reach the ruins of an old bridge where they are greeted by around thirty more monks! Naturally, Asian and Alan scarper.

Now an extended and superb chase sequence kicks off. Getting into their flashy Mitsubishi, Asian and Alan escape, only to be followed by the monks in Jeeps and on motorbikes! The chase is on and they weave in and out of the narrow idyllic streets of Yugoslavia, destroying several restaurants and the local marketplace. There are countless stunts to enjoy here as bikers are sent flying through the air, or Jeeps are sent crashing down flights of steps or into parked vehicles. After one biker is electrocuted when completing a stunning stunt over a flyover, Asian and Alan are trapped on a bridge by two Jeeps. As the Jeeps attempt to crush our duo, Asian uses another of his special gadgets to get them out of trouble. Pressing a small button, the duo escape in a minicar, whilst the bad guys are promptly blown up!

This scene is both exhilarating and stylishly handled, and another fine example of Jackie Chan's gift of making edge-of-the-seat set pieces interwoven with moments of comedy. Some of the stunts leave you shaking your head at their sheer audacity, and the fact that none of the extras or stuntmen got killed!

During the evening the trio arrive at a small restaurant situated in the town. Here they bribe a camp waiter into revealing details about the sinister monks. He informs the trio that they are disciples of a monastery located in the hills nearby, and that once a month they arrive in the town to pick up food and girls! Alan enquires about how to reach the monastery, however the waiter claims that he does not know its location.

Next we see Asian and Alan loitering in the town market, where they beat up two monks and steal their robes before jumping on the back of their truck. The truck is filled with young girls as well as, to Asian's surprise, May, who has disguised herself as a prostitute. After a picturesque drive they reach the monastery.

Once inside, the monks' leader talks in front of his followers about the amount of money they have made from the harvest. However we are not talking crops here, but opium, cocaine and morphine! At this point Asian, Alan and May arrive with the call girls. However, unbeknownst to our heroes, the monks have been expecting their arrival and the leader is duly informed, and he advises that no-one is to stop them. At this point another monk takes over and begins to pray, although not about the good things in life, but sickness, plagues and the pleasures women bring! Suddenly all the monks get up and run off with the prostitutes. Poor old May gets caught up in this fiasco.

Next we learn about the evil scheme the monks have to retrieve the Armour of God. We see Laura tied to a chair, where she is injected with a sinister drug that will make her join allegiance with the monks and become a willing slave. The drug lasts for three days, and she is informed in that time she should steal the Armour of God and inject the drug into Asian Hawk.

Next we see May sprawled out on a large sofa with a monk on top of her. Trying to scupper the advances of the sex-crazed monk, May tries to whack him on the head with a wine bottle. Catching her in the act the monk becomes suspicious, and his initial suspicions are confirmed when an informant knocks on his door to advise him that she is a spy. Upon learning this, the monk fakes that he is drunk and leaves the monastery keys on the bed for May to steal.

Meanwhile Asian and Alan are prowling around and chance upon Laura's cell, which is heavily guarded. As the monks play cards, Asian passes Alan a large wooden plank. At this point they attack, and in a comic moment Alan hits one monk across the back of the head with the plank. This has no effect and as Alan falls to the floor, Asian steps in and knocks out the remaining three monks. At this point they reunite with May. She shows them the keys to the cell, and they quickly rescue Laura. Disguising Laura as a prostitute, Asian and company quickly escape from the monastery back to the village, all under the watchful eyes of the monks, who have actuallly knowingly 'let' them escape.

Back at our heroes' retreat, May informs the party that the earliest flight they can get back home is the following day. Laura and Alan retire to bed, and May and Asian spend a delicate moment together. Asian ruins the mood with an off the cuff remark that results in a hard smack around his chops. At this point Asian retires to bed too!

Meanwhile Laura asks Alan whether she can see the Armour of God. Suspicious of her behaviour, Alan speaks to Asian on the matter, however he reassures Alan that everything is okay. They proceed to May's room, where the Armour of God is stashed. When they reach May's room they discover she's not inside. Alan creeps into the room and attempts to take the Armour of God. At this point May returns with a glass of milk and spots Asian loitering outside her room.

What then erupts is a typical Jackie Chan comic sequence that is both funny and well executed. Asian does his best to stop May spotting Alan in her room, as Alan hides in cupboards and behind doors to avoid his cover being blown. Asian pretends to apologise and takes May off to his room, saying he has something to show her. A relieved Alan finally manages to leave.

When Asian enters his room, he is shocked to find Laura already in there, and naturally May isn't too chuffed either! May storms off and Laura then attempts to seduce him. Luckily for Asian, Laura pops into the bathroom when moments later Alan arrives! He slumps in a chair before moaning that he can't find Laura. Alan then spots movement in the bathroom, and goes to investigate. Quickly stepping in, Asian claims that it's May, and that they have recently got together. Satisfied, Alan and Asian leave the room.

The situation takes another twist as they leave Asian's room when Alan spots May at the top of the hall. The smart-thinking Asian tells Alan that their bathrooms are connected and that May doesn't want anyone to know about the affair. May suddenly comes down the hall and confronts Asian on the matter with Laura. Obviously Alan has no idea about Laura being inside Asian's room, so when May asks Alan about the situation he replies he has no problem with it - he thinks they are talking about Asian and May's relationship! May calls the pair of them "beasts" before again storming off to pack her bags.

Whilst Asian talks May out of leaving, Alan discovers their bathrooms are not connected and, creeping into Asian's room, Alan is accidentally injected with the evil drug by Laura, who has emerged from the darkened shadows.

It is not until the next morning that Asian discovers that the pair have stolen the Armour of God.

Intent on rescuing his friends, we see Asian first motorcycle up steep sandy woodland before abseiling down a rocky cliff above the monks' monastery. Halfway down the cliff face Asian crawls into a cavern, and is attacked by a load of bats!

This scene sets Jackie apart from other action stars as we can clearly see it is Jackie himself performing all the stunts, just confirming why he is the world's best action star. At one point when we see Jackie abseiling, the

camera pulls back to reveal how high this cliff-face actually is! How often in Hollywood films do we have stunt doubles, not the star, undertaking these shots? The fact that Jackie is prepared to risk life or limb in order to capture the required shot is testimony to him and his films, and why he is so widely supported by his fans.

Once inside the cavern complex Asian dodges numerous wandering monks, and at one point he only just manages to dive for cover in time. Then as the monk passes Asian, he jumps out but misses him. Turning quickly, Asian then creeps up behind the monk, and as the monk turns, Asian unleashes his fist into the monk's mouth and then beats him to the floor. From here Asian finds Alan and Laura's cell. Before he can save the pair, Asian is forced to hide in the cavern's rafters when a group of suspicious monks investigate the kerfuffle. Once they have gone, Asian climbs into the cell and unties the two, whereupon Alan and Asian begin bickering over Laura. Once their differences have been set aside they all set about escaping from the monastery.

As they blindly creep around the dark dingy caverns, Asian accidentally knocks Alan down a small shaft that leads to the monks' dining hall. Unfortunately all the monks are having lunch at this point, and they immediately recapture Alan, despite his lame attempts to escape.

Arriving on the scene, Asian realises his friend's predicament, grabs a large wooden pole and douses it with red wine. Placing the end in the open fire, the pole is suddenly engulfed in flames, and Asian runs at his enemy swinging the pole like a Samurai wielding a blade. Freed, Alan quickly runs for cover behind Asian with Laura, before Asian orders them to escape. After a couple more swipes at the monks, Asian promptly follows the others, hot-footing it as the monks throw a large wooden table at him!

Just as Asian is about to make his escape the door closes and the satanic monks suddenly surround him. What erupts from here on is an electric fight sequence that sees Asian defeat monks, whether it be by fist, kick or even by throwing large wooden objects at his foes. At one stage Asian is reunited with Alan and Laura and they begin throwing plates at the monks, only for the monks to return fire with vegetables, bowls and cups!

From here the hapless duo of Alan and Laura manage to get themselves locked up again, whilst Asian single handedly defeats the remaining monks before himself escaping.

By this point the action has really kicked off big time, and it is great to see Jackie on top form again. The scene boasts some lightning moves from Jackie that are made even better by the way he uses objects as springboards or ramps to perform them. In one standout moment, Jackie unleashes a deft double kick to one of the monks and we see him summersault backwards in slow motion onto the stone floor.

Leaving most of the monks battered and bruised, Asian wanders around the caves, searching for the Armour of God. Again Asian is attacked, however he easily dispatches their feeble efforts with a bevy of quickfire kicks to the chest. Asian spots a red glow and when inspecting it discovers the resting place of the Armour of God. However, before Asian can grab the items the cave lights up and the sinister head monk (played by Ken Boyle) confronts Asian. Asian informs the head monk he will take the Armour of God at all costs as the money the items can bring him drives him to reclaim them. The head monk then kindly informs Asian that he will die!

Suddenly Asian is confronted by a quartet of monks. However, as they disrobe we soon learn they are the 'Sisters of Mercy' - an evil foursome who are decked out in high heels, leather and frizzy hair! These girls mean business, and resemble something out of the seventies Shaft movies. Like a pack of jackals the women attack Asian, at once delivering a number of brutal blows. After an initial beating, Asian soon fights back. Gliding around the cavern, Asian hoists himself up onto a staircase where he beats one of the women into submission. Then he throws another of the hapless vixens down a banister, before throwing a third off the staircase onto the hard floor below. The final sister is dispatched with a stunning backward kick as she mis-times a flying kick.

This scene represents all that Jackie is capable of. Instead of fighting the women independently, Jackie takes on all four at once, making it harder to choreograph. However Jackie makes the impossible look easy, and we are rewarded with an excellent battle that features many of his trademarks. Jackie also replaces the female actresses with male members of his own stunt team, due primarily to the fact that the ladies would not have been able to keep up with his lightning reflexes. Although it is hilarious watching his stunt team dressed up in wigs, high heels, black face paint and make-up, this does not detract anything from the sequence.

Turning to the monks' leader, Asian declares he's taking the Armour of God, and he reveals he is wired up with dynamite! After bluffing that he will set the fuse alight, Asian accidentally does so, resulting in the caverns being blown to pieces. Scrambling to his freedom, Asian stumbles onto a small ledge where he jumps off into a passing balloon manned by Alan, Laura and May (heaven knows how both Alan and Laura got in there)!

Cue credits and outtakes of that infamous stunt.

Although some Jackie Chan fans consider the film too slow, *Armour of God* remains one of Jackie's most enjoyable adventures, despite the often glaring nods to *Raiders of the Lost Ark.* Although admittedly perhaps not as good as the sequel, *Armour of God* is memorable for more than just being the film that almost killed Jackie. In retrospect, *Armour of God* ranks up there with the *Police Story* series, *Project A*, *Drunken Master* and its sequel, *Rush Hour* and *Operation Condor* as essential Jackie Chan flicks.

THE NORTON EFFECT

By Lisa Clemens

Jackie's fans may know Richard Norton best for his roles as the bad guy in such films as *Twinkle, Twinkle Lucky Stars*, *City Hunter* and *Mr Nice Guy*. But the talented martial artist and actor has close to sixty roles in his filmography, starting with the 1976 film *Last of the Knucklemen*, where he doubled the lead actor in a fight scene.

Born in Melbourne, Richard Norton started as a young martial artist in Croydon, Australia. Judo and Karate were not well known in the area at the time. He became involved in the martial arts when he noticed that a neighbor's teen son would disappear a few nights a week and he became curious to find out where his friend was going. His friend told him about the Judo school he had been attending and invited him to check it out. Soon he started two years' training in Judo and earned a junior brown belt.

When a Karate school opened up closer to his home, Richard joined up with instructor Tino Ceberano to learn Goju Kai. One of the things that drew Richard to Karate was the fact that height and weight were not important to be successful. For the skinny youth that Richard was at the time, this was a bonus. While training with Tino Ceberano, Richard met Bob Jones, who was also a student.

He and Bob Jones are credited with initiating a new style of martial arts called Zen-Do-Kai. Zen-Do-Kai is best described as a martial art that includes Karate, but also includes locks, holds, throws, vital point striking, grappling, and principles and practices of boxing, kick boxing and Muay Thai boxing as well as more traditional weaponry.

Zen-Do-Kai was developed after he and Bob Jones split from the Goju system.

When training bouncers and bodyguards they needed a form that was designed to develop these bouncers and give them a more practical approach to fighting. Richard was a head instructor of this style until 1979. He and his partner worked hard at their schools, keeping them running while training six days a week. This experience was beneficial to Richard because the bouncers he trained were constantly pushing him to become more innovative as, with each class, they would get better and

more skilled, wanting to learn more challenging moves and skills. Richard says, "It helped me to grow so much because I had to think for myself, find my own knowledge and express different ways of teaching the knowledge that I had found. I had to internalize it and make it my own."

Already working with Bob Jones, by 1972 Richard also began working as a bodyguard at local arenas when rock bands came on tour to his home town.

At his official website (http://www.richardnorton.net) he tells this story about working at a Rolling Stones concert: "I remember that Mick had just built the crowd into a frenzy. The song set was building, and each song was seemingly getting louder and more energetic. Suddenly a crowd of around 3000 who were outside the stadium

Richard with Stevie Nicks

Pretty soon, Richard Norton was becoming well known in rock and roll circles as someone who would put himself on the line for his clients. And so he found himself working as a bodyguard for such notables as Fleetwood Mac, David Bowie, John Belushi, James Taylor and more.

By 1979, Richard left Australia for America and became a bodyguard for singer Linda Ronstadt while continuing to train in boxing, Aikido and kick boxing. He also had the opportunity to train with the likes of Benny 'The Jet' Urquidez and other top martial artists based in America.

While in the US, Richard had not given much thought to getting more involved in films. He considered himself a martial artist, first and foremost. After all he had been working as a chief instructor of over 200 Zen-Do-Kai schools around Australia...

But enter into films he did. Back in 1977 while still in Australia, Richard and Bob Jones invited Chuck Norris to town to appear at some tournaments they were holding. Chuck Norris was known to Richard mostly from martial arts magazines in which he was featured. Having Chuck Norris come to his tournaments was exciting for him. He considered Norris a legend. The two got along well at this time and Richard was told that if he was ever in California, he should get in touch with Norris again so they could train together.

And so when Richard moved to Los Angeles in 1979, he called on Chuck Norris and soon began training with him. Norris cast Richard in his next film, *The Octagon*, in which he played Kyo and also worked on fight choreography and stunts. Chuck Norris knew that Richard was good with weapons, including the sai, and he asked him to work with his brother, Aaron, to create some fights for the film using these weapons.

Richard decided that he liked making films and continued to do so, working with Chuck Norris at first and then going on to appear in such films as *Twinkle, Twinkle Lucky Stars*, his first Hong Kong film. He was actually on tour with Linda Ronstadt when he got the call to appear in the film.

While working with Sammo Hung, Yuen Biao and Jackie Chan, Richard was introduced to a whole new way of making movies. He has said: "It was my first Hong Kong movie and I didn't really know what to expect. What an eye-opener. When the fight scenes started we were shooting around the clock.

"You'd only get an hour to an hour and a half's sleep a day and that was on the set. That went on for three weeks, seven days a week. Remember, that's just for one fight scene. I lost 18 pounds and ended up an absolute wreck. I was in a Golden Harvest studio in Hong Kong that was never under 115 degrees with no air conditioning - and man did you have to fight hard."

and couldn't get in started playing up. Fueled by alcohol and the frenzied atmosphere they began to push towards the stage. Only a rickety wood retaining fence was keeping them back. We could see the fences beginning to bow inward and we knew they wanted to take the stage over. We of course feared for the band (and maybe ourselves - but just a little, heh!). There were biker gangs and kids hitting cops and each other with whatever they could pick up, they didn't care. There were only five of us on the other side of the fence and we knew we were the last lines of defence. So as they started coming over the fence we would take them out and then throw them back over. I was taking on two or three blokes at a time."

This must have impressed the Stones' front man, Mick Jagger, as Richard soon found himself giving Jagger some basic Karate lessons in his hotel room, sometimes into the wee hours of the morning.

Something else Richard had to get used to fast was Sammo and Jackie's way of not pulling punches. In *Twinkle* there are quite a few kicks and punches that he takes with little or no padding, and at times the hits were directed to his face. As it turns out, Richard prefers full contact, stating that it gives the fights more of an edge.

And he also learned a great lesson from Jackie, not about film-making, but about how to be a gracious host and about treating fans with patience and kindness. During an exclusive interview with *Screen Power*, Norton told Richard Cooper that while he was working on *Twinkle, Twinkle Lucky Stars* Jackie was "such a gracious host, taking me shopping and sightseeing around Kowloon... It was a real lesson for me to watch Jackie and how he is with his fans."

In Hong Kong, he was often cast as the Western baddie. And while some might lament that he never got to be the hero who gets to plant a kiss on a love interest as the credits roll, you have to admit that he does play a wonderful bad guy. Not only that, but he really seems to enjoy playing the heavy, especially in roles where he can play it a little over the top.

He told Richard Cooper that the most appealing factor in working with someone like Sammo Hung or Jackie is that he always gets to perform in fight scenes that are quite different from anything done in Hollywood. "These guys

can certainly bring out the crazy in you." He was taught that in their films, gestures and mannerisms were better when played broadly rather than subdued.

His character Colonel MacDonald in *City Hunter* is certainly a great example of this. Based on an anime, one would expect the villain to be over the top, and Norton performs perfectly. He strikes the right balance, not letting the character go too broad but still making him one of the most entertaining characters in the film. He delivers his lines with a twinkle in his eyes and an evil smirk on his face that makes him the perfect villain for the film. His character knows he's bad and he's loving it.

Richard made several Hong Kong films, such as *Millionaire's Express*, where he was reunited with Sammo Hung and Yuen Biao. The film also boasted an impressive cast and cameo list including Jimmy Wang Yu, Rosamund Kwan, Hwang Jang Lee and many others. Richard also appeared in *Jade Crystal*, directed by Wong Jing and starring Andy Lau, and *Fight to Win* with Cynthia Rothrock.

Richard has also continued to work with Chuck Norris, appearing on the TV show *Walker, Texas Ranger* eight times. Other US television appearances include *The New*

Richard in *Amazons & Gladiators*

Adventures of Robin Hood, a Warner Brothers production that aired for three seasons from 1996 until 1998 on TNT network. He played Rossamar in an episode titled 'The Legion' and Lord Chilton in another called 'Assault on Castle Dundeen', in which he played a devious uncle intent on laying siege to the castle. He also worked as the 2nd Unit Director and Stunt Co-ordinator for the shows. He was also involved in the made-for-TV movie called *Fugitive X: Innocent Target*. The plot concerns a blackmailed advertising executive who becomes human prey for wealthy thrill seeking hunters.

In Australia, he worked on a 1992 TV mini series called *Good Vibrations*. It was a film somewhat like *Poltergeist*, where a family discovers their house is a portal to the spirit world.

Richard had the opportunity to be reunited with his co-star of *Fight to Win* and *China O'Brien* in the movie *The Redemption*. The star of this film is three time WKO World Kickboxer Champion Don 'The Dragon' Wilson, whom Richard last worked with on the film *Cybertracker*. In *The Redemption*, Richard plays a S.W.A.T. team member who is somewhat jealous of Wilson's higher rank but still maintains his integrity. Chris Penn (*Rush Hour*) also appears as a mob boss.

An interesting project that Richard was involved in was a DVD interactive video game/movie called *Tex Murphy: Overseer*. A game where players would navigate through live action scenes and interact with characters as well as look for clues in 3D generated rooms and locations. Along with Richard, cast members include Michael York and Clint Howard. Another video game he worked on was *Supreme Warrior* where he was credited not only as a cast member in the video game, but also as the stunt co-ordinator.

Although he has played several mean and nasty villains, fans who came to Los Angeles in October of 2002 were shown just how much of a 'Mr Nice Guy' he really is. Everyone was treated to a two day event that included a question and answer session and a viewing of a few of Richard's films the first day.

The second day's events included an autograph/photo session with fans, and a martial arts seminar where Richard taught fans some self defence one might use on the streets. Richard even had several fans learning via a hands on method, grappling with him personally for demonstration purposes. He also answered more questions from the fans about different styles and forms of martial arts. Lastly was a dinner with the star at a Chinese restaurant where Richard answered even more questions, posed for more photos and then enjoyed turning a video camera belonging to Richard Cooper onto the fans and making some funny comments. Hope we all get to see this footage on a future *Screen Power* Video Magazine DVD release!

Although he has become well known for his films, Richard Norton still considers himself as a martial artist first and an actor second. He is a Dan Zen-Do-Kai expert whose hope is to continue to learn and grow. He has earned a black belt in Brazilian Jiu-Jitsu after training with his coach Jean Jacques Machado. Richard has also become instrumental in helping to get Machado Jiu-Jitsu set up in the United States.

This quote from his official website sums up Richard Norton's feelings in regard to himself and martial arts: "I don't know where I'd be without my training. It just keeps me grounded and sane. Even without the movies and my career, as long as I had my martial arts, I reckon I'd be pretty happy. The arts just give you such a sense of mateship and belonging. Many of the friends I've made through my training have turned out to be some of the most influential people in my life and are just like family to me. Because when you get right down to it - when you really think about it - the only thing that really matters in life is your honor and integrity and the relationship and love of your wife, family and friends."

The New Adventures of Robin Hood

RICHARD NORTON
INTERVIEWED

Screen Power editor Richard Cooper talks to everyone's favourite Western Hong Kong action movie villain - Richard Norton.

Despite the fact that Richard Norton played the bad guy in 'reel' life in numerous Hong Kong action pictures, including three of Golden Harvest's Jackie Chan productions, thankfully but not surprisingly Richard is a nice guy in 'real' life.

Being *Screen Power*'s biggest critic, I have always said in the past that we'll not publish an interview with someone unless it is justified - well on this occasion, and like so many other interviewees in the past, Richard Norton more than justifies this interview.

Personal bodyguard to the stars, actor, martial artist, stuntman, Hong Kong movie veteran now turned Hollywood performer - and hey, he has a cool name too! So here's what we talked about:

Dream Warrior

Screen Power: Richard, let's start at the very beginning. Where were you born and raised?

Richard Norton: I was born in Melbourne, Australia and grew up in the Melbourne suburb of Croydon. I have a twin sister and an older brother. My father was born in England and died in 1963. My mother is still alive and a wonderfully healthy eighty-six years old.

SP: When did you first get into the martial arts? What styles have you studied, and what attracted you to study martial arts in the beginning?

RN: I started training in Judo at twelve years of age, and Karate at age fourteen. My Karate style was a Japanese system called Goju-Ryu and my instructor was a Hawaiian born Philipino by the name of Tino Ceberano.

My initial attraction to the arts pretty much started with ads in the back of comic books. You know, "Defeat five attackers with one finger!" Of course on starting my Judo

training I soon realised that nothing was further from the truth. You see, as a child of twelve, I was incredibly skinny and quite short for my age and therefore ended up resembling one of those cartoon characters being pitched from one end of the Dojo to the other. (Laughing) I was just "cannon fodder" for the older Brown Belts in the class. So much for my defeating five attackers with anything, let alone one finger. I felt I would be lucky to defeat my twin sister at this rate. I should mention by the way, that I had a great upbringing in a typical neighbourhood with a couple of wonderful boyhood friends. We were always wrestling and play fighting and extremely physical, but I was not in an environment where I was being beaten up by neighbourhood gangs every other day. In other words, learning how to fight out of necessity was not my reason for taking up the arts in the beginning. Back then, the martial arts still conjured up thoughts of an Eastern discipline so mystical and with mysterious powers available to the avid disciple. This notion, I remember, absolutely intrigued me.

I honestly believe in retrospect that being involved in the martial arts was what I was meant to do with my life, and that I was drawn to it by somehow recognising that fact. I mean, everything great that has happened in my life, like travelling the world as a Rock and Roll bodyguard and doing martial arts movies, has come as a result of just wanting to be the best martial artist possible. Hey, you can't beat that.

Anyway, back to the Judo. I met another student in my class who told me about a Karate school being run by Tino Ceberano that was opening up near to where we lived. So we went and watched a class of students that had been training for about six months or so. They demonstrated a basic kata, or form, known as Taikyoku Jodan, Chudan and Gedan. They also did some controlled sparring called Jyu-Kumite. Well, that was it. I knew this was the art for me, as I immediately saw it as something not necessarily relying on size or strength. I trained with Tino for about five years before leaving with a Goju student/friend of mine, Bob Jones, to initiate a new kind of eclectic style we called Zen-Do-Kai, which basically translates into "The best of everything in progression". I remained head instructor of Zen-Do-Kai until 1979, when I left Australia to go to America to work as a personal bodyguard for rock singer Linda Ronstadt. I also trained during this time in various Okinawan weapon systems, Aikido, boxing and kick boxing. Since living in the US I have trained on a daily basis in kick boxing with Benny 'The Jet' Urquidez, Machado Jui-Jitsu with Jean-Jacques Machado, and a whole host of top ranking martial artists based in the US, most notably of course my mentor and best friend Chuck Norris.

SP: You have appeared in numerous martial arts and action films, but how did you get into acting in the first place? Was it your dream to become an actor?

RN: My first experience of working in movies was back in 1976 in a film called *Last of the Knucklemen*, when I doubled one of the lead actors in a brutal fight scene. Despite the dubious title, the movie was a critically acclaimed story about opal miners in outback Australia. The actor I fought was a professional wrestler, who you might recognise in the *Crocodile Dundee* films. He plays one of Crocodile Dundee's home town friends, Donk. He's the big guy with the tank top and crewcut.

Apart from that start, no, I had no aspirations to be an actor. I was a martial artist and that was that. You see, in Australia, I was Chief Instructor of then over 200 schools throughout the country. I was also working as a personal bodyguard and had been since 1972, looking after bands such as The Rolling Stones, Joe Cocker, Abba, James Taylor, Fleetwood Mac and David Bowie, to name a few.

In 1977, my partner Bob and I bought Chuck Norris out to Australia to do some appearances at some tournaments we were holding. Chuck and I immediately struck up a great friendship, so when I ended up in Los

Angeles in '79, you can guess who was the first person I called. I began training with Chuck every day at his house in Torrance and when he went onto pre-production on one of his earlier movies, *The Octagon*, I was cast in the role of his evil Ninja heavy, Kyo. This was due to the fact that Chuck knew of my expertise in Japanese Kobudo, or weaponry. I helped choreograph a lot of the fight scenes and was also one of the four 'stunt Ninjas' throughout the movie. In fact my claim to fame is that I died eight times in that film. Pretty good, huh? One life to go I guess (laughing).

So that was my beginning in action films. I had such a good time that I found myself saying, "Hmm, not a bad way to make a living." I then did a couple more movies with Chuck before auditioning for one of the leads in a movie called *Force Five*, produced by the legendary producer of *Enter the Dragon*, Fred Weintraub, and directed by Robert Clouse, who of course directed the classic Bruce Lee film. That experience, incidentally, was the catalyst for a whole change in attitude as to whether or not I thought I was worthy of competing in the US market for roles in martial arts movies. When I auditioned

Force Five

for *Force Five* I was up against probably a hundred or so of the best martial artists in the US. I remember thinking, "No way. There is *no way* they are going to hire an unknown Australian in the lead role for this American movie." Then, when I ended up in the final ten actors to be decided on, I thought, "You know what, instead of thinking 'Why me?' I'm beginning a new attitude of 'Why *not* me?' I have trained just as hard as anybody else here - why not me?" Anyway, I ended up being cast as one of the leads, and my career was off and running. Since then I have worked in over fifty movies and I'm still going strong.

SP: *The Hollywood movie business is very different to the Hong Kong movie business. Which do you prefer? I assume there is more work for you in Hollywood?*

RN: Yes, there is definitely more work for me in Hollywood and probably one of the obvious reasons is the language and the fact that I don't speak Mandarin or Cantonese. Also, for some time now, the Hong Kong movie industry has not been nearly as healthy as it was when I was last there a few years ago. After the change-over, a lot of the good directors and actors left for places like the US and Canada. The industry in Hong Kong basically went into a slump. I also know that the only roles I would be cast in, in Hong Kong movies, would be that of the Western heavy. I think the idea of a bigger

Western foe being one of the baddies beaten up by a Chinese hero is a lot of the appeal of using someone like myself.

As far as which I prefer, it is definitely easier doing a Hollywood movie. Most times in Hong Kong I would be the only Westerner on set, which can make it a pretty lonely place when you can't speak the language. Also, in Hong Kong there is usually no English language script, so you are pretty much in the dark as to your character or storyline. In fact, in the majority of cases, the script is being written daily as the film is being shot. This of course can make it difficult on the actor. On the other hand, I think the good part about this is that it enables film-makers like Jackie to be able to be completely spontaneous as to the direction they can take their story-line and characters. Take a Hong Kong fight scene for instance. There is no such thing as shooting a 'master' like they would do in a Hollywood fight scene. In other words you are not locked in by the 'master' take in a Hong Kong fight scene. The fights are worked out in small sections as you go, with no particular idea of how the fight will end, or how long it will be. Jackie will look at the dailies that night and decide if the fight needs to be longer or whatever, and continue on the next day, sometimes for weeks or even months on one fight. This, by the way, of course, is why their fights are so amazing - it's because they put all their priorities into the action, which, of course, is what the kids want to see...

Promotional shot for *City Hunter*

In a Hollywood movie you would be lucky to spend a day on a fight of the same screen time, and it shows. So, obviously, I must say then that the most exciting reason for me to work on a Hong Kong movie, especially a Sammo Hung or Jackie film, is that I will always end up doing fighting scenes that are so totally different to anything I might do in Hollywood. These guys can certainly bring out the crazy best in you. You see, for a start, nothing is under played. All mannerisms and gestures are larger than life, and of course the length and breadth of the fight scenes are legendary, and because directors like Jackie and Sammo are the masters of choreography, you also know you will do fights that leave the Hollywood fight scenes for dead. I mean, what a lot of people don't realise is the amount of incredible thought Jackie and his team will put into an action scene, even to the point of working out what colour clothes the fighters should wear to stand out against the colour of the background and best highlight the fight. Then there's decisions on camera speed, depending on whether the action is being shot as a long shot or in close-up, camera positions and shooting angles...

This is just a small example of the kind of artistry I have never experienced in Hollywood. Lastly and most importantly of course there is the masterful choreography. Need I say more? It's literally poetry in motion. I remember when I first saw *City Hunter* - I was nearly on the floor laughing! It was so great, as it was as though I was watching myself as a completely different person. I'm telling you, if anyone can make you look great in a fight scene, it's these guys.

Oh yeah, one other reason though for maybe preferring Hollywood movies, is that I have so much more chance of playing a good guy. You see the problem with always being a baddie is that you always get beaten up and you never ever get the woman. Ah well, such is showbiz (laughing).

SP: (Laughing) Very true! It's nice to get the girl some of the time... How did you get into the Hong Kong movie business then?

RN: I was recommended to Jackie by an American stunt co-ordinator, Pat Johnson. Pat was a good friend of mine and had worked with Jackie on *Big Brawl*. When Jackie's people first called me, I was in a little hotel in Fukuoka, Japan. I think I was on tour with Linda Ronstadt. God only knows how they found me. Anyway, this voice on the phone says, "Jackie Chan wants you to work on his next movie. What's your price?" I said, "Whoa, hold on, when would I have to start?" So the voice says, "You would have to be here in two days. What's your price?" I said, "Look, it doesn't really matter what my price is as I'm committed to this tour for another six weeks and can't possibly come to Hong Kong on such short notice." Anyway, some time later they contacted me again, thank goodness, and that was to work on a movie called *Twinkle, Twinkle Lucky Stars*.

Shanghai Express

SP: Yes, you worked with Jackie on Golden Harvest's Twinkle, Twinkle Lucky Stars back in 1985. What was it like working on that movie?

RN: Wow, what an experience. Of course working with Jackie was a phenomenal experience, as was working with Sammo Hung for the first time. You must realise that to go and work on a Hong Kong movie for the first time after only having done cozy Hollywood movies is an eye-opener to say the least! Listen, the absolute hardest thing a martial arts actor can be asked to do is a fight scene with Jackie Chan. This is mainly because of the level of excellence Jackie will demand of you, and especially of himself. I mean I had no idea what I was getting into. Like I had mentioned previously, there was no script for me to read and we were on the set a minimum of eighteen hours per day, often seven days a week. When we started the fight scenes, the choreography was so different to what I was used to, in that the timing and techniques were very unique to Hong Kong-style movies. Then there was the contact.

Ah yes, the contact. What a lot of people don't realise about Hong Kong-style action is that what you see is probably what's happening when it comes to the actual impact of the blows. Doing the fight with Jackie was

great though. He was so helpful in helping me get my 'Hong Kong feet' wet. We fought hard and had a great time. Actually I joke about the 'contact' in the fights, but I was in terrific shape going into the movie and I've never had a problem with hard physical contact, in fact I prefer it, as it gives the fight such an edge.

Aside from on the set, Jackie was also such a gracious host, taking me shopping and sight-seeing around Kowloon. He has such a warm and friendly nature that it's hard to imagine anyone not getting along with Jackie. Of course you already know that yourself, working with Jackie. But it was a real lesson for me to watch Jackie and how he is with his fans. I remember on *City Hunter*, a whole heap of Japanese fans had bought tickets to be on the cruise ship while we were shooting exteriors around Tokyo. One day I saw him spend literally hours taking pictures with each of them, literally a hundred or so. He was so patient and gracious, and I always remembered how cool that was of him, to take the time to do that. His fans really mean a lot to him.

SP: Jackie must have been impressed with you because you later joined him for City Hunter in 1992. What was it like working on this movie? Any funny stories on set?

RN: *City Hunter* was a terrific shoot. What a funny, zany movie. Actually, I got the role in *City Hunter* not

only because of my friendship with Jackie, but also because of having worked in the past with the director, Wong Jing. That was in one of Andy Lau's first screen movies, *The Magic Crystal*. Cynthia Rothrock was also in that movie.

I think also at this stage that, aside from my having done a good job on *Twinkle* and having a friendship with Jackie, he knew that I understood how a Hong Kong movie and especially a Jackie Chan movie worked. I knew to just shut up and do the job, no matter how many takes it took. I think a lot of Westerners would want to come to Hong Kong and do things their way and basically strut their stuff. But what I realised is that this is their movie and fight action is what they do better than anyone in Hollywood. Better to be quiet, do the absolute best you can and, most importantly, learn.

I must say I loved my character in *City Hunter*. I know it's not one of Jackie's favourite movies but I liked it. You know it took six weeks to shoot that end fight scene just with Jackie and myself. Wow, what a marathon.

SP: Well, you must have also impressed Sammo Hung as well as Jackie, as you later joined them both for Mr. Nice Guy in 1996 on your home turf of Australia. Sammo directed Twinkle, Twinkle Lucky Stars and also Mr. Nice Guy. What was Sammo like to work with?

RN: Sammo is the best. He, of course, aside from Jackie, is the most creative action director I have ever worked with. Sammo is just so incredibly creative and, boy, what an athlete. Jackie once described Sammo as being built like an elephant but moving like a monkey - which by the way is an incredible compliment to the Chinese. I think I got Sammo's respect when we did our fight scene in *Twinkle, Twinkle Lucky Stars* and he saw that I could take the gruelling schedule and especially not complain about the contact. In my fight with Sammo, I was being hit with bare fisted uppercuts under the chin, with only a little cotton wool I found to put between my teeth to act as a makeshift mouth-guard, and that side kick he hit me with. Wow! He sent me flying into that wall at a hundred miles per hour.

Also, the temperature in the Golden Harvest studios was never less than 115 degrees, what with all the lights and no air conditioning. Again we were on the set eighteen hours a day, seven days a week for three weeks shooting my fight with Sammo. I remember as plain as day getting back to my hotel room after the first full day of shooting and getting battered by Sammo and saying out loud, "If I can get through this, I can get through anything!" I tell you though that Sammo also got my complete respect, as no matter how hard he hit you, he wanted you to hit him back just as hard.

You have to remember by the way, that here's me complaining, but these guys do this kind of thing, movie after movie, day-in and day-out all year long, year after year. So what does that say about how the guys in Hollywood really are? One other thing I remember vividly about Sammo is the advice he gave me during the shooting of *Mr. Nice Guy*. We were at a restaurant one night and he suddenly starts talking about how long we have been friends, and having seen a lot of my other movies. He went on to say that although he thought I was okay in a lot of them, the problem he had with the characters I played was that I played them too normal. He went on to say that the problem with playing normal is that nobody remembers you. He then gave the example of Mel Gibson's character in *Lethal Weapon*. He said he wanted me to be totally over the top as 'Giancarlo' in *Mr. Nice Guy*. You know what? He was so right. I have always tended to underplay my characters in other movies. I thought that was such great advice and I really appreciated Sammo taking the time and interest to give me that input.

SP: On the subject of Mr. Nice Guy, were you surprised at getting such a big role in the film?

RN: Well, yes and no. No, because of some of the reasons I already mentioned earlier, like my relationship with Jackie and Sammo. But yes, I was a bit surprised, especially considering the fact that I had already played the bad guy in previous Jackie Chan movies and I didn't think they would want to use me again. Of course, them knowing that I am Australian and that they were shooting in my own back yard would have helped a lot. They also knew I could handle the punishing work schedule.

You know what is so flattering to me is that, aside from Benny Urquidez, I think I am the only Westerner to ever be asked back to star in more than one Jackie Chan movie. I treat that as such a huge compliment from the biggest and best action star in the world.

Richard on location with Jackie in Melbourne for *Mr. Nice Guy*

SP: *Any funny stories from making Mr. Nice Guy?*

RN: Probably the funniest is when in the opening scene I am seen burying this beautiful young lady in a mining pit beneath twenty tons of coal. Well that young lady is actually my wife and on the day we shot that scene, a beaming Jackie and Sammo both came up to me and asked, "Why you look so happy today?" I said, "I don't know, but just get that mining truck over here!" Just a joke of course sweetie, when you're reading this (laughing).

I must say that the one disappointment for me in *Mr. Nice Guy* was that I didn't get to do a major fight scene with Jackie. I think they ran out of time. Shame though, as I felt it was a bit of a waste using me with no major fight. I know as an audience member I would have wanted to see Giancarlo get his comeuppance and get his ass kicked at the end of the movie.

SP: *True! Well now, judging from the amount of letters and e-mails we have received about your good self from all over the world, you are clearly the fans' most favourite Western villain in Hong Kong movies. What do you think about that?*

RN: I am so flattered Richard, like you can't believe. I have trouble believing this to be the case, but in case it is, thank you so much! I feel truly honoured. I just hope I can hang in there for a few more years and keep working at it. Incidentally, for those interested, I have a new website with the web address of 'richardnorton.net'. I'd be thrilled if some of the readers would check it out.

SP: *I'm sure they will. Now, I remember you in Sammo's 1986 movie, Shanghai Express. That was a great film. All those stars and a big production. The only thing missing from that movie to make it even better would have been Jackie's involvement.*

RN: I couldn't agree more. I had a lot of fun shooting *Shanghai Express*. I especially enjoyed working and fighting with my Japanese actor friend from *Twinkle, Twinkle Lucky Stars*, Shoji Kurata. What a fine gentleman and a joy to work with. Of course, I was also with my dear friend Cynthia Rothrock, which is always fun for me.

SP: *Richard, you haven't always played villains in movies have you? You are well known in the West for appearing in Golden Harvest's international hits, China O'Brien 1 and 2. Do you have good memories from those films?*

RN: Absolutely. Any chance for me to work with my friend Cynthia Rothrock is great. You know an English martial arts magazine once described Cynthia and me as "the Ginger Rogers and Fred Astair of martial arts movies". I thought that was really cute. Of course after that we also starred together in *Rage and Honor* one and 2.

SP: *I can remember seeing you in a film called Sword of Bushido. That film had a few good fighting sequences in it, but it did lack in certain areas didn't it?*

RN: Yeah, I guess, but I kind of liked it. I especially loved the chance to do some traditional swordplay and work with such a master as Sensei Toshishiro Obata. I thought that end fight with him turned out really well. You know a good deal of that sword fight was done using 'live' or real swords that were razor sharp. That was because props ran out of fake bamboo swords. Pretty hairy stuff I'll tell you...

The worst part of the movie for me was that I was made by the producer to go back into the studio after we finished to re-voice all my dialogue. The delivery was fine but he insisted on having me sound more American. That was difficult for me then with my Aussie accent, and I think it really spoiled the end result of how I sounded. Oh well, we live and learn...

Boy, it was sure nice shooting in Phuket, Thailand, though. I also got to work again with my wife. She was the Navy Captain I got to seduce in the beginning of the film. See, it's not all hard work! (Laughing) By the way, my favourite Western movie that I have done is a movie I actually produced myself called *Ironfist* [aka *Under the Gun*]. We virtually shot it with no money, but I really liked how it turned out. I was very happy with all the fight scenes. They are not particularly Hong Kong style but still very rough and gutsy. My co-star in the movie was five-time kick boxing world champion Kathy Long. Check it out if you get a chance.

SP: *I will! One American film where you play the role of the villain was in the movie Gymkata. I remember that classic scene when you pulled out the pair of sais and started twirling them around. That was really fantastic.*

RN: Thank you. Except for Kurt Thomas' line of, "Stick your hardware back in your pants." Cheeky blighter! (Laughing) Actually the sai scene could have and should have been a lot better if it wasn't so cold when we shot that scene, and my hands weren't so frozen!

SP: *You are good friends with Chuck Norris, as you mentioned earlier. And you are helping out on Chuck's popular American TV show, Walker, Texas Ranger too, right?*

RN: Yes. Chuck is one of my best friends here in America. When *Walker* first started I put the fights together for the first three shows. It was meant to be an ongoing job for me, except it wasn't really what I wanted to do. I still had a desire to keep on with the acting side of things, and doing the *Walker* series would have been a full time commitment, so I turned it down. I have probably done at least a dozen acting roles though in the

Rehearsing an action scene for *Mr. Nice Guy*

show over the years. Chuck and I still work out together whenever he's in town or I'm in Dallas.

He really is a wonderful person and a great friend. Actually, Chuck was best man at my wedding to my wife, Judy. We got married at the Bel-Air Hotel in Los Angeles in 1993. In fact, speaking of Chuck, I'm actually leaving for Dallas on Tuesday to do a Guest Star role on an episode of *Walker* being directed by Chuck's son, Mike.

SP: Tell Chuck I said "Hi" (laughing). What other projects have you been involved with recently? And what projects do you have coming up?

RN: I had the lead in a sci-fi movie called *Nautilus*. That just came out in the video stores in January this year. I also recently completed a lead in a drama/thriller called *Shells*. It was shot on Trinidad and is a straight acting role for me. No fight scenes. I'm a sensitive, married, new age kind of guy. Go figure. I actually had a good time with the role, as it gave me a chance to play a very different character in a movie that doesn't rely on fight scenes. I'm not sure when that one will be released. I also co-ordinated all the action on a movie of the week/pilot for a new series for The Norris Bros called *The President's Man*. Chuck Norris stars in it and it was done for CBD television.

The most exciting thing coming up for me though is the lead in a new series called *The Sam Hill Chronicles*. The series is set in 1902 and is kind of like *The X-Files* but set one hundred years ago. I play the lead character Sam Hill, who travels the world investigating unexplained phenomena. Each week you will find me in a different part of the world investigating mysterious deaths, apparitions, ghosts and the like. The stories will be based on real life urban myths. We have the funding to be able to shoot twenty-two episodes, starting in January. I'm so excited, as the story ideas so far are terrific. My character will also have a background of Eastern martial arts, though the show will not be an action fight show as much as a show with a bit of an Indiana Jones feel to it, but spooky. I would love your readers to look out for the show sometime next year, as any support will be much appreciated.

SP: Well I'm sure all our US and Canadian readers will look out for The Sam Hill Chronicles, and as it may take a while for it to be shown on UK television, do me a favour and tape it and send me a copy! Tell me something: which film did you enjoy working on the most between City Hunter and Mr. Nice Guy and why?

RN: Well, I enjoyed them both, but for different reasons. The best part about *Mr. Nice Guy* was that it was shot in Melbourne, which of course is where I live a lot of the time. I must say it was so much nicer shooting on my home turf as opposed to Hong Kong or Taiwan, Ha, sorry Jackie. But I guess as far as movies go I would have to say I enjoyed working on *City Hunter* more, mainly because of the fact that I had a major fight scene with Jackie. I mean you have to understand that for a martial arts actor to get a chance to work with the world's top action star is such an honour and a chance not to be missed. Boy, it was a long shoot though. During shooting, Jackie fell off a skateboard and injured his ankle, which of course lengthened the shoot.

Our fight scene together took over six weeks and was pretty gruelling, but fun, I guess. Ha, again, as I said earlier, I kind of liked our fight because it was so different and funny, and I also enjoyed certain scenes in *City Hunter*, like when my character was playing cards with all the hostage passengers on the ship and shooting them as he beat them in cards. Goofy fun!

SP: You have worked with Jackie on three of his movies. What is your impression of him nowadays and his Hollywood success?

RN: I think his success is so deserved and so overdue. You see, the thing about Jackie, aside from being such a phenomenon in the action movie scene, is that he is first and foremost a wonderful human being. He has always been so gracious and friendly to me, but more importantly, it's his caring for his legion of friends and fans across the world that I have noticed and admired. As I have said earlier, to see the time and patience Jackie puts into his fans is, I think, a rarity amongst stars of his stature and the greatest thing is that he hasn't, at least to my mind, changed since the first time I worked with him some fourteen years ago.

It's kind of funny to me to think that the person who, to us, has *always* been a legend, is suddenly an 'overnight' success in Hollywood. Remember, this is also the star that I have seen, on my shoots with him, sweeping floors, moving light stands and basically doing anything and everything he can do to move things along and be part of the film-making team. Tell me another star that would chip in and sweep the floor of the set he happened to be working on. I absolutely respect him for things like that.

SP: I have just returned from Istanbul where Jackie is making his new Golden Harvest movie called The Accidental Spy, and he was regularly assisting the crew with the lighting and the camera equipment, so he hasn't changed. Let's talk about the martial arts. You have fought Jackie on screen many times. Were you impressed with his martial arts skills?

RN: Oh, of course, who wouldn't be? Jackie can do it all. He can do traditional martial arts, he can box, he can do Muay-Thai, grappling and whatever else a fight scene will call for. He is always in phenomenal shape

and, importantly, is constantly updating his training skills to meet the times. I think though the most important thing about Jackie is his timing. You see if you don't have an acute sense of timing, you will never be able to deliver your repertoire of skills effectively to your opponent. This with Jackie of course has come from performing just about every fight scene imaginable over a huge span of years.

Timing, by the way, is the most important requisite to doing a fight with him. All of Jackie's fights have a very particular rhythm to them, and it is the downfall of many a Western fighter who attempts to do battle with him on screen. That is why you will see the use of fight doubles so much when Jackie fights a Western foe. It's not so much about the person's technique, which of course is important, but all about the opponent's timing.

This is probably the most frustrating thing I see Jackie deal with when fighting a new screen villain. He comes up with the most brilliant choreography, and when his opponent is not able to understand the timing Jackie wants, then sparks start to fly (laughing). Not a good thing...

SP: (Laughing) And on that note we'll end it here. Richard, thanks so much for talking to Screen Power. Good luck in your career, and keep in touch with us.

RN: Thank you so much for the opportunity to speak with you, Richard. I will definitely keep in touch, and again, thanks so much to the fans out there who so kindly follow my career. By the way, keep up the great work with the magazine. I am so impressed with the quality and content. I truly believe that you do such a good thing in officially promoting one of the greatest martial arts movie legends of our time. I just give thanks that I have been lucky enough to have been involved in a part of, even if only in a small way, the Jackie Chan legacy...

THE MEDALLION

A Review by Trish Evans

After waiting for what seemed like years, *The Medallion* has finally opened in the USA. Wait a moment, it *was* years! *The Medallion* began shooting in 2001 and was originally called *Highbinders*, an Irish term referring to a mythological super being. Shooting of the film started off strongly and then was interrupted. Jackie stopped working on *Highbinders/The Medallion* to fulfil his commitment to star in *The Tuxedo*. He then returned to finish the film, which wrapped at the beginning of 2002. Then just when it looked like we might get to see it, there were more delays.

Columbia Tri-Star was unhappy with the product and asked for re-shoots and added scenes. That certainly sounded promising. More Jackie! Not less, which is what usually happens. But alas, we hoped too soon. Scenes were added but others were cut, plus the film spent a little time in movie detention having a CG redo. In the end the movie was chopped down from 116 minutes to 89 minutes and the CG shots went from 400 to 300. This Hong Kong production, directed by Gordon Chan, is the most expensive Hong Kong production ever filmed,

costing HK$300 million (US$38 million).

Jackie stars as Detective Eddie Yang, a Hong Kong cop, and Lee Evans (*There's Something About Mary*) co-stars as Arthur Watson of Interpol. The lovely Claire Forlani (*Meet Joe Black*) portrays Nicole James, Eddie's former love interest. John Rhys-Davies (*The Lord of the Rings*) appears as Commander Hammerstock-Smythe, the Chief of Interpol. The evil Snakehead is played by Julian Sands (*Warlock*). Other cast includes Anthony Wong as Lester the #2 bad guy, and Christy Chung as Charlotte Watson, the wife of Arthur. Opera School 'big brother' Sammo Hung did the action choreography.

The basic plot of the film steps heavily into the supernatural. We begin with a long-haired, leather-clad Eddie working a case in Hong Kong with Interpol's Detective Watson. They are after a creepy criminal called Snakehead, who is searching for a mysterious device that will make him immortal, give him super powers and make him even more creepy! The object in question, the Medallion, is in the hands of a special child named Jai

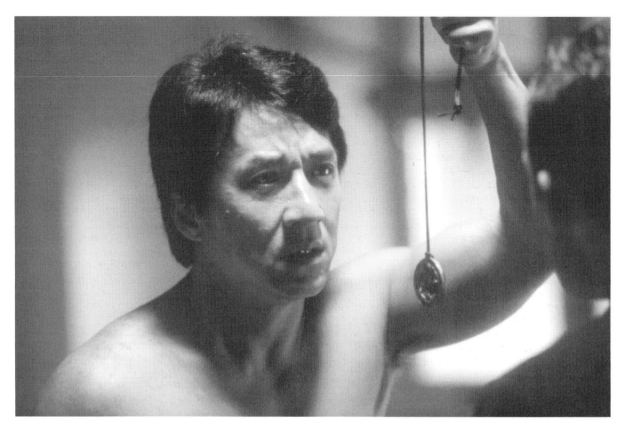

(Alex Bao), and the evil Snakehead makes a grab for the child and the magic talisman. Fortunately Eddie saves the child, but Snakehead slithers away.

Later, while working a case, Eddie sees Jai being abducted by one of Snakehead's men, Lester Wong. Eddie follows, ends up in Ireland and is reunited with Watson and old flame Nicole. They go in search of the boy and Eddie does manage to save the child's life, but in the process Eddie drowns. But all is not lost. The Medallion Jai wears brings Eddie back to life and transforms him into a super version of his former self, an immortal. He has mystical powers, but has no idea of what's going on, or how to use his new gifts. But Snakehead doesn't give up in his quest for immortality. He makes another grab for the child and the Medallion, and succeeds in acquiring powers of his own. Eddie, Nicole and Watson set out to rescue the chosen one, Jai, and destroy Snakehead.

I have to admit, my expectations about this movie had more ups and downs than Jackie being dangled by a wire. I went from expecting something wondrous to fearing the worst. So going in, I have to say I was more than pleasantly surprised. I love Hong Kong movies, yet wire work, when it's glaringly obvious, has never wowed me. Give me something that leaves me in awe of the performer's ability, or wondering how they did it, and I'm much happier. After *The Tuxedo* I wasn't ready to see Jackie doing more wire-fu.

I enjoyed the action at the beginning of the movie very much. Jackie had some great moves that should hopefully quieten those who still wonder if he has somehow lost some of his ability. His moves looked awesome, and I thought the action choreography by Sammo was top notch. Jackie did lightning-fast kicks and punches along with a fair measure of acrobatics, such as his leaps over fences and walls. Nice mix of Jackie's confident kick-butt action with some humor added in. The one thing I would have liked to see different in the opening sequence is when Jackie and his team jump up onto the cargo containers. They made these huge supernatural leaps that were very obviously done with wires and beyond normal ability. I think anything superhuman should have been left to Jackie after he was endowed with superpowers. Having him do something superhuman beforehand diminished what came later.

When Watson was first introduced on the screen I found myself wondering what his problem was. Why the attitude? It took me a bit before I realized he was supposed to be bumbling and funny. The attitude seemed a bit forced to me, and left me wondering where it came from. Later on Lee Evan's character seems more cohesive and his humor is actually quite funny.

The reunion of Eddie and Watson in Ireland was quite a funny moment, as those listening to their discourse got a totally wrong idea of the type of partnership they actually had. My eleven year-old son laughed and then said, "Well, that was awkward!"

The relationship between Eddie and Nicole was something I was eager to see. Jackie with a romantic interest is not something we get a lot of. Claire Forlani did an excellent job as Jackie's former paramour. Her eyes and facial expressions made me believe she cared for Eddie. Jackie slipped into romantic gear quite well, albeit a bit stiffly at times. I didn't feel his discomfort like I did during his kiss with Roselyn Sanchez in *Rush Hour 2*. I did get the sense that Nicole's feelings were stronger than Eddie's. Later, as Eddie comes to grips with his feelings for Nicole, it's a much more equitable romance. The long-anticipated kissing scene was nicely done, though Jackie seemed more amused than passionate, and could have relaxed a bit more.

The scene where Eddie saves the child Jai and then drowns was subdued yet emotional and well done. I could hear sniffling from the audience members around me. The shots in the morgue are among my favorites. When Eddie comes back to life and casually walks up to Watson the fun really begins. Lee Evans' shocked fear and stammering realization was one of the funniest parts of the movie. Jackie did a fine job of being confused and funny at the same time. Later Eddie realizes he is immortal and attempts to prove it to Watson by stabbing himself with a knife. Incredulous, Watson repeats the action in what could have been a gruesome scene, but

instead had the whole theater howling with laughter and groans.

Snakehead's gang goes in search of Eddie and finds him at Watson's house. Here Christy Chung shines as Watson's wife, who has a hidden arsenal of weapons and can whoop on bad guys with the best of them. There is never any explanation as to why she knows how to do this, or why she is armed with riot gear. Maybe the answer is someplace on Columbia Tri-Star's editing room floor. Eddie leads Snakehead away from the house and into the forest in pursuit of the Medallion. It seems Snakehead is only semi-all-powerful, and must have both halves of the Medallion in order to achieve the same level as Eddie. Here the use of wires and the Hong Kong style really worked for me. The leaves blowing as they ran through the forest and fought was artsy and fit with their new-found powers. Some of the blurry shots both here and in the final fight between Eddie and Snakehead left me squinting and trying to make out what was happening. Tight shots, quick edits and the blurring to indicate their speed all detracted from the action for me.

Later, inside the castle, Watson continues to jump around corners brandishing his gun and never quite seems to catch up with the action. However, Nicole is right in the middle of it and does a decent job of laying a few more of the snake man's minions to waste. The final face-off between the two immortals was pretty good. Some of the effects as they used their new powers were

fun and entertaining, and the CG shots were put to good use. At least I didn't sit through it counting CG shots like I did during *Matrix Reloaded*.

One of the things that appeals to me in *The Medallion* is that Jackie plays a more confident person. He wasn't portraying a bumbler or a fish out of water. Even with new powers he seemed in control and assured, displaying some of the "don't mess with me" attitude that he so charismatically oozed in *Police Story* and *Crime Story*. This character Eddie kicked butt with no apologies and was still a hero. Jackie's action at the beginning of the movie proved to me - not that I had any doubts - that he is still as capable as ever, and just because he is trying new things, doesn't mean he still can't do the old ones. Sometimes I think in a few years people will look back on *The Medallion* and *Shanghai Knights* and appreciate all the more how good Jackie really is in them. No matter what we as fans like to see Jackie do, whether it's straight unaided Kung-fu, or wire work to the tune of *Crouching Tiger, Hidden Dragon*, or even kissing scenes, Jackie gives us his best. He is expanding and re-tuning what he does. This movie won't please everyone, especially those who want to see him return to *Police Story*, but if you go to the film and sit down and watch it without expecting it to be something it's not, you will be entertained.

Guest shots in the film are also fun to watch for. I'm

pretty sure I saw Sammo Hung's face in the water next to Jackie in the Hong Kong harbor. It reminded me of *Project A* and gave me a smile at the memory. Also keep an eye out for Nick Tse and Edison Chen, as well as Jackie's dialog coach Diana Weng. Other cameos include Brad Allan and Paul Andreovski (who has a few lines), Nicky Berwick and Anthony Caprio.

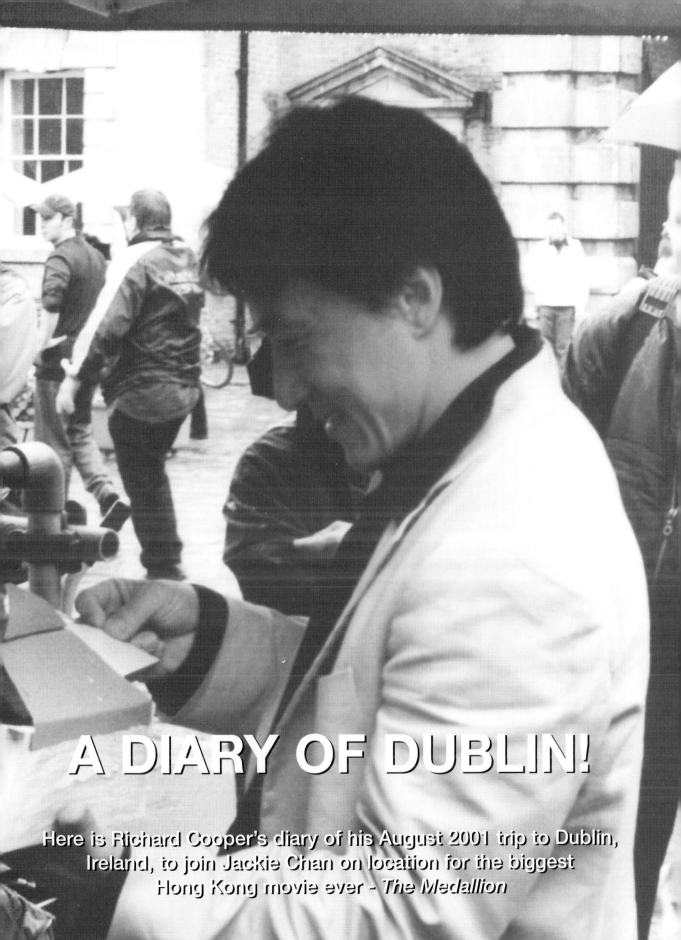

A DIARY OF DUBLIN!

Here is Richard Cooper's diary of his August 2001 trip to Dublin,
Ireland, to join Jackie Chan on location for the biggest
Hong Kong movie ever - *The Medallion*

Sunday 12th August 2001

Leave Bath for Bristol Airport at 11:10. Arrive Bristol Airport at 11:45. Depart Bristol Airport for Dublin at 14:25. Arrive in Dublin at 15:15. Free time remainder of the day.

Monday 13th August 2001

9:30 - Call Dorothy on her mobile (Dorothy Wong - Jackie's Personal Assistant/Secretary) and inform her and Jackie that I am in Dublin. Dorothy gives me directions to the location. I am told the set is outside the Clarion Hotel apartments on Dublin's North Quay Wall. I grab a taxi from our hotel and twenty minutes later I arrive on set. The set is very big - or at least it's much bigger than any of the previous Jackie Chan movie sets I have been on.

One thing that does surprise me is the amount of passers-by watching from behind the barricades. Of course it doesn't help matters that the whole location is based on a main road outside one of the most famous hotels in Dublin either! Cars, trucks, motorbikes and pretty much every other mode of transport you can think of sound off their horns as they pass by. I never really did find out whether they were trying to grab Jackie's attention as they passed by, or just trying to annoy the crew when the cameras rolled...

Soon enough I hook up with Dorothy and then duck under the barricades and wander onto the set. Two Irish security guys run up to me and tell me I am not allowed to be on set and I have to stand behind the barricades with all the other general public... I present them with a copy of Screen Power and they seem happy enough to let me proceed.

I spot Jackie in a corner of the set resting on a wall. He's on his mobile talking in Cantonese. Once he puts the phone in his pocket I make my way towards him... One of the Irish security guys stops me and asks who I am! (Not again!) I look over his shoulder and shout Jackie's name out - Jackie turns around, sees me, waves okay to the security guard and beckons me over just before his mobile rings in his pocket! Ha!

I stand a little distance away from Jackie as he takes his call. Not that it really matters as I cannot understand fluent Cantonese anyway, so it's not like I will be eavesdropping! Still on his phone, Jackie walks past me and punches me in the arm... Shortly after, his call ends and we make our pleasantries with a handshake and a hug (I am hoping most of the security see this and will stop trying to kick me off the set!).

Jackie is preparing for a rehearsal, so he tells me to grab a coffee and sit back and watch. Sammo Hung, Hong Kong movie legend and action director for *The Medallion*, sits in a chair and barks out orders to the young stunt boys to hurry up and set up the shot before it starts raining again!

The whole morning and part of the afternoon is taken up with filming numerous takes of the same shot. I won't give too much away and photos will indeed speak louder than words, but the scene revolves around Jackie's character Eddie falling from a roof (six floors high), landing flat on his face, and then getting up! It's then that his character realises he is not of the living any more, and possesses amazing powers!

Fan favourite Brad Allan arrives on set. Yesterday he got hit on the head by a camera and was out cold, he tells me. After being stretchered away and given an X-ray at a nearby hospital, he's been given the all clear. Despite looking like he's done a few rounds with Jackie, Sammo and Ken Low at the same time, he's in pretty good spirits and wanders off to relax and sit down with his copy of the *Screen Power* "Best Of" book Volume 1.

Around 3pm the cameras are moved upstairs to the roof adjacent to the apartments. The scene being filmed is where Jackie jumps about ten feet in the air, clears the roof edge and lands softly on his feet! Five strong, highly skilled stunt boys are the ones responsible for Jackie's huge flight. "Easy! Wire, crane, harness and mats. Stunt crew make this stunt easy - but you still must have the skill and strength to do the jump too!" Jackie says with a grin after he does the stunt ten or more times!

The next scene to be filmed is Jackie's character clearing the roof and then proceeding to climb up a fifteen-foot wall with his bare hands! All in a day's work for Jackie Chan! Or at least all in a day's work for Jackie's character - Eddie Tang - a "Highbinder"...

Shooting concludes well after 7pm. We depart back to the hotel. Free time.

Tuesday 14th August 2001

10:00 - We arrive at a vet college! This is the location for today. They are filming in one of the rooms - but in the film it will double as a morgue. This is the scene where Jackie's character realises he's actually dead!

Jackie's in good spirits today. I ask him why... His reply is, "Shooting going well, no rain today and also this white make up on my face I look dead is so funny!" At 11:00 we go into an empty room and set about interviewing Sammo Hung. The interview went on for about forty minutes and it was hilarious! Sammo, just like Jackie, is so much fun and has some great stories to tell...

Lunch is soon over and it's back to filming the morgue scene again. As with all Jackie Chan Hong Kong movies, the same scene is shot a number of times so during editing the best of the scenes shot can be used. Unfortunately, with many other Hong Kong movies they shoot a scene only once, and if it's bad then it's still used in the finished print... but those companies are only interested in quick and easy money. A Jackie Chan Hong Kong film is quite the opposite - it's excellent quality and maintains a constant high standard throughout, and if that means it goes over budget and over schedule then so be it! The most important thing is quality!

The sun is certainly out in force this afternoon. It's easily the best day for weather we've had since we got here. I spot Jackie in a corner of the set, he's wearing a blue overall of some kind. "This is what you wear when you are dead in a morgue!" he tells me. "This is the easiest scene for me in the whole movie! Why? I just act dead with no dialogue!" he shouts out over his shoulder as he returns for a final rehearsal.

There is no action scene planned for this afternoon so director Gordon Chan handles the morgue scenes whilst Sammo sits outside relaxing in a deckchair reading... Filming ends at around 7pm. We head back to the hotel. Free time.

Wednesday 15th August 2001
Same location as Monday - the Clarion Hotel apartments. The morning is taken up with shooting the high fall stunt with Sammo directing and the stunt boys testing the weight of the wires. Jackie himself will do the stunt later that day.

What a surprise! You guessed it, it's raining again! Still the rain will not deter me from gathering some more interviews for the two best magazines in the world

(*Screen Power* and *Jade Screen* to be precise, just in case you are a new reader!).

With all the hustle and bustle going on around I decide to just sit back and relax. I get talking to a young Chinese guy. He sees a copy of *Screen Power* and asks to have a look. "Feel free!" I say while I hand him the magazine before introducing myself and shaking his hand. Now, here comes the bizarre part! This young guy by the name of Carl has a small role in *The Medallion*. Nothing bizarre about that - after all, Jackie is a strong supporter of new and up-and-coming Asian talent. The bizarre thing is that Carl has a very well known Dad - or at least well known if you are a big Jackie Chan and Hong Kong movie fan. Carl's Dad is Richard Ng - star of films such as *Winners and Sinners*, *My Lucky Stars* and *Miracles* to name but a few...

Carl tells me that his Dad, who now resides in London, is currently in Hong Kong and the following week would be coming to Dublin to visit him. How typical that I will have left by then!

It's about 2pm and lunch is over. Sammo is still working on the same stunt, Gordon Chan is in a meeting with the production crew and Jackie is hiding in the nearby hotel from the Hong Kong paparazzi who have been following him all week (poor guy!). Around this time I interview the most talented John Rhys-Davies, who is a co-star in *The*

Coffee break: Jackie with Sammo Hung

Medallion. John is a veteran actor of numerous films, including the cool *Raiders of the Lost Ark*. John is a real pleasure to interview. In *The Medallion* his character is Commander Hammerstock-Smythe.

UK comedy star Lee Evans plays Arthur Watson in *The Medallion*. Quite honestly, Lee is hilarious and the interview can only be described as *strange*. As soon as the tape recorder stopped, Lee was as normal as one can get and he couldn't have been any friendlier. Like John, the interview with Lee was a real pleasure.

At around 3pm I am told to head straight over to the Clarion Hotel Coffee Bar as *The Medallion* director Gordon Chan is ready for his interview. Gordon is one of the most respected directors in Hong Kong cinema today. He's the guy behind Jackie's *Thunderbolt*, Jet Li's *Fist of Legend* and Media Asia's *2000AD*.

The most remarkable thing about Gordon is how softly spoken he is, and how flattered and confused he gets when you refer to him as one of Hong Kong's most famous directors.

Gordon leaves the coffee shop as soon as the interview is over and heads back to join Sammo on set - but not before quickly reminding me to send a copy of his interview in *Screen Power* and *Jade Screen* to him in Hong Kong when they are available. "No problem at all!" I say as we shake hands.

I step outside to see what is going on - the rain is easing off now so shooting can commence. Jackie will attempt

the high fall stunt himself a little later on. I hear from some of the Hong Kong crew that the Hong Kong paparazzi are nearby with huge camera lenses. They have heard about Jackie's attempt at the stunt and are waiting to take pictures...

Jackie is in a meeting with *The Medallion* producer Albert Cheung back in the coffee shop, and also trying to keep out of the way of the Hong Kong paparazzi. I receive word that I am to go back to the coffee shop immediately and wait for Jackie to finish his meeting and then we can conduct a short interview for *Screen Power*.

Relaxing over a lovely cappuccino with my tape recorder ready, Jackie doesn't keep me waiting long and bounds over to my table. As always with our interviews, I just let Jackie talk about whatever he wants to, and I am very proud to be able to say that the interview reads as a conversation between two friends and not a reporter/journalist and a very famous movie star.

Sometimes with Jackie the interview will go in one particular direction and sometimes it will go in many directions. It really depends on what kind of mood Jackie is in. On this particular occasion Jackie wanted to talk about making films in Hollywood, and the difference between making a Hong Kong and a Hollywood Jackie Chan movie.

Immediately after the interview Jackie walks outside to the set to attempt the high fall stunt. Many of the Hong Kong and Korean stunt boys are on hand giving Jackie tips on how to handle the stunt. After all, these guys have

A not so soft landing for Jackie in Dublin

Jackie prepares for his big jump

the stunt boys to prepare for another take and Jackie is yet again hoisted about twenty-odd feet in the air before the cameras start rolling again and Jackie is dropped from the skies above... Another perfect take!

It's getting late now and my colleague Paul and myself are very hungry and thirsty. It's time to flag down a taxi and get back to the hotel and enjoy the evening. "OK! We go again... one more time!" shouts Sammo, and Jackie is again raised into the air. Sammo's words echo in my ears as the taxi speeds off back into Dublin City...

Thursday 16th August 2001
10:30 - Taxi to the Clarion Hotel apartments location again. What a surprise! It's raining again! Jackie isn't on this location right now, he's filming a small car chase scene some twenty-odd miles outside of Dublin and will be back later. Apparently this car scene was to be filmed a couple of weeks ago but they ran out of time for some reason, and are filming it today instead.

Time is of the essence for the Dublin shoot of *The Medallion* because Jackie is leaving for Toronto, Canada, at the end of August to start shooting his next Hollywood project, *The Tuxedo*. Jackie will conclude *The Medallion* in Hong Kong and Thailand in December and the early part of 2002, once he finishes *The Tuxedo*.

While Jackie is away filming the chase scene, we stay at the familiar location and watch Sammo and the Hong Kong crew rehearse another stunt scene. Many of the stunt boys (a mixture of Sammo's Hong Kong and Korean stunt group and the familiar JC stuntman and bootmaster Brad Allan - one of Sammo's sons is also in this group) are attached to wires and a harness supported by a huge overhead crane.

Each of the stunt boys takes a turn to take a high fall to test the weight and speed, and each time notes are made and procedures are met, so by the time Jackie arrives on set he can do the stunt himself at the lower risk factor.

"When Jackie does the high fall stunt we have the blue screen behind - so then our special effect department will create something amazing and show Jackie Chan like never seen before - a ghost with special powers!" Sammo informs me over a coffee break while the stunt boys re-set the shot for another rehearsal.

It's well into the afternoon now and no sign of Jackie! We later hear that the car chase scene is taking longer than expected and so Jackie won't be back until late. We depart the set to our hotel about 5pm.

Friday 17th August 2001
No filming today! It's a day off for the cast and crew, so free time for the *Screen Power* camp too! Jackie spent the day shopping for antiques and then training back at his apartment. We spent the day and night exploring

experience with this stunt now from performing it so many times themselves, before 'big brother' Jackie tries.

There is a huge crowd of the general public watching from the outside street, and no doubt the Hong Kong paparazzi are amongst the crowd of onlookers too! For safety precautions and for general peace of mind, big shutters are put up shielding Jackie and the incredible action away from a few hundred prying eyes!

Time is pressing on and Jackie makes a first attempt with the stunt. "Yat, Yee, Samm!" cries Sammo as Jackie is dropped down from above at enormous speed supported by a harness, wires, a huge overhead crane and about ten stunt boys controlling his speed via a cable... The stunt goes perfectly! Everyone on set applauds Jackie!

Jackie gets up off the mat and is grinning. Sammo tells

Dublin City.

Saturday 18th August 2001

On location in Dublin Castle. Absolutely pouring down with rain! Again! Sammo walks by and waves, "Dublin weather is the weirdest weather!" he says. Despite the weather the shoot is going well. The location is in Dublin Castle's courtyard. "In the movie it will represent the outside of a restaurant/bar," Jackie tells me before his mobile rings and he answers.

In fact this location is for an action scene, or a chase scene to be exact - hence why Sammo is here on set. In this scene Jackie chases one of the main villains of the movie, played by an actor called Johann Myers. As I look closer on the monitor behind Sammo's shoulder I can see the whole scene captured. With Sammo's experience and knowledge of what 'younger brother' Jackie can do, the scene is explosive!

To me it looks reminiscent of the chase scene with Jackie and Alan Tam in *Armour of God* - but in this case, no cars and no Alan Tam! Jackie chases Johann (and sometimes Johann's stunt double) through the plastic white chairs while drinks are flung everywhere!

This scene is shot a number of times. In one take Jackie tries to run faster and jump higher over the chairs to give the scene more excitement and as Sammo shouts "Cut!" Jackie hobbles back as he has pulled a muscle in his leg... But he laughs it off, and with a few axe kicks with his right leg the martial arts expert is good as new!

While the crew set up the scene again (with new glasses and drinks!) Jackie takes time out to meet with some young fans who have flown over especially from Germany to meet him. However, these three young men are no ordinary fans - these three young adorable guys are seriously ill and their one wish in the world was to meet Jackie. As I stood by and watched these kids with Jackie many a tear came to my eyes. The size of their smiles and the expressions on their faces when Jackie sat next to them and talked to them was unbelievable... words can't describe it. It made me feel so proud inside to know that I work with Jackie. Watching him talk to these kids, play with them, pose for photos with them and give out autographs and then stand up and push their wheelchairs around the set with an umbrella over their heads was incredible. It's something that I will never ever forget...

I guess it's very easy to assume that Jackie has all the time in the world and is a very famous and successful man who only makes amazing movies for millions of adoring fans. It's times like this that you actually realise that Jackie has no *real* time to himself - if he's not filming then he's being interviewed, or he's in a meeting, or he's on a plane thousands of feet in the air, or he's doing some charity event, or he's somewhere on a gruelling promotional tour, or he's spending his more than valuable time meeting and talking to special people or young kids such as the ones who came today...

In between takes for the next rehearsal, Jackie can be seen talking to Xavier Lee high on top of the roof of a truck. Xavier, never really seen without a digi-cam, is busy filming the new and up and coming *Making of The Medallion* documentary.

The rain is pouring down even more! Filming is delayed. Everyone is sheltering one way or another. It's a prime excuse to sit down for a coffee. Jackie and Sammo are already sitting down with a coffee in a tent, watching the previous scenes on a monitor. It's incredible watching them together in a working environment. When you see them together talking you can't help but think of them in *Project A*, *Wheels on Meals*, *Dragons Forever* and many other classics...

Rain is delaying filming considerably. Everyone breaks for lunch at 13:00.

14:00 - It's still raining and shooting cannot commence. All the extras for the scene hide in one of the castle alcoves. There surely must be a few hundred coffees drunk and cigarettes smoked since filming was put on hold.

Our flight back to the UK is at 17:45 so we stand around until 15:00 to say our goodbyes to Jackie, Sammo and everyone else. The rain is still thundering down as we jump into a taxi and head back to the hotel before heading straight to the airport.

Arrive back at Bristol Airport at approximately 6:30pm.

JOHN RHYS-DAVIES

The Tallest Dwarf!

Interview by Richard Cooper

Welsh-born actor John Rhys-Davies, better know to audiences as the character "Sallah" in the Hollywood hits *Raiders of the Lost Ark* and *Indiana Jones and the Last Crusade*, was a complete gentleman and a real find on location in Dublin for Hong Kong's biggest and most expensive movie ever - *The Medallion*.

Screen Power: *John, who is your character in The Medallion?*

John Rhys-Davies: Well I play Jackie's Interpol boss. My name is "Commander Hammerstock-Smythe". In fact the scene that we were just shooting and you were watching is where Jackie's character is officially dead and then drops in on us from a great height and then gets up and convinces us that he is in fact still alive! (Laughing) It's a scene with some shock!

SP: *Yes it looks like it! What is the story of The Medallion?*

JRD: Am I allowed to tell you? (Laughing)

***SP:** (Laughing) Of course! This is the Official Jackie Chan Magazine after all...*

JRD: Well that's completely different then! (Short pause) *The Medallion*. Well it's about good and evil. It's about mortality and resurrection, and certainly audiences that enjoy the elements of comedy, action, fantastic martial arts and of course Jackie Chan will not be disappointed...

SP: *How's the filming going here in Dublin?*

Planning the next scene: John Rhys-Davies and Lee Evans

JRD: It's going wonderfully well. It's a wonderful facility here with this incredible international cast and crew and it's a lot of fun. I believe the weather is causing a little concern with the shooting but I don't think it will delay filming or do any real damage.

SP: *What's it like working with Jackie?*

JRD: Well, you're in fact talking to an "official Jackie Chan fan". (Short pause) I regard him actually as the finest physical actor and comedian that I certainly have ever worked with, and I think he's actually, at the end of the day, certainly in my opinion, one of the greats and is up there with the likes of Buster Keaton, Harold Lloyd and Chaplin. I think Jackie is the most underrated actor of our day and I put him at the top of the highest ladder. It's a real pleasure to work with him and also observe him while he works.

SP: *John, get your own plug in - apart from The Medallion what else can moviegoers see you in soon or what projects do you have coming up?*

JRD: Well the next project for me is publicising a little film called *The Lord of the Rings* which is released this December 2001, 2002 and 2003. I play the dwarf, "Gimli" - certainly the tallest dwarf you'll ever encounter in your travels around the world, I'm sure (laughing).

SP: *(Laughing) I don't doubt that at all, John.*

JRD: *The Lord of the Rings*: brilliant cast, brilliantly directed, and it will be the biggest film of all time! *The Medallion* a close second, of course. (Laughing)

SP: *(Laughing) Having worked on Hollywood films such as The Lord of the Rings and, of course, not forgetting Raiders of the Lost Ark and the third Indiana Jones movie, you are now working on a Hong Kong movie - in fact the biggest and most expensive Hong Kong movie ever. What do you see as the noticeable differences between a Hollywood and a Hong Kong film?*

JRD: Working around the world you will always find greater or lesser standards in proficiency. The differences between a Hollywood and a Hong Kong film are incredibly small. Really. I mean you seldom work with a bad crew. Sometimes you work with a crew that are having to work with inefficient equipment, like in Russia sometimes. I mean stuff that really hasn't been seen in the West for forty-five or fifty years. But by and large all crews - American, Chinese, Irish or British - are equally competent. Some may have more flare or bravado than others. It's one of those films. When you film, you go to a strange location, you grumble about your hotel or you get a wonderful hotel, you get treated wonderfully, you have a lot of fun with the people you choose to be with and work with, and you get paid! (Laughing) What is there to bitch about?

SP: *(Laughing) Very true! John, thanks a lot for talking to Screen Power in between scenes, and all the best with all your projects.*

JRD: My pleasure.

LEE EVANS

Interview by Richard Cooper

The first thing you notice about Lee Evans after a chat is that he is exactly like the person you see on the screen – he's interesting, strange (in a nice way!), charming and incredibly funny! Looking from behind the scenes you can quickly tell that Jackie and Lee get on well. Jackie is the physical comedian and like fellow co-stars before – aka Chris Tucker and Owen Wilson – Lee Evans is just excellent cast as the verbal "motormouth" comedian.

Certainly out of all the people I have interviewed around the world for *Screen Power*, Lee Evans was the most difficult person to chat to, but it was definitely one of the funniest interviews I have ever done, which in many ways more than made up for it.

I don't know if Lee is ever serious about interviews or whether he just wanted to make my job difficult on the afternoon of August 15th, 2001, but either way, it was a great experience and a lot of fun! Let us begin:

Screen Power: Lee, how's filming going?

Lee Evans: It's a nightmare! A real nightmare! (Laughing) Every day it's Kung-fu this and Kung-fu that! Personally I am a good runner - I can run from trouble. I'm good at Karate but not much good at Kung-fu!

SP: *Did you have any special martial arts training for The Medallion before any of the filming?*

LE: (Short pause) I done some "martial" but no "arts". I haven't really got an artistic bone in my body! But "martialing" is great. What you do is kind of get this small badge like a small sheriff's badge and you kind of go around high streets - any high street will do - and martial people... You know martial them into shop doorways and everything...

SP: *(Laughing) I see! I can tell you really enjoy being interviewed, don't you?*

LE: I've been interviewed many times over the years... but yeah, I'm enjoying this interview best, so well done - and you are so young too! So talented!

SP: *(Laughing) Thanks - I think! So, you have worked on UK television, Hollywood movies and now a Hong Kong movie. What's the difference in your opinion about working on a Hong Kong production? You knew I was going to ask you that, didn't you?*

LE: (Laughing) Yes, I did know that question was coming. There's isn't that much difference to be honest. I turn up every day, I'm an idiot, I make strange faces, I have huge ears and people laugh! That's what I am used to in whatever I do, whether it's on British TV, a Hollywood film or something else. But the crew and the cast on *The Medallion*, no matter where they are from, are highly skilled and professional.

SP: *What is your role in The Medallion?*

LE: I play "Watson", who is Jackie's sidekick. Jackie does all this incredible Kung-fu and stunts in the film and I just stand there with my ears and pull strange faces. I think fans of Jackie Chan and me will certainly enjoy *The Medallion*...

SP: *Do you have any new funny faces for this film or are they your usual style faces?*

LE: (Laughing) Nope! There are a couple of new ones - but I can't talk about those in case anyone steals them...

SP: *Fair enough! Will you show me one though?*

LE: (Lee pulls a face) What do you think?

SP: *Yep! Not bad. Bet that looks great on film (laughing).*

LE: Thanks!

SP: *You're welcome! Well thanks for taking time out for a chat, and I shall send you a copy of Screen Power, OK?*

LE: Really? OK then, that will be great.

SP: *Personally, from what I have seen over the last couple of days, you and Jackie look great together on camera, and I also enjoy your other work Lee, so I think The Medallion will do very well.*

LE: Thank you very much! And Merry Christmas to one and all...

Strike a pose: Lee Evans in Kung-fu mode for *The Medallion*

GORDON CHAN

Screen Power Editor Richard Cooper sits down with Director Gordon Chan in Dublin, Ireland, on the set of the most expensive Hong Kong movie ever - Jackie Chan's *The Medallion*.

Screen Power: We are here in Dublin on the new Jackie Chan movie, The Medallion. How's it all going?

Gordon Chan: Up to now it's been going really smoothly and I am so surprised about the Dublin crew. I was always sceptical about coming here - you know, the working attitude of the Western crew compared to the Chinese crew. The main thing that worried me was because you know Jackie moves very fast, and he gets kind of p****ed off when things are going slowly and dragging on. If that happens he will get fed up. But it's not like that here at all. The tempo, the crew, the working conditions really make me happy and it gives confidence to a Chinese Director and company that you can make Hong Kong or Asian movies in the West and work with a Western crew without any problems.

SP: How did you get to be Director of this movie for EMG?

GC: It was kind of an accident! I wasn't going to be Director of *The Medallion*, mainly because I was the "Executive in Charge of Production". I lined up everything... To me it was going to be the biggest and most expensive Hong Kong movie ever starring Jackie Chan. For me at that time I was more concerned with all the administration, dealing with all the foreign companies associated with the film at that time. We tried to find one Director from the States, and after a while we thought everything was set and we can start the movie, but then suddenly there was some creative differences between the Director and Jackie. So that Director was no good. Then Jackie turned to me and said, "I think we should find a Director that really knows me and what I can do!" I agreed with him and then he said to me, "Why don't you do it?" I thought about it and then agreed because we didn't have a lot of time left. So I agreed to be Director of *The Medallion* because Jackie asked me to do it.

SP: What was the main

It's all on tape: Gordon and Editor Richad Cooper

problem with the previously announced Reginald Hudlin as Director of The Medallion?

GC: For a start we did not need him telling us what to do and also it's not good to disagree with Jackie on one of his films. Basically the Director just tried to turn Jackie into something he wasn't! That would not work - a successful Jackie Chan film is a film that has Jackie playing himself. But I am Director now and I am happy that Jackie wanted me to be Director.

SP: You are a very famous Director in Hong Kong and Asia, and also very well known in the West by Hong Kong movie fans. You directed Jackie in Thunderbolt. Did you enjoy directing Thunderbolt?

GC: That one. That was really the first time I actually got to direct a big budget movie in Hong Kong. You can't get much bigger than directing a Jackie Chan movie for Golden Harvest. That was also the time that Jackie and I really started to become friends. I can remember being on set watching Jackie and Sammo [Hung] trying to work out all

this action. We did have a little problem, mainly disagreeing on how to shoot some drama and also the big ending race scene which was directed by Frankie [Chan]. But when *Thunderbolt* was made Jackie and I remained close friends. I was very grateful to him for letting me direct that movie.

SP: Were you happy with the finished cut of Thunderbolt?

GC: (Short pause) Yes! I tried my best. But mainly I was grateful to Jackie for supporting me and giving me a chance.

SP: Looking back now at the finished print of Thunderbolt, what would you change to make it better? Or would you leave it as it is? Would you have done anything different?

GC: Something different? Well I certainly would have liked one of those cars (laughing).

SP: (Laughing) Me too!

GC: Actually looking back at it now I really would change the end racing scene. The scene in the finished movie is not how I envisioned it to be. I would have made it differently. Also the night with the two cars side by side - I would change that too...

SP: A lot of Hong Kong movie fans in the West really wanted a big fight scene at the end with the main villain, Cougar, and maybe Ken Low Wai-kwong.

GC: Yes. I can understand this. The structure of the whole movie did change a lot while we were shooting. Mainly the story was serious and it was heavy drama. That was my direction. It was a turning point for Jackie to suddenly realise that it's difficult to have all this heavy drama and then be able to suddenly kick back and relax and do comedy and fighting. *Thunderbolt* was a drama with good

action. It was not meant to be a *Police Story* kind of movie. Actually, I'll tell you, now that I look back on *Thunderbolt* after a few years, I have some good new ideas on the cars and the racing...

SP: Oh! So maybe a future Jackie Chan movie will be directed by Gordon Chan and the movie will be about racing...

GC: Yes, racing. I hope to do it one day. I have some very good ideas... My ideas have improved from *Thunderbolt*. My new ideas involve more action and fighting as well as good racing scenes.

SP: That sounds excellent, Gordon. I am sure that project would be very well received. Jackie is not only the number one star in Hong Kong and Asia but also now

a successful Hollywood star too. What's your opinion of Jackie? Jackie and I were talking in London last month in his hotel when he was promoting Rush Hour 2 and he said some good things about you!

GC: It's strange. He's not only a star, he's a legend already. The thing I find the most amazing about him is that he never acts... he's always just him! The Jackie Chan everyone sees in movies is the same guy in real life. Jackie Chan doesn't need to pretend to be successful, he just needs to be himself. He's a nice guy. He's one of a kind. Very funny and always very loyal to his friends and people who work with him. Jackie Chan is great because he is GREAT. He's my "big brother" and we have been good friends for many years now.

Gordon with UK comedy star Lee Evans

Hanging Out With Sammo

On location at Dublin Castle

Richard Cooper talks to *The Medallion* action director Sammo Hung about working with
Jackie on so many incredible movies we have all come to love

*Screen Power: It's very well known that you are "big brother" to Jackie Chan and Yuen Biao in the respect of
growing up with them and training with them at the Peking Opera School in the 1960s. For the benefit of new
readers and people unsure of what it was like at the Peking Opera School, tell us about it...*

SP: *Sammo we are now in Dublin, Ireland, on the set of the latest Jackie Chan movie. You last worked with Jackie on Mr. Nice Guy back in 1996 in Australia. What was it like shooting Mr. Nice Guy?*

SH: I was very happy to be the Director on that movie. It was good that we could take our time with everything. We had a lot of time so we could work full time on that movie and also be very comfortable too. We were very lucky with that film. We shot on location in Melbourne, Australia. It was a good shoot and I had a good time working with Jackie.

I liked it and it was a successful film too. After *Mr. Nice Guy* I knew that I had missed not working with Jackie and so we said that we would do lots of solo projects but we would continue to work together on projects too. Now, I am very happy to be in Dublin as the action director of *The Medallion*.

SP: *The Medallion is the most expensive Hong Kong movie ever. How is the filming going in Dublin? I've only been here for a couple of days so far...*

SH: I like it here! We only started filming about two weeks ago and it's going fine, except for the weather. Never seen weather so strange as this before (laughing). Everything looks fine... but sometimes we cannot film for a whole day because of the rain or we can only shoot for eight hours at a time. Only thing is that we must be on schedule and finish on time because Jackie's schedule is

Sammo Hung: It was very serious at the Peking Opera School. You know, the training, the discipline, the learning, everything. We trained every day. We got up very early in the mornings every day, something like five o'clock, and then didn't stop until eleven at night. Very tough. Of course in the middle we have the lunch break and after lunch break we have the teacher for the normal lessons... you know, the painting, the talking, reading and writing. But really the main training was martial arts, acting, singing, acrobatics and those kinds of skills. Lunch, normal lessons and sleeping was only for half the day – the rest of the time was training (laughing). I was at the Peking Opera before Jackie and Biao. I was the "big brother". After three years, if my master was not there in the school, I would be master! I would beat them! (Laughing) Just like Jackie Chan... people say I'm his devil! I would kill him! (Laughing)

Waaahhhh... Sammo does Bruce Lee in 'Skinny Tiger, Fatty Dragon'

Twinkle, Twinkle Lucky Stars

very tight and he will leave Dublin at the end of the month to start his new movie in Canada [*The Tuxedo*]. So we must hurry. Everything is hurry, hurry, hurry…

SP: *Let's talk about Dragons Forever then, which was released in 1988. What can you tell the readers about that movie?*

SH: That movie… I remember that we had such a short time to create that movie. One day the boss at Golden Harvest, Raymond Chow, he called me and said, "Hi Sammo! Do you think we have a chance to make a movie for Chinese New Year?" It was only three months before Chinese New Year, so it would be very difficult, especially when I had no idea for a story, characters, stunts and fights. I tell Raymond Chow, "OK! Let me try!"

Then I stop working on one of my own movies for my own company and then go to the hotel with the writers and just think of the movie. We stay in the hotel for one week and then we have some good ideas and then we go. Then wait for one month for the script to come out – then we start shooting. *Dragons Forever* – we shoot in one and a half months! (Laughing) But we did it!

SP: *That film was hugely successful and is a firm favourite among fans in the West. I think fans enjoyed the fact that it wasn't the same kind of characters. Usually the characters would be policemen but in Dragons Forever we have Jackie playing a lawyer, you are an arms dealer and Yuen Biao is a cat burglar. So, good characters and a good story.*

SH: Yes! Because it's a Sammo Hung idea! (Laughing)

SP: *(Laughing) The story and the characters did work well though…*

SH: Yes! But it was a difficult situation, especially with Jackie's character. At that time I was bored of the usual cop character, I wanted different characters. For a start everyone knows that Jackie Chan can fight. If you had Jackie play a character and he doesn't fight, no one will believe it! How can you say, "Jackie Chan – he can't fight and just knows love story"? No! It won't work! So it was very hard to think of new characters for us, especially three characters that were not policemen but could fight and people would believe too. Same as me. How can people believe, "Sammo, you can't fight you just good at love story"? No! (Laughing) Now I get tired of fighting. I don't want to make action films anymore, I want to make a love story (laughing)…

SP: *Sounds good! (Laughing) Let's talk about Thunderbolt. You were one of many directors involved in that movie back in 1995. You were action director on Thunderbolt weren't you?*

SH: Yes. That film is not bad. Not great but not bad. The trouble with that movie is they were always hurrying for the release. The company set the release date too soon without even telling any of us! So it could have been a lot better. On *Thunderbolt* they were having problems and everything was rushed so they called me and asked if I would help them with some big action scenes. One of my action scenes was the container with the house and another was the big gambling room at the end.

SP: What about the comedy classics of the 80s: *Winners and Sinners; My Lucky Stars; Twinkle, Twinkle Lucky Stars? They were hugely popular in Asia and found great success on video in the West. Did you enjoy those movies?*

SH: Yes. That generation is very difficult, you know. Very different. Films like *Prodigal Son*, *Magnificent Butcher*, *Warriors Two*, these films really had only one tone: fighting, fighting, fighting. The comedy films – the *Lucky Stars* films – these films were something else. Totally different. In those films you have a lot of good actors, but you have to make sure that you control the timing with the joke, then you can have a good movie.

With the *Lucky Stars* movies I just wanted… I didn't want people thinking… If you think too much about a film, a story, you can't enjoy the movie. I didn't want any pressure on the audience. Each shot in those movies, I wanted people to laugh and be happy. That's why most of the scenes are shot very quickly. Don't have scenes or the joke going on too long. If you do people will get confused or bored. Just relax and enjoy the movie. Sit back and laugh. No pressure at all.

I am happy about those movies. We were lucky that we had so many talented funny people working on the films. The tempo, the timing, they show everything, the jokes… We had so much fun making those films. The films were made for Asian audiences only. I was happy and surprised to know that the Western markets wanted to release them.

SP: *You starred in Project A with Jackie and Yuen Biao. What can you remember about that movie?*

SH: That's a long time ago! (Laughing) *Project A* was a big responsibility for Jackie as a Director and star. It was also a big risk for Golden Harvest too, as so much money was spent on the set and the props. I was happy to star in that movie.

Jackie, myself and Biao – when we work together it's never really work, it's fun! *Project A* was a good film. I helped to direct some of the film too. Every time you see me on the screen in *Project A* I'm also directing all the scenes too. The scene with me gambling was one of the scenes I directed. Jackie did a good job with *Project A*, and I was happy to star in the film and also help with some of the directing.

SP: *Another fan-favourite is Wheels On Meals. Why did you decide to shoot on location in Barcelona, Spain, for that one?*

The nunchucks are out

SH: *Wheels on Meals*? I decide to shoot outside Hong Kong because at that time I was getting bored with the same locations. I wanted to give the film a more international flavour. We had a good idea for the story and when we thought about the location we decided Spain would be good. The shooting went well and the film made a lot of money for Golden Harvest. I think *Wheels on Meals* was the first film to really start a new trend for Hong Kong movies shooting outside Hong Kong and Asia. The fighting in the movie is also very good, as well as the story and the comedy.

SP: *What about the film Heart of Dragon (aka First Mission)? That was a very different film wasn't it? Very serious drama. You both directed and starred alongside Jackie didn't you?*

SH: I like that one. The script was very different, but I just wanted to try it. I wanted a different film. Not comedy at all. With that movie I wanted to show that I could act well and I didn't have to fight to make Sammo look good. For Jackie, he showed he can act seriously in drama and still fight and look good. It was a big gamble for Golden Harvest and it didn't do as well as our usual movies at the box office but we had to try. Yuen Biao was working on another movie at the time we shot *Heart of Dragon*, but he still came to the set and helped choreograph great action. You can tell his choreography and action – lots of kicking and acrobatics.

SP: *Yes, the end fight scene with Jackie and Dick Wei was very realistic.*

SH: Yes! So that movie didn't do as well as the others, but it can still be remembered for some great action and good drama.

SP: *Lastly Sammo, what is your message to all the fans all over the world who will read this interview?*

SH: One thing is that I hope that my fans around the world continue to have good health and peace. I really hope there is no war anymore. You see every day that people kill people and so many people die. I hope we can change that. No more war and hurt. Everyone be happy.

SP: *Sit back, relax, watch a Sammo Hung movie?*

SH: Yes! That's most important (laughing).

SP: *(Laughing) Sammo, it has been an absolute pleasure talking to you. Thanks for your time. Good luck with everything, and we'll be sure to keep everybody up to date with your projects and activities.*

SH: (laughing) You're welcome. Thank you. I really enjoyed talking to you.

ON-LOCATION WITH JC!

**SCREEN POWER EDITOR RICHARD COOPER
FLIES TO DUBLIN, IRELAND, TO HANG OUT WITH
THE ONE AND ONLY JACKIE CHAN IN BETWEEN TAKES
FOR THE MOST EXPENSIVE HONG KONG MOVIE
EVER – THE MEDALLION.**

Wednesday August 15th 2001 and I am standing outside Dublin's famous Clarion Hotel. Dublin very much reminds me of my own home city of Bath. It must be because of the tall old buildings and the weather... Yep, it's pouring down with rain! Still, I don't really care as I am not here on holiday and I am quite well sheltered enough from the dreaded weather anyway...

It's a little after two in the afternoon and the Hong Kong crew are busy setting up the next action scene with a series of wires and a harness. This is one of Jackie's big action scenes in *The Medallion*, so the crew make sure everything is working alright before Jackie comes out to film.

Jackie can relax though as *The Medallion* Action Director and Hong Kong movie legend Sammo Hung Kam-po is on hand taking care of everything behind the scenes.

As with all his stunts, Jackie needs his own private time to prepare for them. In fact that's what he's doing right now in the Clarion Hotel Coffee Bar. I make my way to the coffee bar and leave all the hustle and bustle of the set behind me...

Inside I sit down to a gorgeous cappuccino, and after a few minutes Jackie bounds over to my table to join me for the following exclusive interview for the world's supreme mag!

Screen Power: Jackie, we are in a quaint little coffee bar in Dublin. You're here filming The Medallion - so how is the filming going?

Jackie Chan: You know what? At first I am very surprised. When I first heard we are coming to Dublin, Ireland, I think, "Wow! So many terrorists and bombs going off!" That's how Asian people think. But actually it's not. Dublin is totally different. The people are very nice and I am very surprised with the Irish crew. They are all very professional. You know, no matter where I go, the word of mouth about shooting in Ireland is good! When I go back to America to talk about *Shanghai Noon* and *Shanghai Knights*, the production company - it's called Spyglass [Entertainment] - they just finished a movie here. So when I hear from them... So this is why we are thinking of coming back here to make *Shanghai Knights*. I'd really like to do the same thing in Hong Kong. Why? It's like after ten years everyone talks about Ireland, talks about Dublin: "Yes! Very good! Good professionals! Good place to shoot!"

SP: Good pubs? (Laughing)

JC: (Laughing) No, I never go to the pubs. Well, I just go once because one of the producers have a birthday - then I go to the pub. But Dublin is good. Except the weather. Strange!

SP: Same as Britain's weather.

JC: (Laughing) Yes! But it's quite comfortable here. The people, they don't bother you. It makes me very comfortable when you shoot on the street. You saw today on set... they wave and shout, "Hi Jackie!" and smile but don't bother me. They support me. I'm very happy to know this.

SP: The whole of Dublin certainly knows that Jackie Chan is filming here doesn't it?

JC: Yes! I like it - even the production office here, they signed all kinds of things for me when I arrive, "We love you Jackie! Welcome to Dublin!" It makes you feel very good inside.

SP: So filming for The Medallion is going well. But what's it like working with Lee Evans? He is more well known in Britain as a comedian than an actor. Have you seen any of his work before?

JC: Yes. I see only two movies: one is *There's Something About Mary*, and also *Mouse Hunt*. When I work with him on this movie I find out he's really a comedian. Totally different to Chris Tucker. How can I say it? (Short pause) Different jokes and style, and even different to Owen Wilson. Owen is more quiet and then will say something. He [Lee Evans] is more body language and more acting... You know, all kinds of physical things. Chris Tucker is more dialogue and the voice - "Aaaahhhh!!" (Laughing)

SP: (Laughing) I saw Rush Hour 2 just before I came to Dublin.

JC: What do you think? Like it?

SP: Yep! Better fight scenes this time around as well.

JC: Yes! Much better fight scenes. I am in total control this time. Because in *Rush Hour* part one, the DP [Director of Photography] really gave me a lot of problems. His job is to make sure the movie is smoothly going on, save a lot of money, and make everything quick and keep to the timing and schedule. He's a good photographer for drama but not for action! When it comes to action he's just like the kindergartener - even though he's seventy years or sixty years old. If you talk about action scenes, I'm the master!

SP: I would assume that the DP would help you and assist you.

JC: No! First day, no. He won't move the camera. He won't listen to me. He give me the 'face' [Jackie pulls an angry facial expression], you know, "Jackie Chan, who are you?" (Laughing) "Don't you dare move my camera!" (Laughing)

SP: (Laughing) Really?

JC: Yes! Of course I don't dare move the camera because of the union and those kinds of things. So for [*Rush Hour*] part two I said, "He's a good cameraman, a good DP, good for drama but not for action scenes!" Then we change for some other DP who really knows action. The new DP for *Rush Hour 2* - he knows what I am doing. He watched my documentary [*Jackie Chan: My Stunts*]. So I say, "Put the camera over here," and he says, "OK!" But for dialogue scenes I say, "Whatever you want to do!" So it's a collaboration. Right now it's not like a one man show anymore. In Hollywood now they listen to me and I listen to them. So for dialogue scenes I listen to Chris Tucker and for action scenes everybody look at me. For drama scenes I listen to the Director. But that's the work. It works very well.

SP: Before you agreed to star in Rush Hour 2 did you say to Brett Ratner, "I am in charge of all the action scenes"?

JC: No I don't have to say that, he knows.

SP: So you work well with Brett Ratner?

JC: Yeah. Now it's like team work. On the set I am happy that for action everyone looks at me, but for dialogue scenes Brett Ratner talks to Chris Tucker and Chris Tucker talks to me.

SP: What about Rush Hour 3? Will that happen?

JC: I don't know... I mentioned Egypt for the location and Chris Tucker mentioned South Africa, but I said, "South Africa? No!" Why? Because there are a lot of black people in South Africa and Chris is black, so it's not us as the fish out of water anymore. If we film in South Africa only I am the fish out of water, but if we film in Egypt both of us are the fish out of water. That's funny, it works better! Egypt would make the story more interesting for part three.

SP: Is there a lot of action in The Medallion?

JC: (Short Pause) Yes! Why? Because Sammo [Hung] is in charge of the action. But after I look at *Rush Hour* - the box office - I believe we have to be very careful about the action. Because I really trust the American producer. For me, I always want to make more Hong Kong-style action. I believe all the fans and everybody who will read this interview in the magazine also want to see more Hong Kong-style action. But the producer told me, "Jackie, if you want to make a Hong Kong-style movie, Hong Kong action like Jet Li - 20-something million. If you want to make a Hollywood movie - over 100 million!" I didn't believe it then! I said, "No! I want to make a totally Hong Kong-style film!" But then after *Rush Hour 2* came out, I believe in Hollywood films! Even though I believe *Rumble in the Bronx*, *First Strike*, *Accidental Spy* are much better than *Rush Hour* one and *2*. Do you agree?

SP: Yes! I think they work much better than the Rush Hour films.

JC: But what is the box office of these films compared to *Rush Hour*? See? So much difference in the box office. But it depends on what kind of market you want. You cannot make one movie for the whole world market - especially me and Jet Li. If we make a movie in Hollywood, then only make it for the American and the western market.

SP: So you will still make Hong Kong movies as well as Hollywood movies?

JC: Yeah. This is why I came back to make *The Medallion*, aimed at the Asian market not the American market. So now I am making *The Medallion* for the American market? No! At the end, this type of film doesn't work in Hollywood. When I make *Gorgeous* - totally for Hong Kong market and Asia. What's the box office of *Gorgeous* in Asia? Twenty times better than *Rush Hour*. But *Gorgeous* cannot release in American or western market. Instead it goes directly to the video and DVD markets. It's different. So it depends what kind of market you want. Now I know and understand that you cannot take Hong Kong style to Hollywood. I never used to believe it but now I know it's true. The tastes between east and west are too different. It will always be that way. So now I don't argue with that anymore - instead I just make two different movie styles for the two markets.

SP: That will please all your fans though, Jackie, knowing that you will still make Hong Kong movies as well as Hollywood movies.

JC: Yes, so this way every year I will still make one Asian movie and one Hollywood movie. For me there is no Hong Kong movie anymore! For me it's like an Asian international film. Asian first! And if we have an American market, western market for that film, and someone wants to buy it - that's a bonus! But when I make *Rush Hour* and *Shanghai Noon* - Asian market is a bonus. Hollywood doesn't care about the Asian markets. They don't really need or have to rely on them to have a successful film anyway. Understand?

SP: Absolutely.

JC: The audience is totally different. I'm not like Tom Hanks... Western actors only have one audience. For the western market that's the way to be - Tom Hanks. Jackie Chan? No! When I look at Asian films they're not like that! In *Rush Hour 2*, the action scenes are like, "Bam Bam Bam!" - for me it's a piece of cake! But the audience like it and it's not violence.

SP: So Jackie Chan for the next twenty years and the future will be just an actor - drama and comedy and no action and martial arts?

JC: You can tell, all those years, the action star's career is so short! Very short. And so I hope I can become an actor now. The actor who can fight. I don't want to be the action star who can act. Jackie Chan is the actor who can fight, do comedy and stunts.

SP: *That sounds ideal. And it will work well. One great thing about the fans is that they will still watch your movies and support you even if you don't do any more big stunts and fight scenes.*

JC: Yes, I am so happy about that. All these years you can see I've tried to vary my characters. I don't always want to do *Police Story 1, 2* and *3*. OK, *Crime Story* - serious, right? Then *City Hunter* - cartoon! Then *Drunken Master 2* - Kung-fu and martial arts. Then, *Supercop* - action. See? I have been changing. I want to show everyone that I can be like Gene Kelly, and then I can be very serious too.

SP: *Well, either way you certainly have arrived in Hollywood and are making your mark in Hollywood.*

JC: You know, it really surprised me. I think the Hong Kong films I make are much better than *Rush Hour*. But of course in Asia no one mentions or talks about *Rush Hour* or *Shanghai Noon* (laughing), they mention *The Accidental Spy* and these kind of things. But in England, Europe, America - wherever I go everyone shouts out, "Hey! *Rush Hour*!" You know they are very funny, they shout out to me and sing, "War! Huh! What is it good for!" (Laughing) You just can't get away from it! I always tell them, "No! *Accidental Spy* is better." They say, "What? *Accidental Spy*? Where can I see that movie?" See? Very difficult situations. Being Jackie is not easy (laughing).

SP: *I think the west is starting to appreciate that now, Jackie, at last.*

JC: Yes, very hard. Strange too. But I am so happy that the west accepts me now, and I have power and so have more control over the Hollywood films that I do.

SP: *Jackie, we shall end it here. Good luck with The Medallion and congratulations on the fantastic success of Rush Hour 2.*

JC: Thank you, Richard. To all the fans who read the magazine - I wish you all good health. I am happy you are enjoying *Rush Hour 2*, and I hope you like my new projects *The Medallion* and *The Tuxedo* too.

THE TUXEDO

Review by Lisa Clemens with Gail Mihara

Entering the theater, I knew I was in for something different from Jackie Chan, and I was not disappointed. The man who has reinvented himself time and again, who isn't afraid of trying new things, has done it again with *The Tuxedo*.

During his stint in Hollywood, Jackie has specialized in playing characters that always know (for the most part) how to fight, what to say and, when there's a romantic interest involved, how to get the girl.

His latest character, Jimmy Tong, is a sharp contrast to his previous incarnations: Jimmy doesn't know how to fight, has no idea what to say, and hasn't the faintest notion how to even talk to a girl, let alone win her heart.

Jimmy is just your average (or quite possibly below average) guy. When we first meet him, he is working up the courage to approach his dream girl by practicing dubious opening lines on a fellow cab driver. Decked out in a "Hooters Girls Dig Me" T-shirt and a "soul patch" goatee, he is fairly content with his lot in life, but obviously there is much room for improvement. [Cultural Note: "Hooters" is a well-known American restaurant chain staffed by scantily uniformed but generously endowed waitresses.]

Jimmy's lack of confidence is not limited to his dealings with pretty women, but rather includes an aversion to conflicts of any kind. Awkward and easily flustered, he deals with an angry bicycle messenger not with an amazing display of Kung-fu prowess, but by cowering under his cab.

He may not be able to fight, but one thing Jimmy can do is drive. It is his skill as a driver that brings him to the attention of millionaire playboy Clark Devlin, played to perfection by Jason Isaacs (*The Patriot*). Suddenly, Jimmy the taxi driver becomes Jimmy the chauffeur, getting a taste of Devlin's glamorous lifestyle of the rich and famous.

But there is only one rule Jimmy must follow in this newfound paradise: Do not touch the boss's tuxedo.

Once this little glitch is overcome, Devlin, a friendly, down to earth sort beneath all the sheen, soon becomes Jimmy's idol, the embodiment of everything the driver dreams of becoming.

After watching his impeccably tuxedoed boss sweep the latest gorgeous conquest off her feet, Jimmy asks, "How do you do it?" Devlin tells him that it's ninety per cent clothes and ten per cent heart, "And you have plenty."

Nominally just a prelude to Jennifer Love Hewitt's appearance later in the film, this initial relationship between Jimmy and Clark Devlin is one of the highlights of the film. In just a few scenes, Isaacs takes the throwaway part and manages to instill the character of Devlin with a complete, full-blooded personality. When the inevitable *Tuxedo* sequel does come along, the filmmakers would do well to consider keeping Isaacs on as a major member of the mix.

After bonding with Devlin over shopping trips and visits to the drive-through, Jimmy soon learns the truth about his boss when they are attacked by an exploding skateboard. It turns out that Devlin is a top CSA agent investigating industrialist Diedrich Banning (Ritchie Coster), an evil villain who is fostering a nefarious plan to poison the world's drinking water sources and gain control of the bottled water market.

Then Devlin is taken out of commission and must recuperate incognito, leaving orders with poor confused Jimmy to wear the sacred tux.

Back at the mansion to gather a change of clothes for Devlin's extended hospital stay, Jimmy puts on the tuxedo and discovers just why it is so important. Not only do the new threads self-size to fit the wearer, but they also enable Jimmy to do all sorts of amazing physical feats, from dancing the tango and lighting a lady's cigarette, to climbing walls and chopping much socky.

In over his head, he passes himself off as Clark Devlin to Devlin's new partner, CSA water expert and newbie field agent Del Blaine (Jennifer Love Hewitt). A work obsessed lab nerd who doesn't know what the millionaire looks like, Blaine is perpetually perplexed and exasperated by Jimmy's unprofessional, un-spy-like behavior. As both characters try to prove they know what they are doing - without knowing anything - it is close to the blind leading the blind.

Hewitt surprised me in this film. Having seen her in *I Know What You Did Last Summer* I really didn't expect much from the young actress, but the chemistry between her and Jackie works well. Unfortunately, she does not fare so well with the script, which primarily calls on her to be constantly annoyed (when the camera isn't indulging in lingering shots of various body parts for the benefit of the boys in the audience). On the plus side, Hewitt reportedly trained with award winning JC Stunt Team member Andy Cheng. Between this and Jackie's coaching, she manages to hold her own during the action sequences.

Hewitt is not the only one who comes out looking good doing something different: Jackie gets to shake his booty more than we've seen in quite a while. From the out of control "Sex Machine" sequence, to the scenes where Jackie and Jennifer dance their way around Banning's party in search of his secret lab, Jackie shows he is more than a Kung-fu fighter.

Other welcome surprises to look for include cameos from Colin Mochrie of *Whose Line is it Anyway?* as the gallery owner, and Jackie's dialogue coach, Diana Weng, as a CSA agent at the end of the film.

Does the plot have holes you can drive a truck through? Definitely. However, *Tuxedo* is not meant to be a plot driven, serious drama. It's a wild, fun, irreverent adventure with lots of laughs and plenty of action. This is what we expect from Jackie Chan.

Jackie takes the role of director in *The Tuxedo*

ΛROUND THE WORLD
IN 80 DΛYS

SCREEN POWER EDITOR, RICHARD COOPER, TRAVELS TO BERLIN, GERMANY AFTER A PERSONAL INVITATION FROM JACKIE CHAN TO GO BEHIND THE SCENES OF DISNEY'S US$100 MILLION ACTION COMEDY BLOCKBUSTER – "AROUND THE WORLD IN 80 DAYS"

Make-up test for *80 Days*

Wednesday 11th June 2003

It is a little after 11am. This is our first day on set. One thing that I am excited about, apart from the fact that we are on a Jackie Chan film set, is that we are in Germany. I have been to Germany before a couple of times but only as a stopover before connecting to another flight. From my own experience and Jackie Chan knowledge, I know very well that Jackie is HUGE in Germany! In fact I receive many e-mails and letters from German Jackie Chan fans most days! It will be interesting to see how the fans treat him here...

The set is an abandoned slaughterhouse just on the outskirts of Berlin's city centre. It's filthy inside. I should have perhaps checked the location in more detail before pulling up in the car - I feel somewhat overdressed, shall we say!

One thing I am impressed by before we even drive onto the set is the security. Having been on numerous film sets before, I have marvelled at how easy it has been sometimes to just walk on, but in the case of *Around the World in 80 Days* it has proved very impressive.

On this particular set you have to drive through a main entrance first of all, which comprises of a couple of chaps with walkie-talkies. "Let's see how easily we get

in," I tell Rebecca as we pull up to the main gates.

Our car is stopped dead in its tracks as soon as we bank into the entrance and we are then asked who we are and what we want. From my past seven years experience of Jackie Chan worldwide film sets I know that it's always a good idea to bring along a few copies of the supreme mag! In most cases, if you just say, "I am here to see Jackie!" it usually does nothing for you!

Upon entering the main entrance, we wind down the car window and show the security guys a copy of *Screen Power*. They take the magazine and then speak into their walkie-talkies in their native German tongue and after a few minutes we are ushered on through to the main carpark not too far up ahead.

If I was asked which Jackie Chan film had the worst security, then I would have to say *Shanghai Knights*, shooting in Greenwich, London. On that particular set, over two days in the summer of 2002, anybody could and did walk onto the set and take photos galore!

The carpark is huge - although on closer inspection it isn't a carpark, but just a big concrete wasteland surrounding a huge warehouse which must be the abandoned slaughterhouse.

Rehearsing the end fight scenes for *Around the World in 80 Days*

The weather is really beautiful today - shame they are filming indoors. I bet Jackie is thinking the same thing! Today will be our first time meeting the film's publicist, Julia. Up until now she has been so nice and helpful to us. Sometimes publicists for films are not so nice and not so helpful.

Soon enough we meet Julia and get our first impressions of her. Our first impressions last through to the day we leave - she is great! A real pleasure to work with.

This will also be our first time meeting Jackie here in Berlin, although we have been here three days already. Quite understandably though, while we have been sightseeing and enjoying the sun, Jackie has been working so hard and pretty much non-stop. Time for us to get down to some work too!

As soon as we hook up with Julia, we walk down to the set's main entrance. It takes around ten minutes to walk from where the car is parked to where the set is. We pass a number of motorhomes on our way. It is easy to identify Jackie's, as not only is it the biggest but also there is a Mitsubishi Pajero parked outside it! A few smaller motorhomes are situated next to Jackie's with various "JC Team", "JC Action, Power, Sport" stickers on. These are no doubt for Jackie's stunt team.

On the way to the set's main entrance there are also various food and drink tables and we stop for a quick coffee before we go on in. As with all Jackie Chan film sets, and no doubt film sets in general, as soon as we walk in we get numerous stares and looks from the crew. This is quite usual, and I think it is the case that we are the strangers in their environment. This has always been the case! I guess they are just curious, as it is almost a family atmosphere on set for them, working together for over three months, and then to suddenly receive unknown visitors... In these cases one can only smile back at all who stare!

We walk onto the set and it is all hustle and bustle. One thing you automatically feel when you get onto a set is that you are in the way, as crew are working all around

you. So the best thing to do - and I am a dab hand at this now - is to look for a unique little part of the set behind the cameras and monitors and out of the way of the crew. If you look hard enough on a set you will always find at least one suitable place. This is what I call the "Safe Place" - and this is where you can take off your jacket and put down any belongings and observe all the glory!

I clock a great "Safe Place" over in the far corner of the set behind all the hustle and bustle, and when I get closer I get a nice surprise as two familiar faces are already there! Osumi Yahagi, Jackie's P.A., and Diana Weng, Jackie's dialogue coach. Osumi is giving Diana a shoulder massage in between all our talking. Osumi tells Diana that she remembers me as a young boy! I tell Osumi that that was many years ago, in 1997, on location in Rotterdam, Holland, for Benny Chan Muk-sing's *Who Am I?* - and so much for being a young boy! Next year I will turn 30... although I am still a young boy at heart and by nature!

It is after our initial chat with Osumi and Diana that I suddenly realise that across the room, ten or so feet up, is Jackie! He is in costume - kind of like grey robes - and choreographing a fight sequence with his stunt team. Nicky Li Chung-chi, Jackie's longtime assistant action choreographer and JC Stunt Team second boss is also on hand. When Jackie and Nicky are together working on a fight scene it really is like looking at two masters at work. These guys are the best - the *crème de la crème*!

They are not actually filming yet but merely setting up the correct lighting and moving the cameras into position to film this up and coming fight sequence. Osumi tells me Jackie is in a bad mood because he wants a couple of days extra to shoot the scene and he is not being given them! I tell Osumi that I am used to Jackie's moods by now after eight years! She laughs and agrees.

Jackie never really gets in bad moods, but when he does get into a mood you ought to stay out of the way! All of Jackie's bad moods result from the frustrations of filmmaking - or perhaps I should say *Hollywood* filmmaking! Jackie is a perfectionist. When he doesn't get time to finish a shot, or a particular shot just doesn't go the way it should do, or others working with him are not doing their job correctly or to the best of their ability, that is the time when you see Jackie's mood change from all smiles...

This particular fight sequence should have been shot a couple of weeks ago but they simply ran out of time and they are now picking it up from where they left off. I am told there is a lot of pressure on set because they are three weeks behind schedule, but when I look at director Frank Coraci smiling, laughing and joking in his chair, watching playbacks a few feet in front of me, I think either the pressure is not as bad as they are saying or he is just a guy who hides stress well!

Soon enough I am introduced to the director by Diana. What a loveable character! I give him a copy of *Screen Power* and our sister magazine *Jade Screen* to peruse, and he flicks through them in front of my very eyes and comments, "You're the Editor and Publisher of both? You are very talented!" I tell him he is talented for making films such as *The Wedding Singer* and *The Waterboy*. He smiles back. Anyway, I am very, very flattered by his remarks!

The lighting is now set up, the cameras are in place and they are ready to resume filming. Before they shout, "Cameras roll, and action!" a huge background sheet is lifted down behind Jackie and I am completely stunned. It is a twenty foot replica of the Statue of Liberty, and Jackie is in fact standing on the statue's right arm and ready to fight for his life as the character Passepartout!

This is what they must surely call "Movie Magic". No wonder they say Hollywood is number one at making films. The detail and care to the statue is unbelievable! The cameras roll and Jackie leaps and vaults onto the statue's arm whilst being chased by a black-clad Chinese fighter - a Scorpion Warrior in fact!

"Cut!" shouts the director. "Let's go again!" The same sequence is shot a few times, and Nicky Li watches the scene on the monitors with the director and shouts comments and any feedback to Jackie. They get the shot and then prompt to move the cameras closer to the action.

Nicky passes me and shakes my hand. "Suit? I almost didn't recognise you!" he says laughing. "I almost didn't recognise you either! Where has all your hair gone?" I reply. As Nicky tells me later on during lunch, as well as action choreographer for the movie he is also one of the Scorpions, and indeed some of the other Jackie Chan Stunt Team are also playing Scorpions, including a certain Ken Low.

While the crew move the cameras and all the hustle and bustle begins again, we chat with Diana and shortly we

Jackie being "miked up" on set

end up meeting Hong Kong actress Karen Mok (*Tempting Heart*, *So Close*, *The Twins Effect*). Karen was born in London and despite talking Cantonese most of the time her accent is very British, or at least very London! She is great fun and really into Hong Kong films too. It is rare to find a Hong Kong actress who really enjoys talking about what films are good and what films are not. She asked if she could read some magazines over lunch and said she would bring them back later. I told her she could keep them, and if she wanted future copies free of charge in the future she should e-mail me.

Karen was supposed to be finished on the movie and was going to be flying back to Hong Kong this week but they asked her to stick around a few more days. She tells me that she is pleased she did stick around as she gets to fight Jackie a little more over the next couple of days as her character, Agent Fang, is the chief of the deadly Scorpions!

Soon enough the cameras roll again and Jackie is back in action. The take is good but they continue to film the same sequence two more times. The next part of the fight sequence involves the lower part of the scaffolding under the statue's right arm. This will take a little time to set up and Jackie isn't prepared to wait around for this. He slides down a ladder and walks in between the cameras and over to the director to watch the previous scene played back on the monitors. He laughs and jokes with Frank and is obviously pleased with what has been shot.

A quick chat between Jackie, Steve Coogan and Richard Branson

to keep rolling and go again. This time the kick is good. They go again two more times to make sure that they get that shot!

It is at times such as these that you can understand Jackie's frustrations at time wasting. In Hollywood it takes three men to work the dolly and push and move a camera back and forth. In Hong Kong a guy will push it around on a wheelchair - cheap and cheerful but effective, and it saves valuable time!

It is past 3pm and lunch is soon - all the crew look excited, but Jackie isn't. Once everyone leaves to fill their bellys, Jackie and his stunt team skip lunch and continue to rehearse the next part of the fighting sequence and also work on any improvements and new ideas. They have an hour but that time will go in no time!

Lunch is served buffet style in another warehouse south of the main set. It will be nice to get some fresh air as well. I skip lunch, although Rebecca has a small snack.

Back from lunch, some of the crew look lazy or are just working slower. This angers Jackie and he lets them know about it high up in the air above them. It works. They all start speeding up!

What we didn't notice earlier was that the occasional person on set was wearing a white surgeon's mask covering their mouths. Jackie's other P.A., Dorothy Wong, passes by me, pulls down her mask and smiles. I ask her why she has the mask on, and she tells me she hates the dust and recently they were scared that asbestos was leaking down from the warehouse ceiling. Wow! So much for the glamour of filmmaking!

Cameras are moved again, lighting is changed and moved around and the fight sequence continues. This time Karen Mok gets in on the action, although they just need her face on camera with Jackie's. After a few takes the director is happy and Karen walks on back, sits down and continues her magazine reading.

They have almost finished the main opening fight sequence, but another two or three hours is still needed to make sure of it. We leave around 6pm and head on back into Berlin city where our hotel is based. In this weather and working in a warehouse all day, one certainly looks forward to a shower at the end of the day as well as a nice relaxing meal and a drink or two.

It will be interesting to watch tomorrow's shooting and see how the fighting sequence evolves...

Thursday 12th June 2003
It's the same location as yesterday - the former slaughterhouse. We certainly picked the best week to come to Germany - not only is the weather beautiful, but we also get to see Jackie in action filming a trademark fighting sequence.

We are seated a few feet away behind the monitors and as soon as Jackie finishes with Frank he looks straight at us, smiles and comes on over for a quick chat while they set up the next shot. He doesn't seem to be in that much of a bad mood, although he tells me that he is genuinely annoyed that he has to rush this fight sequence. Jackie goes on to confirm that Hollywood is great at a lot of things, but this is primarily due to the fact that they have big budgets and still, even to this day, Hong Kong style is the best, because it is fast, effective and reasonably priced.

The cameras are in place and shooting is ready to resume. Jackie advises us to move a little closer so we can watch the next shot in more detail. We take his advice. Once again, Jackie climbs on through the cameras and then runs up the ladder to the lower level of scaffolding.

The scene must be finished by tonight and they still have a few more scenes yet. The fighting sequence will continue tomorrow and also Friday, but by tonight they have to reach a certain part of the sequence so they can stay on schedule and pick up where they left off tomorrow.

Cameras roll and the director shouts, "Action!" Jackie flips around the statue and evades an oncoming flying kick. The stuntman's kick falls too short. Jackie signals

The car we have hired to get around in Berlin is great. It has satellite navigation, so once you programme in your current destination and where you would like to go to it tells you every time you need to turn left or right or continue straight on.

Having such a remarkable facility makes me want to explore more and more of Berlin and also the neighbouring Potsdam area. Potsdam is where the Babelsberg Studios are located. These studios are where some of the *80 Days* interior shots have been filmed already and also where some of the last filming will take place later next month.

We arrive on set around 11am. It takes around forty-five minutes to get here by car from our hotel. As this is our second day on set we receive no questions from the set security guards.

Filming won't take place for another hour or so as the crew are setting up the lighting inside. During this break Jackie's stunt team go outside into the sunny concrete wastelands just up from the site carpark to kick a football around.

Ken Low says he will use this opportunity to grab a quick sleep and call his wife instead. Ken has his own private trailer on the lot. To the right of Ken's trailer is Nicky Li's and left of Ken's trailer is a trailer for all the other stunt team combined. Jackie's trailer is double in size and is to the far right of Nicky's.

As he passes our car, eating some late breakfast, Nicky tells me Jackie is in his trailer sleeping. Outside Jackie's trailer is the well known Mitsubishi Pajero. If the Pajero is not outside Jackie's trailer when he is on set it means two things: one, Jackie has given his driver time off, or two, it means that the driver is doing a few errands for Jackie as his free time away from filming is so limited.

It's around 12pm and filming will commence shortly. Everyone walks back to the set and awaits the director. Once on set the director calls for a rehearsal. The scene is an action sequence and a follow on from yesterday's take.

Jackie is under great pressure today - the producers have told Jackie that he has until the end of the day to complete this sequence or the scene has to be cut out completely. Being the world's number one action martial arts movie star, this is something Jackie does not want to hear.

On set, Jackie and his stunt team are working overtime - everything is so fast. He is choreographing the action for the scene literally as he goes along. From what I hear, only Jackie and one other can do this incredible skill in the whole of Asia - the other person is Sammo Hung.

Jackie and his team are working fast, choreographing and rehearsing - it's quite apparent that the western crew are slow in comparison! One time, Jackie asks for a camera to be brought in closer so he can check camera

Waiting to film the balloon scene

angles. It takes two crew members to move the camera even though it is on wheels. Once Jackie has finished with the camera and needs it moved back out of the way, instead of asking two crew members to take it away, he jumps onto the back of the camera and kicks off and rides the whole equipment out of shot. The looks on the faces of the western crew members are priceless. Jackie is not only the master in front of the camera but notably behind the camera as well.

The director wants to start filming and Jackie asks for another twenty minutes to rehearse with his stunt team - he gets the twenty minutes. They are ready to film, so cameras are pushed into position and the lighting is set overhead in the correct position.

Cameras roll and the action begins. Jackie is being attacked by one of the movie's villains, played by one of his Korean stunt guys. Jackie gets kicked and falls to the ground high above, suspended on a platform. The action should continue but the stunt guy trips over during fight mode. Jackie calls, "Cut!" and they go again. This time the scene is a good take and Jackie wants to go again. There is another good take to add to the last one, so things look like they are running smoothly.

The cameras and lighting are being moved closer in for the next scene. While this is being done, Jackie and his stunt team rehearse more and more. The director calls for a rehearsal and Nicky Li, who also appears in the movie as one of the main villains, a Scorpion, comes behind the camera with the director to watch and check camera positions.

Jackie rehearses and Nicky gives the all clear. The trust between Jackie and Nicky is very unique. If Jackie is happy then Nicky is happy. And behind the camera, if Nicky gives the all clear to Jackie, then Jackie is happy with the set-up.

One more rehearsal and the scene will be shot. This time the fight moves down to the lower platform - it's a tight shot so that's why the cameras were moved a few feet forward. The scene involves Jackie evading a jumping kick from his stuntman and swinging down to the lower platform with the aid of some rope.

"Action!" calls the director, and the scene is shot. Watching the action from behind the cameras, it's really like watching a piece of history being recorded for years of further enjoyment. The scene is shot three times and each take is good. Jackie smiles after the last take. He rubs his hands - I think the rope swings must have burnt his hands a little.

Hong Kong actress Karen Mok wanders onto set in full costume. She plays Agent Fang, the film's main villain. Agent Fang is the leader of the villainous Scorpions. Karen is involved in the next scene. She wields a sword and attacks Passepartout, the character played by Jackie.

Jackie and Karen rehearse the next scene along with the JC Stunt Team. Also on hand is the only female member of the Jackie Chan Stunt Team. She is from the mainland of China and her name is Angel. She is an expert in Chinese martial arts and acrobatics, and also is skilled in stunt work involving high falls. Karen will be doubled during the next scenes when they involve heavy action and fighting.

A rare break inbetween filming

The scene is ready to be filmed. As soon as the cameras roll, Karen kicks Jackie and he falls backwards onto the ground. Jackie gets up and tells Karen to kick harder and to make more aggressive facial expressions. The scene is shot again and the take is better. The director asks for one more take and they get it.

The cameras and lighting are moved forward to film the next sequence that involves Karen swinging her sword at Jackie. Jackie rehearses with Karen and the cameras start rolling. Three takes are shot and they are all good. Nicky is behind the camera with the director and gives a thumbs up on each of the three takes.

It's around 3pm and it's lunchtime. Lunch lasts for an hour. It's so nice to get some fresh air outside in the sun during lunch. Everyone else on set obviously thinks so as well, as no one is left lurking around inside. The set is very hot and incredibly dusty - so dusty that some of the crew are still wearing face masks.

Once lunch is finished everyone returns to the set. Jackie and his stunt team are already on set and rehearsing. They obviously had a short lunch break. Jackie's next scene involves Angel, Karen's double. Angel attacks Jackie with a sword, and in the film you would not think Karen is being doubled - Angel is the same size as Karen, they have the same costume and hair style, and the camera is filming Angel from the back.

As soon as the director is back on set, Jackie says he is ready to film and there is no need to spend more time rehearsing. The director looks happy, although surprised, and the cameras roll immediately. The action sequence looks great, Angel attacks and Jackie evades, flips and jumps out of harm's way - on screen it will look incredible.

The scene is filmed the usual three times. Karen is brought back in just so they can get a shot of her with the sword face to face with Jackie. No rehearsal necessary, and the shot is taken, again, three times.

Angel is brought back in and the next scene is rehearsed. This time the action steps up a notch and involves the fight scene being moved up to a platform around twelve feet off the ground.

Jackie and Angel rehearse, the crew move the lighting and cameras into position and, while not in demand on set, Karen Mok very graciously grants us an interview while she has a spare twenty minutes.

Karen is needed back on set. What a charming lady! I am proud that she is of British origin and making such a great success in Hong Kong movies, as well as being such a huge singing star! She is another person that I believe would be successful in both Hong Kong and Hollywood films.

Karen goes in front of the cameras and performs a jumping movement. Once performed and filmed, she walks off set and welcomingly allows Angel to take her place performing dangerous movements high above with Jackie.

It's around 6pm and shooting will go on throughout the night. As long as Jackie gets the sequence today, I am sure he will carry on as long as it takes. For us it is a forty-five minute car journey back to our hotel, not to mention it's rush hour time.

It's back here tomorrow. I hope Jackie nails his shot and this sequence does make it to the finished movie and doesn't get cut out completely. I guess we will know more tomorrow...

Saturday 14th June 2003

It's about 11:30am and I can't believe it took almost thirty minutes to park our car. Even though there is a carpark reserved right next to the location for crew and others with set access, it is rather small and difficult to find any available spaces, let alone think of parking in one of them.

This is our sixth day here in Berlin and today is by far the warmest. Because of the sun, today there are so many people out and about, but then again this is a Saturday as well, and also we are situated at a very well known tourist attraction.

Today they are filming at the Schloss Charlottenburg Gardens, also referred to as the Charlottenburg Castle. This will be interesting because this is the first outdoor location shoot this week - for the last few days it has been the closed set of a former slaughterhouse. This is really great news, because this is my first time visiting Berlin and today I get to do some sightseeing while I work!

The set location is about a twenty minute walk from the private carpark, because you have to walk around the back of the gardens first of all, as the main entrance is closed off and an orange rope surrounds much of the outer grounds.

It has only been a few minutes into our walk and I think I must have seen a couple of hundred people already. Many of the people here are extras in the film as they are dressed in period clothes, but others are just dressed in normal clothes or just casually. Maybe they still work on the film or are simply tourists or even fans of Jackie's. If they are tourists or fans then they will be disappointed, as up ahead a large number of security guards (some even holding fierce dogs on leashes) are waiting to check our set passes. This game is simple: No pass? Go back!

The whole garden will be used as a backdrop in the few shots filmed today. Filming will commence around 1pm and go on until 7pm and even a bit longer if the light holds up.

On set there are so many extras. It reminds me of the extras on the London and Prague sets of *Shanghai Knights* last year. The period of this movie is very close to, if not the same as that of *Shanghai Knights*.

Things are frantic on set today. The director and the producers look more anxious. Their extra pressure comes from two main sources. The first is that Virgin boss Richard Branson has just arrived in Berlin and will shortly arrive on set and they must get his scene done within three hours as he's leaving to go straight back to London. The second reason for today's pressure is that a bunch of German and other European press photographers have been invited to the set to take photographs within a designated boundary a few hundred yards from the set. Once the photographers arrive they are given only five minutes to take photographs before having to leave the location immediately.

Richard Branson will arrive shortly. In *80 Days* he plays the role of a balloon owner - a role in which I am sure he is very comfortable, as it is a role he has played in real life. In *80 Days* many well known faces and celebrities have cameo roles throughout the movie. This is definitely a unique selling point from the filmmakers' point of view, and will also no doubt delight audiences everywhere when it is released in the summer of 2004.

Richard Branson arrives. He is only accompanied by his assistant. He meets the director and producers on set and they exchange pleasantries. Branson looks really excited and happy to be on set and appearing in the movie - as well as being a very successful businessman and famous round the world adventurer, maybe he will also call himself a movie actor as well. I don't blame him!

Steve Coogan appears and joins Richard Branson and others in a chat. While they chat, more and more extras arrive on set and the costume department rushes around to each of them adding a hat or two, or a scarf - anything and everything to make all these German extras look more the part and more suited to the movie's era.

A huge crane enters the location from afar. The crane is an incredible sight to see, and what makes it so special is not only is it the biggest crane I have ever seen in my life, but it is also carrying in front of it half a hot air balloon!

The balloon consists of the passenger basket and the lower half of the balloon. In the scene, Jackie, Steve Coogan and actress Cecile de France get into the balloon and then the crane (which is situated out of shot) will lift them up high into the sky. When you see this scene in the finished movie, a computer generated upper part of the balloon will be put in place! Wow, the wonders of Hollywood!

The crane is now in place and the extras are being instructed on what they should be doing when the director shouts, "Action!"

No sign of Jackie yet though. He must be in his trailer which is located ten minutes away from the set.

It's around lunchtime now and some of the extras look tired and bored. Considering the fact that they are getting paid, they are appearing in a Hollywood film starring Jackie Chan and also they can eat and drink as much as they like on set at the caterer stand, one would think they would look happier!

Located near the set is a river. On the river there are a few people out in small rowing boats. We walk down toward the riverbank and have a closer look. The weather is glorious, and the river and the entire scene looks amazing. I don't think I will ever forget these sights today.

I have been in Berlin for seven days now and I really love it here. I know that I will be back to visit here in the future, whether it involves a Jackie Chan movie or not. Over the last seven years I have travelled to a lot of places to join Jackie on set and because of this I have visited many beautiful cities and countries. I want to thank Willie Chan and Solon So, Jackie's managers, for these opportunities - all these memorable trips really opened up this kid's eyes...

Jackie's dialogue coach, Diana Weng, comes to have a look at the riverbank with her husband Brian and baby son Aaron. They are a lovely family. I first met Diana and Brian in Ireland on the 2001 set of *The Medallion*, although at that time it was called *Highbinders*.

Diana truly is a great person, not only does she always help out if you need her to, but she is always smiling. Diana and I often exchange e-mails from around the world. Her husband is a computer expert and has a great laptop. I must get one of those real soon.

Diana is so busy working on *80 Days* that Brian has also joined her to look after baby Aaron from time to time. We bought baby Aaron a jacket in Berlin city yesterday and he looks cool in it - he should grow into it in about a year!

Also down at the riverbank are some of the Jackie Chan Stunt Team. These five or six guys are in costume and will be appearing in a scene later this afternoon. Their faces are smudged with paint and it looks hilarious.

Ken Low walks past me and tries to wipe some of the paint on my shirt as a joke! I ask Ken what the make-up is for and he tells me that the stunt team are villains in the film and fight Jackie in an art gallery and end up getting covered in paint!

The stunt team, always energetic and searching for fun,

get in a couple of rowing boats and paddle out into the river. There are two boats, in one of them is Nicky Li, the boss of the stunt team, and in the other is Ken Low and stuntman Wu Gong.

It's a race! Nicky rows and is in the lead, and coming up behind is Ken Low's boat with Wu Gong on the oars. Ken is just relaxing in the boat and telling Wu Gong to row faster and faster. Either way, Nicky wins! They get to the end of the riverbank and paddle on back. The scene is hilarious!

What makes it even more funny is, as they start paddling back, Jackie arrives and walks down to the riverbank watching them. The look on his face is difficult to explain, he doesn't smile or look mad - he just looks at them rowing back.

Nicky's boat is the first back. When he arrives back, he's smiling and laughing and gets out of the boat. Then, quite bizarrely, Jackie walks down to him and gets in his boat and rows off himself.

Jackie's boat passes Ken Low's and Wu Gong's coming the other way. Ken and Wu Gong come on back to the riverbank to join Nicky while they all watch Jackie rowing out further and further and eventually disappear completely through the end bushes onto the next river!

When a few minutes pass by, they look quite concerned and Nicky therefore instructs both Ken and Wu Gong to go and find Jackie. They get back into their boat and head off. Just as they are a few feet away from the riverbank, we can see Jackie rowing back into view. Soon enough everyone is back on dry land and the filming will commence soon.

The crane is being tested - it takes the balloon up and up and then down again. This is done several times. Jackie's assistants film this and everything else around them - over the years they must have collected thousands of hours of footage from behind the scenes of Jackie's movies, personal appearances and other such activities. I think in the future there will be some incredible footage available for audiences and fans alike to watch on documentaries, just like there was on *My Story* and *My Stunts*.

Some of the stunt team ask me for copies of magazines to read while the crane is still being tested. I pass them out copies to read. One of the copies of *Screen Power* I pass out has not yet been seen by Jackie himself - after all, it is the latest issue and only just out. Jackie snatches the copy off one of his Korean stunt boys and sits down and flicks through the pages himself.

I always send copies of *Screen Power* to Jackie at his

Hong Kong agency office. However, it seems that he has not seen the last couple of issues. He looks and acts quite frustrated because of this, and promptly gives me another office address to send copies to. He tells me that sending copies to his office in the New Territories will be better, so he will always receive them and copies will not go astray!

While the stunt guys are reading magazines, I get introduced to the latest recruit, who is from Canada. His name is Joe Eigo and he specialises in acrobatics and flips. He demonstrates for me and is quite unbelievable! Certainly the best I have ever seen. We exchange e-mail addresses and he kindly accepts my invitation of an interview for *Screen Power*. Thanks to Jackie, I have made another new friend.

Richard Branson is ready for his scene. They must be quick as he's flying back home in a couple of hours. There is a joke on set between the crew about Branson (it's not a cruel joke because that would be unfriendly and very unfair). The joke is that Richard Branson could not fly to Germany on one of his very own Virgin planes, as Virgin do not fly directly from London to Berlin. Instead he had to fly in on a competitor's airline (in disguise you would assume). Maybe you had to be there to find the joke amusing. Either way, it was all said in good humour by the crew.

The scene will now be shot. The extras are told again what they should be doing in the background while Branson, Jackie, Steve Coogan and actress Cecile de France are rehearsing their scene a few times. In this scene, Jackie, Steve and Cecile run up to the balloon and jump the queue of around a dozen people and then get into the basket and then get launched into the air. Branson is the balloon owner, and he has one sentence to say in French to Jackie and his co-stars when they jump the queue.

I can't quite hear what Branson says, but later Diana tells me he is basically asking Jackie and co what they think they are doing jumping the queue. I guess that makes a lot of sense when you watch the scene.

The scene is performed for real for the camera after director Frank shouts, "Action!" He's happy with the first take but wants at least another five or six takes while they have Branson on set. The scene is shot again and the take is another good one. The scene is shot again and this time more extras are added to the balloon queue to perhaps add more realism.

Everyone is happy with the scene, and Branson says his goodbyes to the set of *Around the World in 80 Days* and also to Berlin.

It's around 3pm and lunchtime is here. While the cast and crew break for lunch, the press department for *80 Days* handle the dozen or so photographers that have just

arrived. The photographers are given publicity information on the movie and then given a few minutes to take photos of the set and the huge crane with half of a balloon suspended from it. The photographers leave promptly.

Lunch is over and everyone returns to the set. Steve Coogan's little daughter has come to visit her Dad working. While the scene is being set up they both throw bread to the ducks down by the riverbank. You can tell she loves her Dad a lot and vice versa...

It's back to filming. The scene being shot is a close shot of Jackie and co running up to the balloon's basket and climbing in. Again, there are multiple takes of this scene, and each time Jackie tries to do something different, whether looking over his shoulder while he runs up to the basket or simply running up to the basket and vaulting in instead of climbing in like the scene before.

Filming will finish in another two hours or so. The light is fading. Everyone will return to this location and will complete the scene on Monday. Tomorrow is a day off for all.

We bid our farewells to Jackie and whoever else is present on set. Another Jackie Chan adventure has now come to an end. I hope you will enjoy this report from the Berlin set of *Around the World in 80 Days* and I hope you will look forward to watching the movie when it opens in the summer of 2004.

SCREEN POWER

Screen Power is packed with exclusive interviews with Jackie, his directors, past and present movie co-stars, stuntmen, bodyguards and staff, on-set reports from Hong Kong and Hollywood movie projects, reviews, detailed articles, past and present projects profiled, readers 'Letters Page', competitions (with top prizes!), worldwide 'fans & pen-pal service', and all the latest news and happenings in the Jackie Chan world!

WORLDWIDE SUBSCRIPTIONS AND MERCHANDISE AVAILABLE ONLINE NOW AT:
WWW.HONGKONG-STORE.COM

We accept the following credit cards online through our secure server :

ALTERNATIVELY SUBSCRIBE BY POST USING THE FORM BELOW.

Sterling/US Dollar Cheques and Sterling Postal Orders made payable to *Screen Power* please. Euros sent cash via registered mail to: :

SCREEN POWER MAGAZINE, SUBSCRIPTION DEPT., P.O. BOX 1989, BATH, BA2 2YE, ENGLAND

SUBSCRIPTION RATES
(For 4 issues - mail order including all postage and packing)

#1 UK: £25.00   **#2** Europe: €50.00
#3 USA: US$45.00   **#4** Rest of World: £30.00

GUARANTEE YOUR COPIES
SUBSCRIBE NOW!